Database Management Systems

FASTTRACK

DATABASE MANAGEMENT SYSTEMS

Patricia Ward and George Dafoulas

THOMSON

Australia • Canada • Mexico • Singapore • Spain • United Kingdom • United States

THOMSON

Database Management Systems
Patricia Ward and George Dafoulas

Series Editors
Walaa Bakry, Middlesex University
Alan Murphy, Middlesex University

&
Middlesex
University
PRESS

Publishing Partner
Middlesex University Press

Publishing Director John Yates	**Commissioning Editor** Gaynor Redvers-Mutton	**Managing Editor** Celia Cozens
Senior Production Editor Alissa Chappell	**Manufacturing Manager** Helen Mason	**Marketing Manager** Mark Lord
Production Controller Maeve Healy	**Text Design** Design Deluxe, Bath	**Cover Design** Matthew Ollive

Typesetter
Pages Unlimited

Printer
Zrinski, dd, Croatia

CONTENTS

The FastTrack Series

Thomson Learning and Middlesex University Press have collaborated to produce a unique collection of textbooks which cover core, mainstream topics in an undergraduate computing curriculum. FastTrack titles are instructional, syllabus-driven books of high quality and utility. They are:

- **For students**: concise and relevant and written so that you should be able to get 100% value out of 100% of the book at an affordable price
- **For instructors**: classroom tested, written to a tried and trusted pedagogy and market-assessed for mainstream and global syllabus offerings so as to provide you with confidence in the applicability of these books. The resources associated with each title are designed to make delivery of courses straightforward and linked to the text.

FastTrack books can be used for self-study or as directed reading by a tutor. They contain the essential reading necessary to complete a full understanding of the topic. They are augmented by resources and activities, some of which will be delivered online as indicated in the text.

How the series evolved

Rapid growth in communication technology means that learning can become a global activity. In collaboration, Global Campus, Middlesex University and Thomson Learning have produced materials to suit a diverse and innovating discipline and student cohort.

Global Campus at the School of Computing Science, Middlesex University, combines local support and tutors with CD Rom-based materials and the Internet to enable students and lecturers to work together across the world.

Middlesex University Press is a publishing house committed to providing high-quality, innovative, learning solutions to organisations and individuals. The Press aims to provide leading-edge 'blended learning' solutions to meet the needs of its clients and customers. Partnership working is a major feature of the Press's activities.

Together with Middlesex University Press and Middlesex University's Centre for Learning Development, Global Campus developed FastTrack books using a sound and consistent pedagogic approach. The SCATE pedagogy is a learning framework that builds up as follows:

- **Scope:** Context and the learning outcomes
- **Content:** The bulk of the course: text, illustrations and examples
- **Activity:** Elements which will help students further understand the facts and concepts presented to them in the previous section. Promotes their active participation in their learning and in creating their understanding of the unit content
- **Thinking:** These elements give students the opportunity to reflect and share with their peers their experience of studying each unit. There are *review questions* so that the students can assess their own understanding and progress
- **Extra:** Further online study material and hyperlinks which may be supplemental, remedial or advanced.

Database Management Systems

This book introduces you to the major concepts and issues in the field of database systems. You will learn how to model databases using a number of techniques and approaches. You will also learn how to write SQL code to query data in a database and to write some more sophisticated coding using Oracle's PLSQL. In addition, you will be made aware of certain issues and trends connected with database software.

The book covers the areas of:

- Relational, object-oriented and object-relational models
- Entity relationship modelling and normalisation
- The standard query language SQL
- Oracle's procedural language, PL/SQL
- Query optimisation
- Transaction management and concurrent access
- Database recovery
- Web database connection
- Data warehousing systems.

Using this book

There are several devices which will help you in your studies and use of this book. **Activities** usually require you to try out aspects of the material which have just been explained, or invite you to consider something which is about to be discussed. In some cases, a response is provided as part of the text that follows – so it is important to work on the activity before you proceed! Usually, however, a formal answer will be provided in the final section of each chapter.

The **time bar** indicates *approximately* how long each activity will take:

 short < 10 minutes

medium 10-45 minutes

long > 45 minutes

  Review questions are (usually) short questions at the end of each chapter to check you have remembered the main points of a chapter. They are a useful practical summary of the content, and can be used as a form of revision aid to ensure that you remain competent in each of the areas covered.

Where computer code is encountered, it is displayed in a different typeface and, where practical, is also provided online (see *About the Website*) – so you are not required to key in very long pieces of code. Do note, however, that the act of keying code is a useful discipline, and your keying errors are a valuable lesson in their own right. If your code does not run, do check the obvious – there is often little visual difference between l,1, I (small 'L', figure one, capital letter 'I' or between 0 and O.

About the author

Patricia Ward

Patricia Ward is a Senior Lecturer in the School of Computing Science at Middlesex University. She completed her undergraduate studies at the University of Edinburgh and earned an MSc in Computing at the University of North London. She has worked in UK universities for more than twenty-five years, initially as a Research Fellow and then as a Lecturer. Her research interests include database design and programming, object databases and the linking of databases to the Internet.

Dr George Dafoulas

Dr George Dafoulas is the curriculum leader in pedagogy for Middlesex University's Global Campus. He is a Senior Lecturer in Business Information Systems for the School of Computing Science at Middlesex and Honorary Visiting Professor at the School of Informatics, University of Manchester. He is the sole organiser of the 'e-Learning Online Communities' international workshop series, a member of the editorial and review board of five international journals and of several organising and programme committees of international conferences. He is the founder and co-director of the Magnum Opus Knowledge Transfer Partnership specialising in e-services for the education sector.

Acknowledgements

The author and publishers would like to acknowledge the contribution made by Dr Wendy Wu in respect of chapter 12.

Visit the accompanying website at **www.thomsonlearning.co.uk/fasttrack** and click through to the appropriate booksite to find further teaching and learning material including:

For students

- Activities
- Multiple choice questions for each chapter
- Source code
- Tools & resources.

For lecturers

- Downloadable PowerPoint slides
- Questions (exam style) with outline answers and grading guidelines
- Discussion topics.

CHAPTER 1

Introduction

OVERVIEW

In this chapter, students are introduced to the basic concepts of database systems. Students are provided with a background of such systems for more detailed discussion in subsequent chapters, and, to this end, we start with a brief **history of database systems**. The next topic concerns the software that manages and controls access to the database, namely the database management systems (DBMSs). We look at how the DBMS interacts with both the operating system and the database itself and examine the functions that a typical DBMS will provide. Some of these functions will be explored in detail in subsequent chapters.

The objective of the next part of the chapter is to introduce students to the process of developing a **conceptual model** of the real world which is of interest and relevant to an application. A top-down approach to designing databases is examined, i.e. **entity-relationship data modelling**.

There are a number of database systems approaches. One approach, the **relational model** underpins most of the major database systems in commercial use today and most of the remaining chapters in this book place a strong emphasis on the relational approach. Relational databases, as the most popular approach, have certain advantages. However, they also have shortcomings, particularly in relation to what is generally termed 'advanced database systems' – described in a later chapter. This chapter looks at these advantages and disadvantages.

| Learning outcomes | On completion of this chapter, you should be able to: |

- Understand the structure of a typical DBMS and the key functions that a DBMS must support

- Describe the structure of the relational model and explain basic concepts of the relational model, including relation, attribute, null value, primary key and foreign key

- Identify the elements in a specific application area that need to be included in the design of a database solution. This includes the entities, the relationships between them, and the data items contained in those entities

- Understand the advantages and weaknesses of relational database management systems.

1.1 A brief history of database systems

Database systems developed because of the need to store large amounts of data and retrieve that data quickly and accurately. For example, a university library stores details about the books held and loans taken out by students. Not very long ago this information about the books and loans might have been stored in a box card index. Nowadays, only a few decades later, students are able to view their loans online and see if any books are overdue. They can check to see if a book is available and reserve it. The library staff can quickly access statistics on overdue books, popular books and books which never leave the shelves.

Another example is a company that accepts customer orders – for instance, orders for spare parts for electrical goods. Originally orders might have been created when a customer telephoned the company to place the order. If information about the customer already existed in a **paper file** then his/her details would be retrieved; otherwise, customer details would be requested and recorded. An order form would have been filled in and copied: one copy being stored in a filing cabinet; the other sent to the warehouse. To complete the order, information on stock held would need to be accessed.

Eventually, the order entry system was computerised so that by the 1960's the data about customers and orders might have been stored in a computer file – a magnetic tape file and then later magnetic disk. These files were processed by computer programs. Other applications programs were used which could create invoices, orders to suppliers and so on. Although different applications software would at times require similar data, the data would be kept on different files. In both types of system, the paper one and the **file system**, processing was slow and problems of inconsistencies of data could easily develop. The introduction of **shared files**, whereby different applications shared some of the same files, solved some of the problems described earlier, and was good for providing routine data. For example, a customer order application and an invoicing application might use both the customer and stock files, and in addition their own files. As only one copy of each file was made available, the inconsistencies were avoided. However, this method was not efficient, as a shared file would only be available to one application at a time. Shared file systems were also not effective in providing data for planning and control of an organisation.

In the 1960s, **database systems** began to emerge, with the release of the IBM product IMS, a system where the user viewed the data as a **hierarchical** tree. In the late sixties, database systems based on a different data model were developed. This time the user view of the data was a network of data records. In both cases (hierarchical and network) skilled programmers were required and users tended to be large organisations. The database approach was an improvement on the shared file solution as the software which was used (the **databases management system**) to control the data (the **database**) was quite powerful. The software consisted (and still consists) of a number of components which provided facilities for querying data, data security and integrity and the ability to access the data simultaneously by different users. Another characteristic of database systems is that the underlying structure of the data is isolated from the actual data itself. The specification of the entire database is called a **schema**. There are various levels of schema – the conceptual schema or model is discussed below. If there is a requirement to change the structure of the data (for example to add a new attribute), the change will be made at the schema level. Such changes are independent of both the physical storage level and the level seen by individual users.

Returning to our brief history, by the 1970s the study of database systems had become a major academic and research area. The **relational model** was first proposed in 1970 by Ted Codd with his series of pioneering papers. The theory underpinning relational databases is derived from the mathematical principles of set theory and predicate logic. The model is based on the familiar concepts of tables, rows and columns and the manipulation of these tables is achieved through a collection of simple and well-understood set theory operators. The query language **SQL**, based on relational algebra, was developed and has become the most important query language for relational databases. The first commercial relational product was Oracle's DBMS and was released in 1980. The relational model has been successfully adopted for transaction processing in numerous organisations and supports most of the major database systems in commercial use today. Its ability to handle efficiently simple data types, its powerful query language, and its good protection of data from programming errors make it an effective model. Most of the remaining chapters in this book place a strong emphasis on the relational approach.

Relational databases, although widely adopted, do have a number of weaknesses which led, in the 1990s, to attention shifting to object-oriented databases. We shall see that these databases became successful with applications which required more complex data structures than simple tables. Examples of such applications include computer-aided design and manufacturing. Some of these ideas were adopted by vendors of relational database systems (e.g. Oracle Corporation). New features were integrated into their products and these became known as **object-relational** databases.

In the mid 1990s the first databases which could be accessed over the **World Wide Web** began to appear. In the late 1990s vendors began to integrate **XML** into their products. Nowadays, the growth of databases supporting websites continues exponentially.

1.2 The database management system

Many of the topics in this module look in detail at particular functions of the database management system (DBMS) so a description of this piece of software is a good starting point. In this section we will look at the structure of a typical DBMS and the key functions that a DBMS must support. A simple definition is given:

> A DBMS is a collection of programs that allow users to specify the structure of a database, to create, query and modify the data in the database and to control access to it.

The DBMS and the operating system

In fact, the DBMS needs to interact with both the operating system and the database. The elements of the operating system that are critical are shown overleaf.

Figure 1.1: The DBMS and the operating system

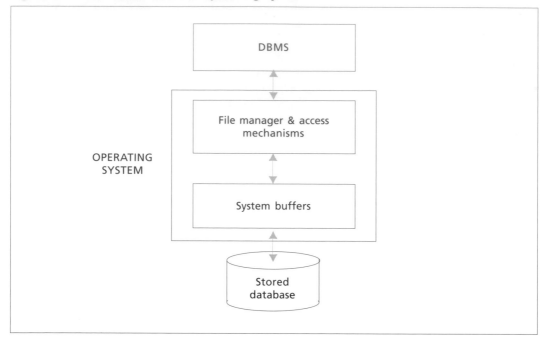

Access to the database is controlled by the host operating system. The DBMS accepts requests for data from the application program and then informs the operating system to transfer the appropriate data. This is done via the file manager which keeps track of the location of the underlying database files on secondary storage (disk). The system buffers (in particular, database buffers) are temporary locations for storing and manipulating data. Reading and writing of data is performed via these buffers. Memory is organised in pages and these pages are read from secondary storage (disk) into the buffer in main memory and then written back to disk.

Functions of a DBMS

Originally, database management systems were large and expensive and were run on large computers. Nowadays, they appear as a common tool for even small machines. Despite this, modern DBMSs are complex pieces of software and although the architecture will vary, there are a number of functions that a typical DBMS will support. These include:

- A **data definition language** (DDL) to define a database. The DBMS must allow users to create database definitions

- A **data manipulation language** (DML) to insert, update, delete and query data in the database

- **Concurrency control** – this allows shared access to the database, with multiple transactions being executed at the same time and scheduled in a safe manner (this will be looked at in detail in subsequent chapters)

- **Buffer management** – this function is responsible for transferring data to and from main memory and secondary storage

- **Query processing and optimisation** – query processing converts queries (typically written in SQL) into a low-level language, which are then optimised by the database manager. Query optimisation determines the optimum strategy for a query execution (this will be looked at in detail in subsequent chapters)

- **Recovery** – the DBMS must take steps to ensure that if the database fails, it remains in a consistent state (this will be looked at in detail in subsequent chapters)
- **Security control** – the DBMS should prevent unauthorised access to the database
- **Data integrity** – the DBMS must include the facility for enforcing integrity constraints whenever a change is made to the database to ensure the database is consistent and correct
- **Data dictionary** – a DBMS includes a repository for storing meta-data. Meta-data is data about the data held and includes the structure of the data items, information about the relationships between the data items, integrity constraints and authorisation privileges.

1.3 The conceptual model

The first step in the development of a database application usually involves determining the major elements of data to be stored. These are referred to as **entities**. Returning to the university library system above, a database for such an application will typically contain entities such as 'students', 'books', 'loans' and 'reservations'. Each of the entities identified will contain a number of properties, or **attributes**. For example, the entity 'book' will contain attributes such as *title*, *author* and *ISBN*; the entity 'student' will possess attributes such as *name*, *address* and *student number*. When we have decided which entities are to be stored in a database, we need to consider how they are related to one another. Examples of such **relationships** for the library system might be that a borrower can borrow a number of books, and that a librarian can make a number of book purchases.

The correct identification of the entities and attributes to be stored, and the relationships between them, is an extremely important topic in database design and is often referred to as **data modelling**. Data modelling is just one process in the development of a database application. After the data and process requirement have been investigated, the information gathered from this initial stage is transformed into a formal model known as the **conceptual model**. This model is derived from a perceived reality – it is an **abstraction** of a complex view which will try to meet the requirements which have earlier been identified. It is a model which is independent of the target database management system software and hides details of how the data will be stored and accessed within a computer.

A number of different methods have been developed to arrive at the conceptual data model. In this chapter we will look at a method which starts with identifying the entities and then the attribute and relationships between the entities. This top-down method is known as **entity-relationship modelling**. Another method, a bottom-up one known as **normalisation** (examined in chapter 2), starts with the identification of the attributes of interest and builds entities using various techniques. This is a formal method, consisting of a number of stages, arriving at data in various states or 'normal forms'. With each stage of normalisation, undesirable properties of the data are eliminated. Normalisation is therefore used to improve the quality of the database design and may be carried out after or in tandem with the top-down method.

The modelling methods described above map easily to relational databases, where data is viewed as a set of relations or tables. Other models discussed in this book map more easily to object- and object-relational databases which we discuss later in this book in chapter 6. In that chapter we will show how entity-relationship modelling can be adapted for object-oriented database design.

1.4 Database design – data modelling

What is data modelling?

Data modelling is concerned with the design of the data content and structure of the database. Process modelling is concerned with the design of the data processing and software applications. The two activities are closely related.

Data modelling gives us a formal model of an organisation which is achieved through the consolidation of the user requirements specification. The information gathered from fact-finding is appraised and the basic data and data relationships are established. The result of the data analysis is a representation of the user's view of the data. It is independent of any DBMS software or hardware considerations.

The model documents the structure of and interrelationships between the data. It is presented as a combination of simple diagrams and written definitions.

Data modelling as part of the development process

The main tasks facing the database designer, at the analysis and design stage of the database system life cycle, are:

Figure 1.2: Database designer tasks

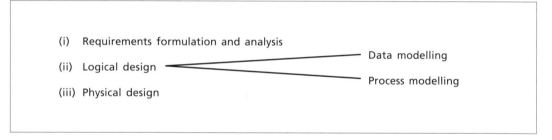

Logical design consists of two parallel activities, **data modelling** and **process modelling**. This book is concerned with data modelling, which incorporates a set of techniques which can be used at a number of different points in the development process. Some systems analysis and design methodologies place little emphasis on this technique, such as Demarco/Yourdon variants. Others balance data analysis with process analysis, for example SSADM. For others, such as in Information Engineering, it is the most dominant of the approaches used.

Data modelling concepts

Entity and attributes

An **entity** is anything relevant to the organisation about which information could be, or is, kept. It can be defined as a group of logically associated data items identified by a unique key. 'Entity type' is used to describe all the entities relevant to the organisation which fit a given definition.

Figure 1.3: Entity examples

Entity type	Entity occurrence
Person	David Beckham, Miss Dynamite
Building	Buckingham Palace, Mansion House
Car	X123 LSO, S234 TJH

Identifying entities

This can be a difficult task. The analyst must gain a thorough understanding of the system environment. The entities could come to light, for example, from the dataflow diagrams produced during systems investigation. Another method is to find the things in the environment which need to be individually identified and referred to. Notional keys can be used to identify a range of other data – for example, a customer number identifies customer name and address, class, credit limit etc, which leads us to identify the CUSTOMER entity. Examples of notional keys could include:

- Customer number
- Product code
- Job number
- Account number.

Figure 1.4, concerned with **attributes**, is a property or characteristic of an entity about which there is a need to record data; it is the named column of a relation. The **attribute type** is the collection of all values of a defined property associated with a given entity type.

Figure 1.4: Attribute examples

Entity type	Attribute type	Attribute occurrence
Person	name D.O.B. sex	John Smith 28.07.60 male
Building	address annual rent	6 High Road £90 per sq. metre

Note: there is no absolute distinction between entity type and attribute type – an attribute type in one context can be an entity type in another.   For example, to a car manufacturer, COLOUR is an attribute of the entity type CAR; to a paint manufacturer, COLOUR may well be an entity type.

Null values

A special value called the **null value** may be created when there is no value for an attribute. Null can be used for one of two reasons: either an entry is not applicable or it is not known.

- An example of 'not applicable' would be the attribute Flat_Number of an Address: this applies only to those people who live in flats; the Flat_Number attribute would be null for those people who live in houses

- An example of 'not known' would be the Height attribute of a Person being recorded as null if the height is unknown.

When a table is implemented (using SQL), nulls are treated in a special way – as nulls rather than 'spaces' or zero. They are either displayed empty, or, if part of a calculated column, the whole record is excluded from the query, since it is not possible to determine the result of a calculation with null.

Relationships

A relationship is an association between entities that is operationally significant to the organisation.

Figure 1.5: Relationship examples

Entity	Relationship	Entity	
At Middlesex University	STUDENTS SCHOOLS	take have	COURSES STAFF
At Ford Motor Corporation	ASSEMBLIES STAFF	have work on	PARTS CONTRACTS

The entity-relationship (E-R) diagram

Entities and relationships can be used to produce a pictorial representation of what an organisation is interested in. This picture is called an entity-relationship diagram. Figure 1.6 shows an entity-relationship diagram for the following scenario:

A University Library keeps information on books held, students who borrow these books and the loans which the students make. In addition, information is held about the authors and publishers of these books. A database designer has established the entities and attributes needed to carry out typical library functions and has produced the following entity-relationship diagram.

Figure 1.6: Example of an entity-relationship diagram

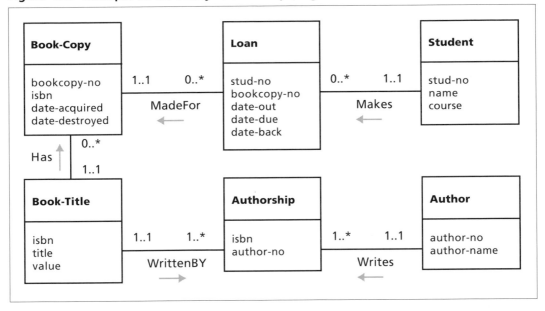

Note that the Book-Copy table holds information on the physical books stored in the library whereas the Book-Title table holds information on a particular publication of a book. For example, there are two copies of *Pride and Prejudice*, with bookcopy-no of 101 and 102. A book may have a number of authors and this is indicated in the authorship table. Also, a book which is still out on loan will have a blank date-back field in the loan table. As copies of books become old, damaged and dirty, the books are removed from the library and destroyed. Destroyed book copies have a date to indicate this, otherwise the date is null.

- Note that, traditionally, entity names are in the singular form
- Rectangles are used to denote **entity types** (named normally as a noun) and lines represent **relationship types**
- The lines are labelled with the names of the relationship (normally as a verb)
- The arrow symbol indicates the correct direction for the name of the relationship to make sense. For example, a *student* makes many *loan records*. This **unified modelling language** (UML) notation will be used for all entity-relationship diagrams throughout this text.

The diagram also shows the maximum and minimum times that an entity occurrence can exist in a relationship. For example, a student can borrow zero or more books. This is called an optional relationship: occurrences of an entity (student) can exist independently of the loan entity. Otherwise, the relationship is mandatory: every occurrence of an entity participates in the relationship. In the book-title/authorship relationship, a title cannot exist without at least one author. The notation used will be explained more fully in the next section. An E-R diagram is drawn because:

- By analysing the entities and relationships of an organisation, many hundreds of entities may be identified. The data model provides a concise summary of the results of the analysis
- The E-R diagram will be used as the basis of database design. The structure of the model will be mapped onto the logical structure of the database.

The cardinality of a relationship

There are several relationship types:

- One-to-one relationships
- One-to-many relationships
- Many-to-many relationships
- Recursive (or involute) relationships.

One-to-one relationship

Here, an occurrence of the first entity type is related to a maximum of one occurrence of the second entity type, and each occurrence of the second type to a maximum of one of the first.

Figure 1.7: One-to-one relationship example

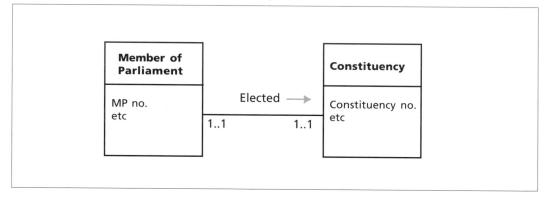

It helps the understanding of E-R diagrams, when stating the relationships between the two entities, to 'read' the diagrams thus:

Examine the relationships firstly from left to right and then from right to left. To describe the relationship, use two sentences, each sentence starting with the word 'one'. In figure 1.7:

> **One** member of parliament is elected to one constituency; **one** constituency has one MP elected to it.

One-to-many relationship

Here an occurrence of the first entity type may be related to several occurrences of the second, but each occurrence of the second is related to a maximum of one occurrence of the first.

Figure 1.8: One-to-many relationship example

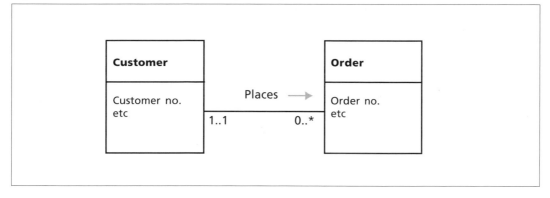

So, in figure 1.8, stated as the two sentences starting with the word 'one':

> **One** customer places zero or more orders; **one** order is placed by one customer.

Many-to-many relationship

Here an occurrence of the first entity type may be related to several occurrences of the second and vice versa.

Figure 1.9: Many-to-many relationship example

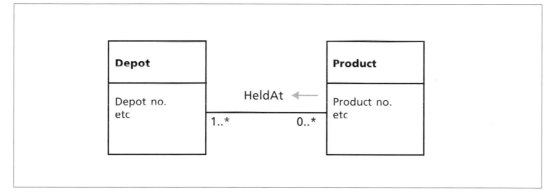

So again, stated as the two sentences starting with the word 'one':

> **One** depot holds zero or more products; **one** product is held at 1 or more depots.

Recursive (or involute) relationship

Here entity occurrences relate to other occurrences of the same entity.

Figure 1.10: Recursive relationship example

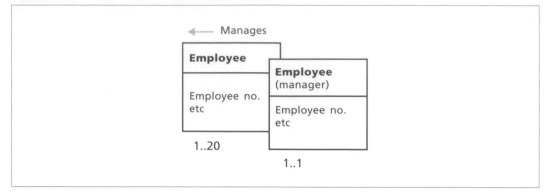

In this example:

> *One* employee (a manager) manages one to twenty employees; *one* employee is managed by one employee (manager).

Decomposition

All many-to-many relationships, can be decomposed into two one-to-many relationships. One reason for doing this is that relational DBMSs do not support many-to-many relationships directly. Also, by eliminating many-to-many relationships, problems in the model become easier to spot.

Figure 1.11: Many-to-many relationship example

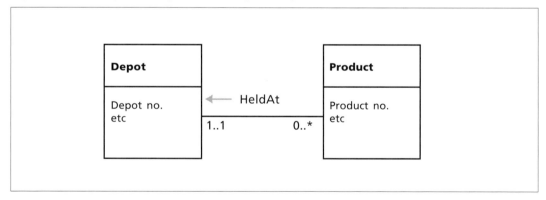

Figure 1.12: Decomposition example

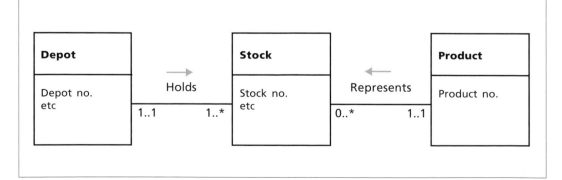

Key attributes

It may be necessary to specify one or more of the attributes of an entity as a 'key' of the entity. This is particularly true of the relational model. Three types of keys are defined here:

- A **candidate key** is a unique identifier for the entity – there may be more than one candidate key (for example, customer-no, customer address)
- A **primary key (Pk)** is also a unique identifier for the entity – that is, an attribute (or combination of attributes) with the property that, at any given time, no two entity occurrences contain the same values for that attribute (or combination of attributes). One candidate key is chosen as the primary key. (Between the two candidate keys mentioned above it is likely that customer-no would be chosen as the primary key as this is more likely to be unique.)
- A **foreign key (Fk)** is an attribute in a relation which is also the primary key in another relation.

Example

An entity **product** may be described by its name and its associated attributes:

Product-no is the primary key. We now introduce two other entities, **depot** and **stock**:

Figure 1.13: E-R diagram for products and depots

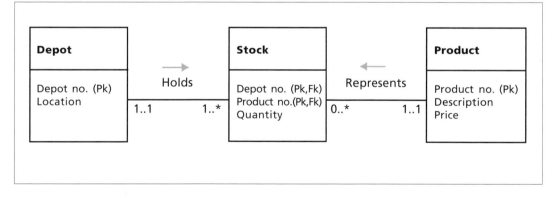

In the relational model these 'foreign keys' link the entities together. In our example the foreign keys are also part of the primary key. This is because the **stock** entity was created after decomposition and the primary key of this entity is created by the concatenation of the primary keys of the other two entities. If we introduce the entity **salesrep** (sales representative) to our model, we now have:

Figure 1.14: E-R diagram for products, depots and sales rep

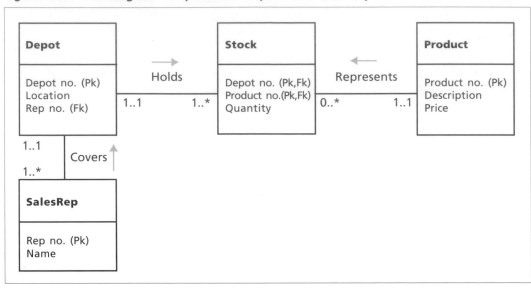

Note that the 'salesrep' entity is linked to the 'depot' entity via the primary key *Rep_no* in 'salesrep' and foreign key *Rep_no* in 'depot'.

Producing the data model: the top-down approach

The main phases involved in producing the data model are:

- Define the entities
- Define the relationships
- Establish the key attributes for each entity
- Identify the initial structure of the data model
- Complete each entity with all its attributes
- Validate the model by checking that the model can support the processing requirements. At the same time, functional requirements of the system are established using another technique called process modelling (e.g. using data flow diagrams)
- Refine the model as necessary. The technique is an iterative one: initial discussion with the user will yield a list of possible entities and an initial E-R diagram can be drawn; this is used as a basis for further discussion with the user. Successive versions of the model will be more detailed, until all concerned are satisfied with the model.

The technique described above is a **top-down approach** to data modelling and is known as entity-relationship modelling. Here we start off by selecting the entities and work down to the attributes. Another approach, the bottom-up procedure, is discussed in chapter 2.

1.5 The relational data model

The origins

The relational model was developed by EF Codd in the early 1970s. Commercial systems based on the relational model appeared in the late 1970s. At present there are several hundred relational DBMSs and most computer vendors support 'relational' software. Examples of well-known products include Oracle, DB2, Sybase, MySQL, MS.SQL Server and MS Access.

Some terminology

The model uses terminology taken from mathematics, particularly set theory and predicate logic. With relational databases, users perceive the data to be stored as tables or relations. In other types of database systems, the conceptual view of the data is different – for example, the conceptual view of the data might be a hierarchical structure (hierarchical and object-oriented databases) or a network structure (network databases). Basic terminology used in relational theory includes:

- A **relation** – this corresponds to a table or flat file with columns and rows
- A **tuple** – a row of a relation
- An **attribute** – a named column of a relation
- A **domain** – the set of allowable values for one or more attributes
- The **degree of a relation** – the number of attributes it contains
- The **cardinality of relation** – the number of tuples it contains.

Figure 1.15: Sample relation – FILM

attributes

FilmNo	Title	Director	Country	Year	Genre
005	Reservoir Dogs	Tarantino	US	1992	Crime
006	Pulp Fiction	Tarantino	US	1994	Crime
008	Trainspotting	Boyle	UK	1996	
009	Titanic	Cameron	US	1997	Disaster
107	Dirty Pretty Things	Frears	UK	2002	Crime

relation

tuple

In figure 1.15, the **degree** is 6 and the **cardinality** is 5. The **domain** for 'year' might be the range of years when films have been made; the **domain** for 'title' might be 'character', size 30. Very often it is required to be able to identify uniquely each of the different instances of relations in a database. In order to do this we use something called a 'primary key'.

Properties of relations

- Relation names and attribute names are distinct
- Cell values of a relation are atomic (i.e. single valued)
- Attribute values in a column are taken from the same domain
- Duplicate tuples are not allowed
- Both tuples and attributes are unordered.

Relational languages

Many high-level data manipulation languages are based on either relational algebra or relational calculus (or on both, as in the case of SQL). They are theoretical languages – formal and non-user-friendly and are both defined by EF Codd. They illustrate the basic operations required by any data manipulation language such as SQL.

Relational algebra operators

Each operator takes one or more relations as its input and produces a new relation as output. Codd originally defined eight operators, in two classes:

Set operators: UNION   INTERSECTION
                                        DIFFERENCE   DIVIDE

The special relational operators: RESTRICT   PROJECT
                                        JOIN   Cartesian PRODUCT

We shall now look at the meaning of each of these terms.

RESTRICT (originally called SELECT)

This extracts tuples which satisfy a given condition from a single relation.

Figure 1.16: Restrict

No.	Title	Director	Country	Year	Genre
005	Reservoir Dogs	Tarantino	US	1992	Crime
006	Pulp Fiction	Tarantino	US	1994	Crime
008	Trainspotting	Boyle	UK	1996	
009	Titanic	Cameron	US	1997	Disaster
107	Dirty Pretty Things	Frears	UK	2002	Crime

For example, in the relation above, the condition would be 'all films directed by Tarantino'.

PROJECT

This extracts specified attributes from a specified relation.

Figure 1.17: PROJECT

No.	Title	Director	Country	Year	Genre
005	Reservoir Dogs	Tarantino	US	1992	Crime
006	Pulp Fiction	Tarantino	US	1994	Crime
008	Trainspotting	Boyle	UK	1996	
009	Titanic	Cameron	US	1997	Disaster
07	Dirty Pretty Things	Frears	UK	2002	Crime

For example, in figure 1.17, 'title' and 'year'.

JOIN

Various forms exist, such as *natural*, *theta-join*, *outer*.

Natural join: If two relations each have an attribute with a common domain, they can be joined over that domain.

Figure 1.18: Example of a JOIN

Film

Film no.	Title	Director-no	Year
005	Reservoir Dogs	*001*	1992
006	Pulp Fiction	*001*	1994
008	Trainspotting	*008*	1996

Director

Director-no	Name	
001	Tarantino	
004	Spielberg	
008	Boyle	

Film no.	Title	Director-no	Year	Director-no	Name
005	Reservoir Dogs	*001*	1992	*001*	Tarantino
006	Pulp Fiction	*001*	1994	*001*	Tarantino
008	Trainspotting	*008*	1996	*008*	Boyle

The result of a JOIN is a new wider relation: each row is formed by joining two rows in the original tables such that they have the same values in the common domain. It should be noted that a row of a relation is also referred to as a tuple. In figure 1.18, the 'film' and 'director' relations are joined to produce a new relation. Other types of joins will be examined later.

UNION

This builds a relation consisting of all tuples appearing in either or both of two specified relations. The two relations must be union-compatible, which means that they must have the same number of attributes and these attributes must come from the same domain.

Figure 1.19: UNION

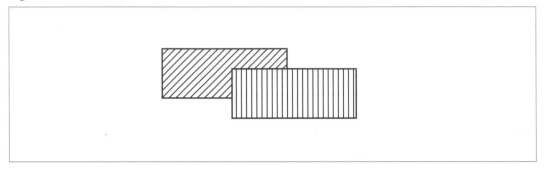

For example, if we had two film relations, one for films made in Canada, the other English-language films, then the union of the two relations is all films made in Canada or English-language films or both.

INTERSECTION

This builds a relation consisting of all tuples appearing in both of two specified relations. The two relations must be union-compatible.

Figure 1.20: INTERSECTION

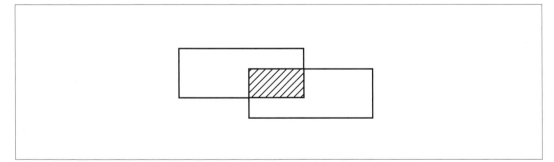

For example, if we had two film relations, one for films made in Canada, the other English-language films, then the intersection of the two relations is: 'all films made in Canada and are (at the same time) also English-language films'.

DIFFERENCE

This builds a relation consisting of all tuples appearing in the first but not the second of two specified relations. The two relations must be union-compatible.

Figure 1.21: DIFFERENCE

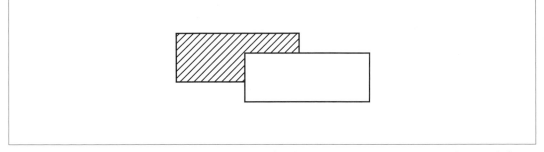

For example, if we had two film relations, one for films made in Canada, the other English-language films, then the difference of the two relations is: 'all films made in Canada but are not English-language'.

PRODUCT

This builds a relation from two relations, consisting of all possible pairs of tuples from the two relations.

Figure 1.22 PRODUCT

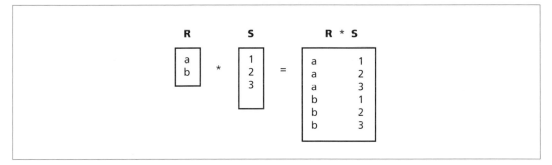

DIVIDE

This takes two relations, one **binary** and one **unary**. It builds a relation consisting of all values of one attribute of the binary relation that match (in the other attribute) all values in the unary relation.

Figure 1.23: Examples of DIVIDE

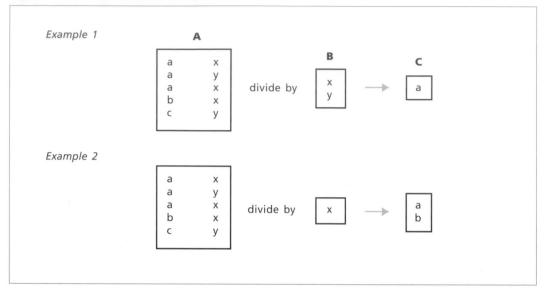

We will look at examples of relational algebra divide in chapter 4, when we study 'Further SQL'.

What is relational algebra used for?

Relational algebra is a collection of operations on relations. There are a number of syntaxes for these operations. In chapter 6 on 'query processing and optimisation', we will look at one particular syntax. Relational algebra is studied for the following reasons:

- Relational algebra is used as the basis for other, higher-level, data manipulation languages including SQL
- The algebra serves as a convenient basis for optimisation. An optimiser is an important component of the database management system. When implementing a query, there is usually more than one way of performing the data access. It is up to the optimiser to decide which strategy to adopt
- The algebra is also used as a measure to compare high-level relational languages such as SQL, and to test if the language is relationally complete – for example, to check if the query language is as powerful as the algebra.

1.6 Strengths and weaknesses of relational DBMSs

Relational database systems are by far the most important type of database around today. There has been a widespread acceptance of this model for the traditional business applications, including payroll, order processing and airline reservations systems. There has also been a widespread acceptance for applications which access databases over the Internet. Well-designed relational databases can provide appropriate data storage and retrieval facilities over a long timescale.

Because of the dominance of relational databases, this book is largely concerned with the relational model, although the object-oriented and object-relational models are discussed in chapter 7. In this section we look at a number of advantages of relational database systems over other methods (including file-based systems and other types of DBMSs) and also several weaknesses that are cited by the proponents of object-oriented database systems:

Strengths

- Relational databases support a **simple data structure**, namely tables
- Relational databases **limit redundancy** or duplication of data. As all the data pertaining to a particular object is stored together, and then linked to related objects, there is no need to store data about the original object in more than one place. In practice, not all redundancy is eliminated – as we shall see (in chapter 2), the process of normalisation will lead to some redundancy, although controlled
- **Data inconsistencies are avoided**. By storing the data relating to an object in one place, it only needs to be kept up to date in that one place. This saves time at the data entry stage and reduces the likelihood of inconsistencies arising
- Relational databases provide **physical data independence** (to a large extent). Database users do not have to be aware of the underlying structure of the objects in the database. The specification of the structure (the tables, attributes and relationships), the constraints, the access methods etc are stored separately and are independent of the application programs that use the data. This makes programming and program maintenance easier
- Relational databases offer **logical database independence**, in that data can be viewed in different ways by different users. With relational databases this is achieved with the definition of the appropriate SQL view
- Expandability is relatively easy to achieve – by adding new views of the data as they are required
- Relational databases support ad hoc queries (one-off or tailor-made) using the SQL query language.

Weaknesses

- **Poor representation of 'real world' entities** and their relationships. When relational databases are designed, entities are fragmented into smaller relations through the process of normalisation (chapter 2). This fragmentation into many relations leads to relations which do not exist or correspond to entities in the real world. Such a design is inefficient, as many joins may be required to recover data about that entity.

  The model is said to suffer from **semantic overloading** in that one construct (the relation) is used to represent two different things (entities and relationships): there is no mechanism for differentiation between entities and relationships. The normalised component, the relation, is not sufficient to represent both the data and data relationships. With relational databases, an entity is broken up into several relations, thus querying becomes cumbersome since project, select and join operations have to be used frequently to reconstruct the entities.

  Also it is **difficult to represent hierarchies** of data. For example, both students and lectures share some of the same data (name, address etc). In a relational database we would have to define three relations: one for the 'super class' person as well as for student and lecturer, and to retrieve the information may well require a join

- **Difficulty in representing complex data types**. As a simple example, consider an attribute 'address'. In a relational database, either we define an address attribute as one atomic value of type string or it could be defined as a number of attributes (one each for street, city, country and postcode). In the latter case, writing queries would be more complicated, as each field would have to be mentioned. A better solution to either case is to allow structured data types – such as the type address with subparts street, city, country and postcode. Now an instance of type address can either be viewed as a whole or as individual subparts.

The limited data types in the relational model cannot represent 'real word' objects that have a complex structure, and this leads to unnatural joins, which are inefficient. Any item in the tuple, i.e. intersection of a row and column, must be an **atomic data type** since it assumes both horizontal and vertical homogeneity. **Horizontal homogeneity** means that each tuple of a relation must be composed of the same attributes. This can be a disadvantage in that it is not possible to store closely related objects in the same category if they differ slightly in the attributes they possess. For example, there may be adult and child aeroplane tickets, with children having the additional attribute 'guardian'. **Vertical homogeneity** means that the values in a particular column of a relation must all come from the same domain.

Relational databases support a small, **fixed collection of data types** and do not permit users to define new types. In many applications the attributes' domains require far more complex data types. Many relational DBMSs allow the storage of binary large objects (BLOBs) – a data value that contains binary information representing images, digitised videos or audios, or any large and unstructured object. Typically, it is held as an attribute in a relational database which references to a file. Storing the data in external files is not a good way of manipulating this data: the DBMS has no knowledge of the structure of this data and cannot perform queries or operations on it. In addition, BLOBs cannot contain other BLOBs. As an example, a picture can be stored as a BLOB by an RDBMS. The complete picture can be displayed but not part of it, and the internal structure is not known to the RDBMS.

We will see in a chapter 7 that relational database systems are not well suited to support certain complex applications such as 'advanced database applications' including computer-aided design (CAD). A clear illustration of the drawbacks of a homogeneous data structure is the so-called parts explosion. Here, some object (such as an aircraft) is composed of parts and composite parts; these latter items in turn are composed of other parts and composite parts, and so on. Data types exhibiting this arrangement cannot be stored in relational databases

- **Difficulty in implementing recursive queries**. For example in the entity-relationship model example in figure 1.6 an example of a recursive query would be to find books which have the same book title as a book entitled *Gardening for Beginners*. This query involves searching the same table twice. We shall see in chapter 4 that recursive queries can be quite difficult to specify and implement

- SQL is **not computationally complete**: it supports only a limited number of operations and does not allow new operations to be defined.

Because SQL is computationally incomplete and cannot provide all of the operations provided by most programming languages, the SQL standard provides embedded SQL to help develop more complex database applications. However, this leads to the so-called **impedance mismatch** problem because we are mixing different programming paradigms (or models).

SQL is a language handling data relations either in rows or columns. The main difference of such a declarative language from high-level languages of procedural or functional programming is that the latter can handle single data relations each time. In other words, SQL handles more than one row of data at the same time. Furthermore, SQL and high-level programming languages represent data in different ways. Especially when attributes of date and time are concerned, SQL has the corresponding data types that automatically 'translate' the value to a meaningful format. High-level programming languages need to convert integer values to the date and time formats. Such type conversion is responsible for as much as a 30% increase in programming effort and use of resources

- There is **no support for domain-specific organisation constraints** in the relational model. Organisation constraints are additional rules specified by the owners of a database that the database must satisfy. For example, an upper limit of 50 may be allowed for the number of employees working in each department of an organisation. In a relational database system there is no support for such a constraint and thus they have to be programmed into the applications using the database – leading to duplication of effort and inconsistent data.

1.7 Summary

This chapter introduced the student to the history of database systems leading up to relational and object-oriented systems. The structure of a typical database management system was described as the basis for exploration in subsequent chapters. Students were introduced to conceptual data modelling and relational database systems. The basic concepts of the latter were discussed, together with the advantages and shortcomings of the relational approach.

1.8 Review questions

 Review question 1.1 For the E-R diagram below, decompose the many-to-many relationship. State the two new relationships as two sentences, each starting with the word 'one'.

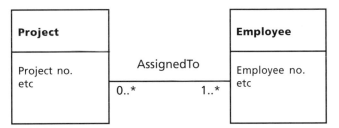

 Review question 1.2 Explain, giving an example, how tables are linked together in the relational model.

Review question 1.3 Middlesex Transport is responsible for running a fleet of buses throughout North London. The buses are housed in one of three depots: Holloway, Hornsey and Islington. Each depot is identified by its depot number; in addition, the depot name and address are recorded.

Each bus is identified by its registration number. Details of the buses' models are also held, for example Routemaster and Spirit of London. The buses run on various routes which are described by their starting and finishing point, for example Camden Town/Hendon. Each route is identified by its route number. Only buses from particular depots will travel on a particular route, so, for example, only buses from the Islington depot will travel on the Camden Town/Hendon route. Buses are classified by various types such as doubledecker, bendy-bus. There are restrictions on some bus types for some of the routes, for example, those with low bridges may exclude doubledecker buses, and bendy-buses may be unable to operate around some corners. For this reason, buses are designated to particular routes.

The bus company employs bus drivers to operate the buses and cleaners who help maintain them. Both the bus drivers and cleaners work at one particular depot. Drivers and cleaners have an employee number, name, and salary. In addition the company holds information on the date that the driver passed his/her PCV (Passenger Carrying Vehicle) driving test.

For cleaning purposes, the depots are organised with cleaners being responsible for a number of buses; each bus has one cleaner who is particularly responsible for that bus. In the case of bus drivers, they can only drive buses where they have completed training for the type of bus, and the date when training is completed is recorded. In addition, bus drivers can only drive buses where they have had practice on particular routes.

Study the case above and then draw an entity-relationship diagram using UML notation, decomposing any many-to-many relationships. Indicate the primary and foreign keys and make any assumptions that you need to make about optional/ mandatory relationships.

 Review question 1.4 Consider a hospital information system with the following characteristics:

- A patient can either be a resident patient who is admitted to the hospital or an out-patient who comes to the hospital for an out-patient clinic

- For both types of patient we will need to hold the patient's name, telephone number, address, date of birth and the patient's family doctor (GP)

- For a resident patient we will need to hold the ward name in which the patient is currently residing, the admission date of the patient, and also information about any operations that the patient has had

- The operation information will have to include the date and time of the operation, the doctor (assume one) who carried out the operation plus the theatre where the operation took place

- For both GPs and hospital doctors we will need to hold the doctor's name and telephone number; in addition we will need to hold the GP's address and the hospital doctor's specialism code (for example, he or she may specialise in ENT, problems relating to ear, nose and throat) – assume one per hospital doctor

- For out-patients we will need to hold information about the outpatients' appointments: the appointment date and time and the hospital doctor who attended to the patient.

Study the case above and then draw an entity-relationship diagram using UML notation, decomposing any many-to-many relationships. Indicate the primary and foreign keys and make any assumptions that you need to make about optional/ mandatory relationships.

1.9 Answers to review questions

Answer to review question 1.1

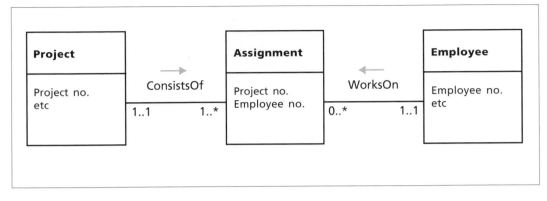

One project consists of **1 or more** assignments;

One assignment relates to **one** project;

One employee works on **zero or more** assignments;

One assignment is worked on by **one** employee.

Answer to review question 1.2 Tables are linked together in the relational model using foreign keys. For example, if we wish to link instances of employees stored in an employee table, with the records of their departments, stored in a department table, we would place the primary key of each department into the record of the employee working in that department (where it will become the foreign key). In that way we can then identify in which department each employee is located. It should be noted that records represent certain data relations that can be in the form of a row or tuple.

Answer to review question 1.3

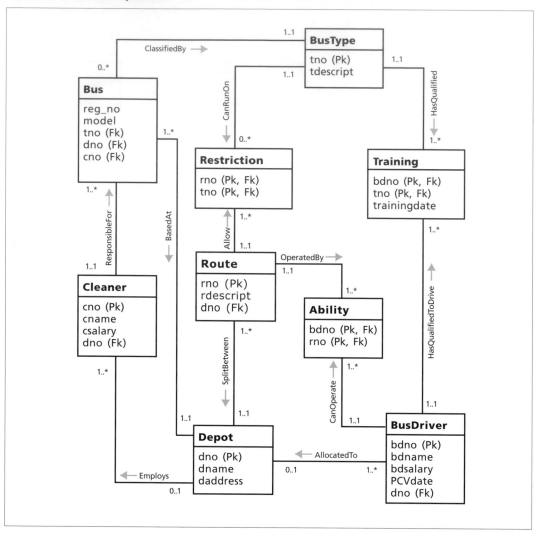

Answer to review question 1.4

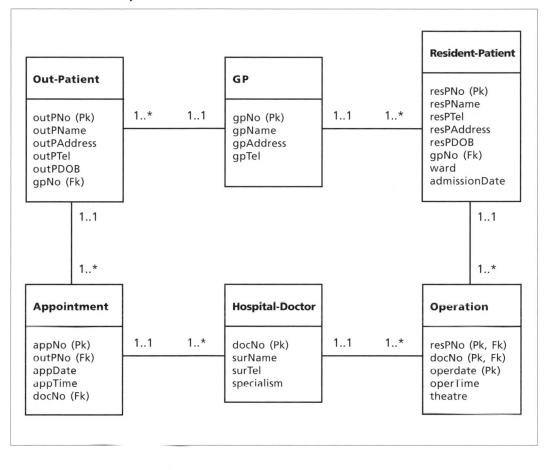

CHAPTER 2

Normalisation

OVERVIEW

Following on from chapter 1 and the discussion of entity-relationship modelling, this chapter focuses on another method of developing a conceptual model, namely **normalisation**. We start by examining a 'bad database design' and the problems or **anomalies** that might exist in such a design. We next introduce the student to an important concept in data design, that of the **functional dependency**. We then show how these anomalies can to a great extent be eliminated with the formal technique of normalisation using a set of rules or guidelines called **normal forms**. In particular, we will examine **first, second and third** normal forms.

Also in this chapter the student is introduced to a case study (the Bus Depots' database) which will be used in a number of chapters in this book.

| **Learning outcomes** | On completion of this chapter, you should be able to: |

- Understand the problems associated with un-normalised data

- Explain and apply the concepts of functional dependency

- Understand of three normal forms for relations (1NF, 2NF and 3NF) and be able to apply these.

2.1 Introduction

We have seen in the previous chapter how relationships between entities can be identified, described and represented in a graphical technique known as **entity-relationship modelling**. This is a top-down method since we use as a starting point the main entities and design a model with its full set of entities, attributes and relationships. We now look at a bottom-up method of database design called **normalisation**.

Normalisation is a formal method for analysing data into its constituent entities and attributes – it starts, this time, with the identification of the attributes of interest and builds the entities from these attributes. It consists of a number of stages, arriving at data in various states or '**normal forms**'. It involves the identification of **functional dependencies**, where we look for attributes that allow the identification of other attributes. With each stage of normalisation, undesirable properties of the data are eliminated. Normalisation is therefore used to improve the quality of the database design and may be carried out after the top-down process to ensure the correctness of the model.

E F Codd originally defined first, second and third normal forms in 1972 in his paper *Further Normalisation of the Data Base Relational Model*. Codd was a British computer scientist who worked for IBM in the 1970's. There are other normal forms including Boyce-Codd, fourth and fifth normal forms, but we shall only consider here Codd's original normal forms.

2.2 The Bus Depots' Database

The examples in this chapter are based on the 'Bus Depots' Database' case which was first introduced in chapter 1, review question 1.3. This case study will also be used in other chapters in this book, particularly the SQL and PLSQL examples in the following chapters. Details of the case and the entity-relationship model are given below.

Middlesex Transport is responsible for running a fleet of buses throughout North London. The buses are housed in one of three depots: Holloway, Hornsey and Islington. Each depot is identified by its depot number; in addition, the depot name and address are recorded.

Each bus is identified by its registration number. Details of the buses' models are also held, for example Routemaster and Spirit of London. The buses run on various routes which are described by their starting and finishing point, for example Camden Town/Hendon. Each route is identified by its route number. Only buses from particular depots will travel on a particular route, so, for example, only buses from the Islington depot will travel on the Camden Town/Hendon route. Buses are classified by various types such as doubledecker and bendy-bus. There are restrictions on some bus types for some of the routes, for example, those with low bridges may exclude doubledecker buses, and bendy-buses may be unable to operate around some corners. For this reason, buses are designated to particular routes.

The bus company employs bus drivers to operate the buses and cleaners who help maintain them. Both the bus drivers and cleaners work at one particular depot. Drivers and cleaners have an employee number, name, and salary. In addition the company holds information on the date that the driver passed his/her PCV (Passenger Carrying Vehicle) driving test.

For cleaning purposes the depots are organised with cleaners being responsible for a number of buses; each bus has one cleaner who is particularly responsible for that bus. In the case of bus drivers, they can only drive buses where they have completed training for that type of bus, and the date when training is completed is recorded. In addition, bus drivers can only drive buses where they have had practice on particular routes.

Figure 2.1: Entity-relationship model

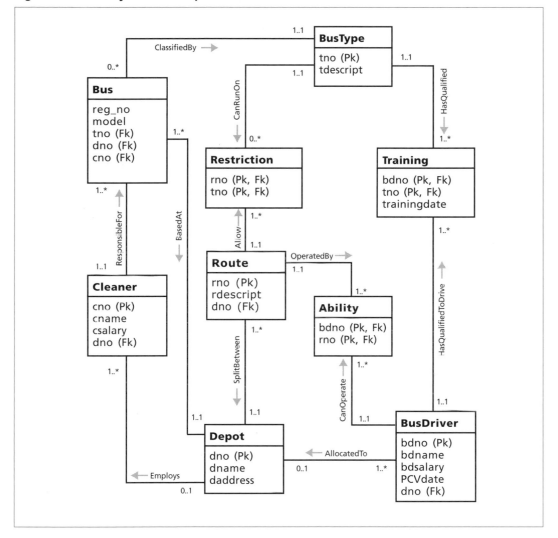

Note that the above model is (arguably) in normalised form and is used as the basis of the SQL and PLSQL practical work. However, for the purposes of illustration, in this chapter on normalisation, some of the examples have been slightly altered from the case study.

2.3 Un-normalised data

Well-normalised databases have a design that reflects the true dependencies between entities, allowing the data to be updated quickly with little risk of introducing inconsistencies. Before discussing how to design a well-normalised database using Codd's normalisation techniques, we first consider a poor database design.

Consider for example a relation 'bus' which includes bus registration number, model, type number, type description, depot name (note that names have changed slightly from the case study for the purposes of this example):

Figure 2.2: Bus relation

registration no	model	type number	type description	depot
A123ABC	Routemaster	1	doubledecker	Holloway
D678FGH	Volvo 8700	2	metrobus	Holloway
H259IJK	Daf SB220	3	midibus	Hornsey
P200IJK	Mercedes 709D	2	metrobus	Hornsey
P300RTY	Mercedes Citaro	4	bendy-bus	Hornsey
R678FDS	Daf SB220	1	doubledecker	
W653TJH	Routemaster	1	doubledecker	

There are several problems with this relation:

- **Redundancy** – the 'type description' is repeated for each 'type number' in the relation. The 'model' is also repeated for a particular 'type description', for example a Routemaster is always a doubledecker bus
- **Update anomalies** – as a consequence of the redundancy, we could update the 'type description' in one tuple, while leaving it fixed in another
- **Deletion anomalies** – if we should delete all the buses of a particular type, we might lose all the information about that type
- **Insertion anomalies** – the inverse to deletion anomalies is we cannot record a new type in our table unless there exists a bus of that type – for example if there is the type 'open top' we cannot store this in our database. To get around this we might put null values in the type number and description components of a tuple for that bus, but when we enter an item for that supplier, will we remember to delete the tuple with nulls?

2.4 Functional dependencies

Determinants

A formal definition for the term **functional dependence** is:

Given a relation which has attributes (x, y, …), we say that an attribute y is functionally dependent on another attribute x, if (and only if) each x value has associated with it precisely one y value (at any one time).

Contrary to first appearances, this is actually a fairly simple concept and easily explained with an example. Examine the cleaner relation in figure 2.3.

Figure 2.3: Cleaner relation

Cleaner no. (cno)	Cleaner name (cname)	Cleaner salary (csalary)	Depot no. (dno)
110	John	2550	101
111	Jean	2500	101
112	Betty	2400	102
113	Vince	2800	102
114	Jay	3000	102

Here attributes cname, csalary and dno are each functionally dependent on attribute cno – given a particular cno value, there exists precisely one corresponding value for each of the cname, csalary and dno.

In general then, the same x-values may appear in many different tuples of the relation; if y is functionally dependent on x, then every one of these tuples must contain the same y-value.

Going back to the cleaner example, we can represent these functional dependencies diagrammatically as:

Figure 2.4: Cleaner determinacy diagram

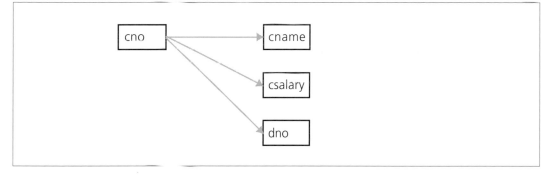

This is an example of a **determinacy diagram**. The arrow line can be read as 'depends on' (reading from left to right). So we say, for example, 'cno depends on cname'. We can also 'read' the diagram from right to left. This time the arrowed line is read as 'functionally dependent on'. So we say, for example 'cname is functionally dependent on cno'.

The attribute or group of attributes on the left-hand side are called the **determinant**. When the value of one attribute allows us to identify the value of another attribute in the same relation, this first attribute is called a determinant. The determinant of a value is not necessarily the primary key. In the example, cno is a determinant of cname because knowing the cleaner's number we can determine the cleaner's name.

Recognising the functional dependencies is an essential part of understanding the meaning or semantics of the data. The fact that cname, csalary and dno are functionally dependent on cno means that each cleaner has one name, has one salary and works at precisely one depot.

Composite attributes

The notion of functional dependence can be extended to cover the case where the determinant (particularly the primary key) is composite, i.e. it consists of more that one attribute. For example, consider the training relation which relates to bus drivers and the types of buses that each driver is trained to drive.

Figure 2.5: Training relation

Driver no. (bdno)	Type no. (tno)	Training date (trainingdate)
001	1	09-jan-2006
001	2	09-jan-2006
006	2	09-feb-2006
007	1	09-feb-2006
••	••	••

Remember that 'bdno' and 'tno' are the bus driver's number and type no (of bus he/she is trained to drive). Here the attribute training date is functionally dependent on the composite attribute (bdno, tno): given a particular combination of bdno and tno values, there exists precisely one corresponding 'trainingdate' value. This functional dependency can be represented diagrammatically as:

Figure 2.6: Function dependency with composite determinant

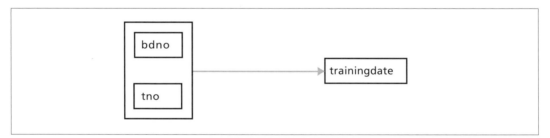

Full functional dependence

We say that attribute y is fully functionally dependent on attribute x if it is functionally dependent on x and not functionally dependent on any subset of the attributes of x where it is a composite attribute.

For example, in the training relation above, training date is functionally dependent on the composite attribute (bdno, tno) but it is not functionally dependent on the bdno or tno alone. A bus driver number can have more than one training dates; a type number can also have a number of training dates. In this case, therefore, training date is fully functionally dependent.

Partial dependencies

The opposite of full functional dependence is partial dependence. Where we have data values that depend on only a part of the primary key, then we have a partial dependency.

So, for example, we might include type descriptions (doubledecker, bendy-bus etc) as a column in the training relation above. Type description is functionally dependent on the partial key tno (type number). The attribute type description is therefore not **fully** functionally dependent on the primary key as illustrated in figure 2.7. Where we have such attributes, we must put them in separate relations.

Figure 2.7: Partial function dependency

Transitive dependencies

We now examine another type of dependency known as transitive dependency.

This occurs when the value of an attribute is not determined directly from the primary key, but through the value of another attribute and this attribute in turn is determined by the primary key.

Consider a relation with attributes a, b and c and where a is the primary key.

If   a determines b and

      b determines c then

      a must determine c – i.e. a transitive dependency.

In this situation, to avoid a transitive dependency, c is removed from the relation, leaving behind a and b and a new relation is created with attributes b and c. This further reduces redundancy.

To illustrate transitive dependencies we will add two further columns to the original training relation concerning the people who trained the bus drivers, i.e. trainer number and trainer name.

Figure 2.8: Extended training relation

Driver no. (bdno)	Type no. (tno)	Training date (trainingdate)	Trainer no.	Trainer name
001	1	09-jan-2006	A123	Tony
001	2	09-jan-2006	G533	Pat
006	2	09-feb-2006	J972	Nawaz
007	1	09-feb-2006	A123	Tony
••	••	••	••	••

Figure 2.9: Transitive dependency

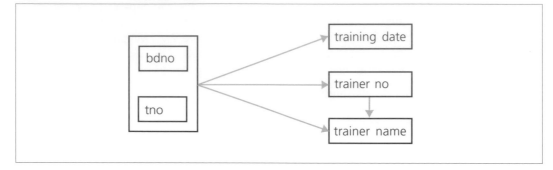

The transitive dependencies are denoted by the vertical arrows in the diagram:

Here the composite key (bdno, tno) depends on training date as before.

Also the composite key depends on trainer no. and trainer name; additionally, we have trainer no. depending on trainer name, which is a transitive dependency.

2.5 Normalisation

The normal forms

Simply put, normalisation is the process of breaking up larger relations into many small ones using a set of rules. The process involves identifying functional dependencies. If there are found to be attributes that are not directly dependent on the primary key, these are extracted to form new relations. The process is carried out until all the data in each relation is clearly and uniquely associated with other data in the same table. This reduces redundancy (although it does not eliminate it) and makes the data easier to maintain.

A number of normal forms have been proposed, but the first five normal forms have been widely accepted. We shall consider here the first three. The normal forms progress from first normal form, to second, and so on. Data in second normal form implies that it is also in first normal form – i.e. each level of normalisation implies that the previous level has been met.

Other normal forms such as Boyce-Codd (BCNF) which is an extension of 3NF, 4NF and 5NF also exist. The following figure shows the correspondence between the various normal forms:

Figure 2.10: Correspondence between the normal forms

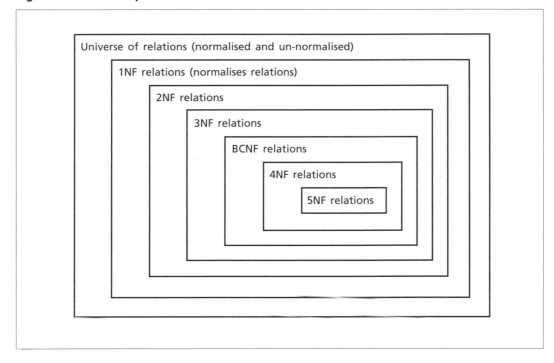

Normal form example

Consider the following example forms that record information about cleaners at the Middlesex Depot and the buses they look after. Note that three extra attributes, roster number, roster date and job complete have been added to the original case study. The cleaner ticks against the appropriate job after he/she has completed the cleaning of a particular bus.

Figure 2.11: Sample rosters

Cleaner Roster

Roster number 1005   **Roster date** 20th March 2006

Cleaner Roster

Roster number 1004   **Roster date** 20th March 2006

Depot number 101   **Depot name** Holloway

Cleaner no 135

Cleaner name Ben Brown

Registration Number	Model	Bustype Number	Type Descripton	Job complete
A123ABC	Routemaster	1	doubledecker	✔
D678FGH	Volvo 8700	2	metrobus	✔
D345GGI	Volvo 8500	1	doubledecker	
G233HGF	Mercedes 709D	2	metrobus	
B683KLH	Daf SB22	3	midibus	
B409NCS	Routemaster	1	doubledecker	

If **Roster** were identified as a relation, it might look like:

Figure 2.12: The un-normalised relation

roster_no	roster_date	cno	cname	dno	dname	reg_no	model	tno	tdescript	status
104	3-3-06	135	Ben Brown	101	Holloway	A123ABC	Routemaster	1	doubledecker	c
						D678FGH	Volvo 8700	2	metrobus	c
						D345GGI	Volvo 8500	1	doubledecker	
						G233HGF	Mercedes 709D	2	metrobus	
						B683KLH	Daf SB22	3	midibus	
						B409NCS	Routemaster	1	doubledecker	
105	3-3-06	166	Lee Zua	102	Hornsey	R123HFD	Mercedes 405G	5	bendy-bus	c
						C189RTB	Mercedes 709D	2	metrobus	
•	•	•	•	•	•	•	•	•	•	•
•	•	•	•	•	•	•	•	•	•	•

First normal form (1NF)

The next step in the normalisation process is to remove the repeating groups from the un-normalised relation. A relation is in 1NF if – and only if – all domains contain only atomic or single values, i.e. all repeating groups of data are removed.

A repeating group is a group of attributes that occurs a number of times for each record in the relation. So for example, in the Roster relation, each roster record has a group of buses (roster record 104 has 6 buses).

Selecting a suitable key for the table

In order to convert an un-normalised relation into first normal form, we must identify the key attribute(s) involved. From the un-normalised relation we can see that each roster has a roster_no, each cleaner a cno, each depot a dno, each bus a reg-no and each type a tno. In order to convert an un-normalised relation into normal form, we also have to identify a key for the whole relation.

You may remember from chapter 1 that a primary key is a unique identifier for an entity. It is an attribute (or combination of attributes) with the property that, at any given time, no two entity occurrences contain the same values for that attribute (or combination of attributes). Bearing this definition in mind, on examination the primary key of the relation is **roster_no, reg_no**.

We now draw the determinacy diagram for the roster relation, showing the attributes which are dependent on the primary key:

Figure 2.13: Determinacy diagram for first normal form

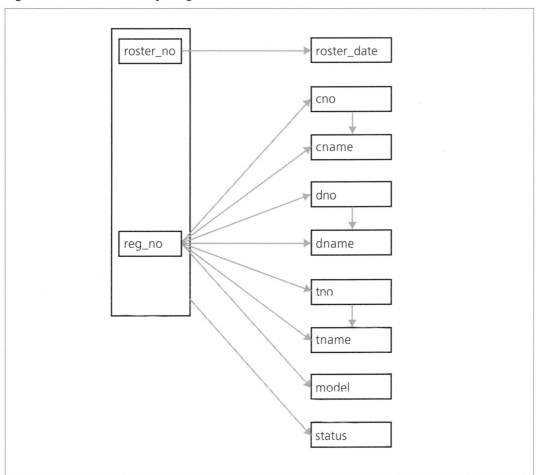

Note that the arrow coming directly from roster_no indicates that roster_date is functionally dependent on the key attribute roster_no and not on the composite key; similarly, the arrows coming directly from reg_no to cno, cname, dno etc indicate that these are functionally dependent on the reg_no. Notice that only 'status' is functionally dependent on the whole of the primary key.

To convert an un-normalised table of data into first normal form we need to remove repeating values, so that there is a single value at the intersection of each row and column. The original table of data is converted into a relation in first normal form as shown overleaf. The relation has the same structure as the determinacy diagram, both being in first normal form.

Figure 2.14: Roster relation in first normal form

roster no	roster _ date	cno	cname	dno	dname	reg_no	model	tno	tdescript	status
104	20-03-06	135	Ben Brown	101	Holloway	A123ABC	Routemaster	1	doubledecker	c
104	20-03-06	135	Ben Brown	101	Holloway	D678FGH	Volvo 8700	2	metrobus	c
104	20-03-06	135	Ben Brown	101	Holloway	D345GGI	Volvo 8500	1	doubledecker	
104	20-03-06	135	Ben Brown	101	Holloway	G233HGF	Mercedes 709D	2	metrobus	
104	20-03-06	135	Ben Brown	101	Holloway	B683KLH	Daf SB22	3	midibus	
104	20-03-06	135	Ben Brown	101	Holloway	B409NCS	Routemaster	1	doubledecker	
105	20-03-06	166	LeeZua	102	Hornsey	R123HFD	Mercedes 405G	5	bendy-bus	c
105	20-03-06	166	LeeZua	102	Hornsey	C189RTB	Mercedes 709D	2	metrobus	
•	•	•				•	•			•
•	•	•				•	•			•

The problems with 1NF are:

- Redundancy – e.g. roster date, cleaner name etc repeated
- Insertion anomaly – a cleaner cannot be inserted into the database unless he/she has a bus to clean
- Deletion anomaly – deleting a tuple might lose information from the database. For example, if a cleaner cleaning a particular bus leaves the company, then we lose information for the buses he cleaned
- Update anomaly – e.g. a change to the cleaner name means it must change in all tuples which include that cleaner name.

Second normal form (2NF)

We now describe the second step in the normalisation process using the relation above which is in first normal form.

Firstly we determine the functional dependencies on the identifying attributes (i.e. the primary key (roster_no, reg_no) and its parts.

If the key is composite, the other attributes must be functionally dependent on the whole of the key. In other words we are looking for partial functional dependencies. In the example, roster date is functionally dependent on the partial key roster_no – there is only one roster_date for a particular roster_no. Also cno, cname, dno, dname etc are all functionally dependent on the partial key reg_no. The attribute 'status', however, is the only attribute fully functionally dependent on the whole of the primary key.

Figure 2.15: Determinacy diagrams for second normal form

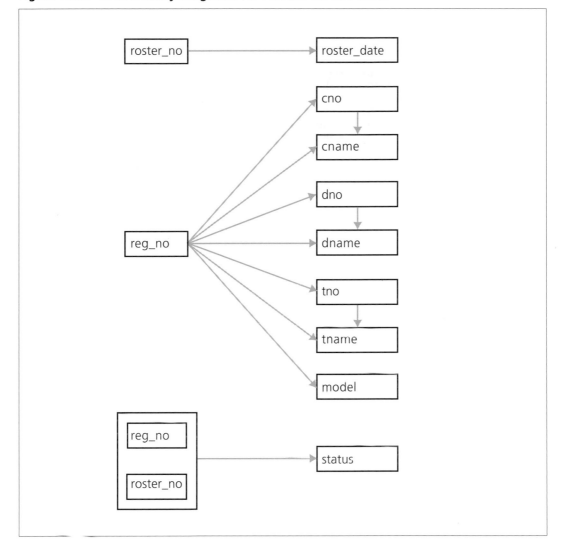

The next stage in the second normal form process is to rewrite the entities so that all the non-key attributes are fully functionally dependent on the primary key, as is reflected in the determinacy diagrams above. Note that this step does not arise for relations that have a single attribute primary key – we only need to consider relations with composite keys as in our example. We thus now have three new relations – see figure 2.16.

Figure 2.16: Relations in second normal form

Bus

reg_no	cno	cname	dno	dname	model	tno	tdescript
A123ABC	135	Ben Brown	101	Holloway	Routemaster	1	doubledecker
D678FGH	135	Ben Brown	101	Holloway	Volvo 8700	2	metrobus
D345GGI	135	Ben Brown	101	Holloway	Volvo 8500	1	doubledecker
G233HGF	135	Ben Brown	101	Holloway	Mercedes 709D	2	metrobus
B683KLH	135	Ben Brown	101	Holloway	Daf SB22	3	midibus
B409NCS	135	Ben Brown	101	Holloway	Routemaster	1	doubledecker
R123HFD	166	Lee Zua	102	Hornsey	Mercedes 405G	5	Bendy-bus
C189RTB	166	Lee Zua	102	Hornsey	Mercedes 709D	2	metrobus
•	•	•	•	•	•	•	•

Roster

roster_no	roster_date
104	20-03-06
105	20-03-06
•	•

Bus-cleaning

roster_no	reg_no	status
104	A123ABC	c
104	D678FGH	c
104	D345GGI	
104	G233HGF	
104	B683KLH	
104	B409NCS	
105	R123HFD	c
105	C189RTB	
•	•	•

The three relations Bus, Roster and Bus-cleaning have primary keys Reg_no, rosterno and composite key (rosterno, reg_no) respectively.

2NF has less redundancy than 1NF as we have removed repeating groups. However there are still a number of problems:

- Redundancy – for example, in the Bus relation, cleaner name is repeated for each cleaner number

- Insertion anomaly – a cleaner cannot be inserted into the database unless he/she is responsible for at least one bus

- Deletion anomaly – deleting a tuple might lose information from the database. For example, if we delete a cleaner who is only responsible for that one bus, then we lose information about the cleaner

- Update anomaly – e.g. a change to the cleaner name means changes must be made in all tuples which include that cleaner name.

Third normal form (3NF)

A 3NF relation is in 2NF but also it must satisfy the non-transitive dependency rule, which states that every non-key attribute must be non-transitively dependent on the primary key. Another way of saying this is that a relation is in 3NF if all its non-key attributes are directly dependent on the primary key. Transitive dependencies are resolved by creating new relations for each entity.

There are three transitive dependencies in the Bus relation above as is illustrated by vertical lines in figure 2.15 above. For example: cno is functionally dependent on reg_no; cname is functionally dependent on reg_no. Additionally, cname is functionally dependent cno.

We therefore have the transitive dependency:

reg_no determines cno and cno determines cname

then

reg_no determines cname

Two other transitive dependencies are identified involving tname and dname. The determinacy diagrams for third normal form are given below:

Figure 2.17: Determinacy diagrams for third normal form

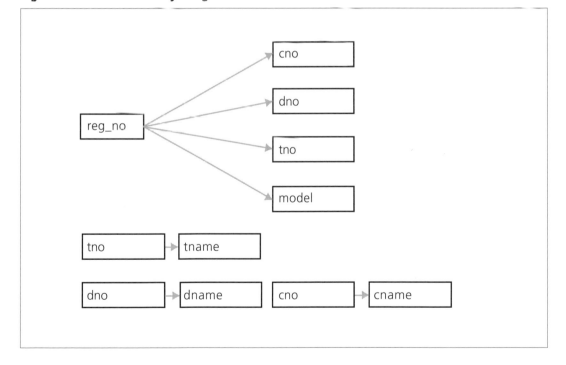

The normalisation of 2NF to 3NF involves the removal of transitive dependencies. This is done by placing the attributes in new relations. The new relation must also include a copy of the determinant (as the primary key) The determinant's attributes (cno, dno and tno) act as a foreign key in the original relation. The original relation is therefore split thus (see figure 2.18):

Figure 2.18: Relations in third normal form

Bus

reg_no	cno	dno	model	tno
A123ABC	135	101	Routemaster	1
D678FGH	135	101	Volvo 8700	2
D345GGI	135	101	Volvo 8500	1
G233HGF	135	101	Mercedes 709D	2
B683KLH	135	101	Daf SB22	3
B409NCS	135	101	Routemaster	1
R123HFD	166	102	Mercedes 405G	5
C189RTB	166	102	Mercedes 709D	2
•	•	•	•	•

Cleaner

cno	cname
135	Ben Brown
166	Lee Zua
•	•

Depot

dno	dname
101	Holloway
102	Hornsey
•	•

BusType

tno	tdescript
1	doubledecker
2	metrobus
3	midibus
5	bendy-bus
•	•

By creating the new entities, we have removed the transitive dependency from the Bus relation. These entities above are now in third normal form (3NF). The complete 3NF model is the above four relations and in addition the two relations which had been created at 2NF:

Figure 2.19: Additional relations

Bus-cleaning

rosterno	reg_no	status
104	A123ABC	c
104	D678FGH	c
104	D345GGI	
104	G233HGF	
104	B683KLH	
104	B409NCS	
105	R123HFD	c
105	C189RTB	
•	•	•

Roster

roster_no	roster_date
104	20-03-06
105	20-03-06
•	•

Review of normal forms

Details of the first three normal forms are given in the table below:

Normal form	What is it?	What does process do?	How is it achieved?
1NF	Relation in 1NF if - it contains scalar (atomic) values only	- Removes repeating groups	- Make a separate relation for each group of related attributes - Give each new relation a primary key
2NF	Relation in 2NF if - in 1NF - all non-key attributes are dependent on the whole of the primary key and not part of it	- Removes redundant data	- If an attribute depends on only part of a multi-value key, remove it to a separate table
3NF	Relation in 3NF if - in 2NF - non-key attributes are dependent on primary key and independent of each other - i.e. non-key attribute must be non-transitively dependent on the primary key - a non-key attribute is changed, that change should not affect the others	- Removes attributes not dependent on the key thereby further reducing redundancy	- Make a separate relation for attributes transitively dependent on the primary key - Give each new relation a primary key - Original relation will include a foreign key to link to new relation

2.5 Summary

This chapter introduced students to normalisation as a bottom-up tool for designing data for a database system. The concepts of determinants and functional dependency are explained. Three normalisation processes are described – first, second and third normal forms. A more flexible design is achieved and the problems of redundancy, update, deletion, and insertion anomalies are removed to a large extent.

2.6 Review questions

Review question 2.1 What is normalisation and what is its purpose?

Review question 2.2 Help At Home is an agency which provides various services such as baby sitting and dog walking. Details of all bookings and a record of the service carried out are kept as in the examples shown below. Assume only one person (employee) is involved in carrying out each particular service. An hourly rate is charged depending on the type of service required. Note that customers will only be able to make one booking for a particular service per day.

Booking record example 1

Customer name: Tel: 081 980 2223	John Smith		Customer no: 111
Date of booking:	11.08.06		
Type of service required:	01	Service required:	Baby sitting
Date service is required:	16.08.06		
Person carrying out job:	Issa Ahmed		
Charge per hour:	£7	Hours:	5

Booking record example 2

Customer name: Tel: 0181-980 2223	John Smith		Customer no: 111
Date of booking:	18.09.06		
Type of service required:	02	Service required:	Dog walking
Date service is required:	30.09.06		
Person carrying out job:	Ben Brown		
Charge per hour:	£10	Hours:	1

Discuss the problems associated with this representation above.

Review question 2.3 Extract the appropriate information from the details given in review question 2.2 and write it in the form of a universal relation (un-normalised form).

Review question 2.4 Identify a primary key for the whole relation in review question 2.3.

Review question 2.5 What is the first normal form rule? Provide a determinacy diagram for the relation in the previous question.

Review question 2.6 Convert the un-normalised table in review question 2.3 into relations in first normal form.

Review question 2.7 What is the second normal form rule? Produce a second normal form determinacy diagram from the above example.

Review question 2.8 Rewrite the relations in review question 2.6 so that all the non-key attributes are fully functionally dependent on the primary key.

Review question 2.9 What is the third normal form rule? Produce a third normal form dependency diagram from the above example.

Review question 2.10 Rewrite the relations in review question 2.8 so that all transitive dependencies are removed.

2.7 Answers to review questions

Answer to review question 2.1 Normalisation is a formal technique for producing a set of relations for an enterprise, given its data requirements. The technique involves a series of steps each of which corresponds to a specific normal form with known properties. The steps involve primary keys and the identification of functional dependencies. As normalisation proceeds, the relations become less vulnerable to insertion, deletion and update anomalies.

Answer to review question 2.2

- Redundancy – for example the customer name, telephone number etc are repeated for each customer number in the relation.

- Update anomalies – as a consequence of the redundancy, we could update the customer name in one tuple, while leaving it fixed in another.

- Deletion anomalies – if we should delete a booking for a particular customer, we might lose all the information about that customer.

- Insertion anomalies – the inverse to deletion anomalies is, if we cannot record a new customer in our table unless there exists a booking of that customer.

Answer to review question 2.3

Relation in un-normalised form:

Cust-no	Cust-name	Cust-tel	Booking-date	service-type	Service	date-required	e-no	e-name	Per hr £	Hrs
111	J Smith	980 2223	11.08.	01	Babysit	16.08	01	Issa Ahmed	7	5
			18.09.	02	Dogwalking	30.09	02	Ben Brown	10	1
112	G Best	678 4455	12.06	01	Babysit	13.06	02	Ben Brown	7	3
•	•	•	•	•	•	•	•		•	•

Answer to review question 2.4 The primary key is cust-no, booking-date, service-type.

Answer to review question 2.5 A relation is in 1NF if – and only if – all domains contain only atomic or single values – i.e. all repeating groups of data are removed. A repeating group is a group of attributes that occurs a number of times for each record in the relation.

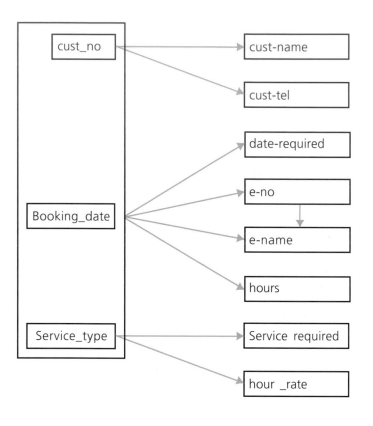

Answer to review question 2.6

Cust-no	Cust-name	Cust-tel	Booking-date	Service-type	Service	Date-required	e-no	e-name	Per hr £	Hrs
111	J Smith	980 2223	11.08.	01	Babysit	16.08	01	Issa Ahmed	7	5
111	J Smith	980 2223	18.09.	02	Dogwalking	30.09	02	Ben Brown	10	1
•	•	•	•	•	•	•	•	•	•	•

Answer to review question 2.7 Relation in 2NF if it is in 1NF and all non key attributes are dependent on the whole of the primary key and not part of it. If an attribute depends on only part of a multi-value key, remove it to a separate table.

Second normal form determinacy diagram:

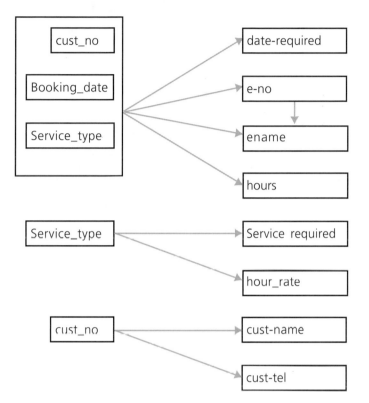

Answer to review question 2.8 The partial dependencies are removed; thus we have:

Cust-no	cust-name	Cust-tel
111	J Smith	980 2223
112	G Best	678 4455
•	•	•

Service-type	Service-required	Hour-rate
01	Babysit	7
02	Dogwalking	10
•	•	•

Cust-no	Booking-date	service-type	date-required	e-no	e-name	hrs
111	11.08	01	16.08	01	Issa Ahmed	5
111	18.09	02	30.09	02	Ben Brown	1
•	•	•	•	•	•	•

Answer to review question 2.9 A 3NF relation is in 2NF and also every non-key attribute must be non-transitively dependent on the primary key. Another way of saying this is that a relation is in 3NF if all its non-key attributes are directly dependent on the primary key. Transitive dependencies are resolved by creating new relations for each entity.

Third normal form determinacy diagram (service and customer diagram as before):

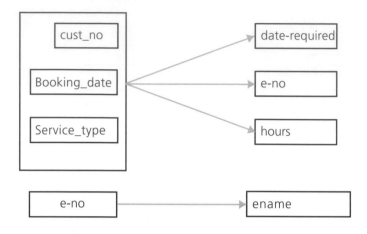

Answer to review question 2.10

Cust-no	Booking-date	service-type	date-require	e-no	hrs
111	11.08	01	16.08	01	5
111	18.09	02	30.09	02	1
•	•	•	•	•	•

e-no	e-name
01	Issa Ahmed
02	Ben Brown
•	•

All other relations as above.

CHAPTER 3

Introduction to SQL

OVERVIEW

In this chapter, students are introduced to the query language SQL, the standard relational database language. Students will learn about the importance of SQL as the standard relational database language. They are presented with some the data definition features of SQL, namely the ability to **create** table definitions. Students are also introduced to SQL data manipulation. The statements available to load data into tables and to change that data are discussed, namely **insert**, **update** and **delete**. We look at how the relational algebra operators project, restrict, product and join are implemented in SQL using the **select** statement.

Note that the example queries later in this chapter have been executed in Oracle10g using the Bus Depots' Database which was given in section 2.2 of chapter 2. You will find details of the sample data used in the Appendix. You should refer to the entity-relationship diagram and the Appendix to assist in your understanding of each query execution code.

Learning outcomes	On completion of this chapter, you should be able to:

- Understand the data definition feature of SQL: create tables

- Understand how to insert data into tables and amend and delete that data

- Understand some further basic data manipulation features of SQL – including simple select, arithmetic expressions, natural join, aggregate functions, sorting and grouping

- Understand how the relational algebra operators are implemented in SQL.

3.1 The SQL language

SQL standards

SQL or Structured Query Language is the standard query language for relational databases. It allows users to create database objects and manipulate and view data. The language was originally developed in the 1970s when IBM decided to develop an experimental database language to support its relational database products. It soon became very successful and was taken up by commercial enterprises, including Oracle, who released the first commercial relational database management system in 1979.

SQL was adopted by the American National Standards Institute (ANSI) in 1987, and the following year the International Standards Agency (ISO, 1987) published its SQL standard. Since then there has been further releases. The first major revision led to SQL-92, with new features such as extra types, operators, integrity constraints and scalar functions. More features were added with the next major release of the standard (SQL-99) and included facilities associated with object-oriented databases. With the SQL-2003 standard, XML-Related Specifications (SQL/XML) were introduced, along with OLAP features, and further improvements to the previous standard such as new data types and generated columns.

At the present time a large number of database vendors are marketing numerous products based on SQL. On the whole, implementations do not conform fully to the ISO standard and manufacturers provide features in addition to this. In the case of Oracle, it supports numerous extensions that go beyond standard SQL. In the examples in this book we will be using Oracle SQL, a partial implementation of the SQL:99 standard.

In our introduction to relational database systems in chapter 1 you were introduced to the formal relational terminology, originally defined by Codd (such as relation, attribute and tuple). In this chapter the ISO terminology will be mostly used (i.e. table, column and row).

Components of SQL

There are two categories of commands in SQL:

1. Data definition language (DDL) which is used to create database objects and to control access to the database.
2. Data manipulation language (DML) which is used to insert, update, delete and query data in the database.

In this chapter and the following we will be examining these in detail.

3.2 Data definition

Creating tables in SQL

The CREATE statement in SQL is used for creating a range of database objects, including tables, views and indexes. The CREATE TABLE statement has a variety of options. We will start with a simple example for creating the busdriver table:

```
Create table BusDriver
    (bdno        varchar2(5),
    bdname       varchar2(20),
    bdsalary     number(6,2),
    pvcdate      date,
    dno          varchar2(5));
```

To create a table, you specify the name of the table followed by a list of column names with their data type. Some data types available in Oracle are illustrated in the table below:

Datatype	Description	Max size (Oracle10g)
VARCHAR2(length)	Variable length character string. You must specify size	4000 bytes
NUMBER(p,s)	This is used to store general numbers. These have precision (the max number of digits to be stored) and scale (optional – the number of digits to the right of the decimal point)	p can range from 1 to 38; s can range from –84 to 127.
DATE	Valid date range. The format is dd-mm-yyyy, for example 19-jan-2006	from January 1, 4712 BC to December 31, 9999 AD.

Oracle provides a number of other data types including char, used for fixed length strings, blobs (binary large objects) and long, used to store large amounts of text.

Integrity constraints

We now expand our Create Table definition to include specifications of the primary and foreign keys thus:

```
Create table BusDriver
    (bdno        varchar2(5)      NOT NULL,
    bdname       varchar2(20),
    bdsalary     number(6,2),
    pvcdate      date,
    dno          varchar2(5),
    constraint pk_bdno primary key(bdno),
    constraint fk_dno foreign key(dno) references Depot(dno)  );
```

These additional clauses are known as **integrity constraints**. Other constraints are possible including Domain Constraints.

The first constraint 'constraint pk_bdno primary key(bdno)', which specifies the primary key, is used to ensure **entity integrity**. The entity integrity rule states that no attribute which forms part of the primary key of a relation can accept null values. This is achieved in SQL by stating the primary key in the clause and by defining the key attribute 'bdno' as NOT NULL.

The second constraint 'constraint fk_dno foreign key(dno) references Depot(dno)' is used to ensure **referential integrity**. This rule states that the database must not contain any unmatched foreign key values. Put another way, a foreign key in a table such as the depot number (dno) above, must match the primary key in another table (Depot) or be of null values.

SQL supports the definition of foreign keys as specified above. In this case if, for example, there is an attempt to insert a bus driver with a depot which does not exist in the related table Depot, then the insert will be rejected.

Dropping tables

To remove a table from the database, the drop table statement is used. For example:

    Drop table busdriver;

3.3 Data manipulation – loading the tables

We now look at some data manipulation statements: insert, update and delete. The data manipulation statement SELECT will be introduced in the next section.

Adding new rows to a table – insert

The INSERT statement is used to add rows to an existing table. The following example inserts a single row into the bus drivers' table:

    insert into Busdriver
    values ('101','Paresh Patel',1900,'09-feb-2006','101');

Note that attributes which have been defined as type varchar are surrounded by single quotes.

Changing data in a table – update

The UPDATE statement is used to change the values of existing data in a table. For example the following query increases James Bond's salary by 10%:

    update busdriver
    set bdsalary = bdsalary*1.1
    where bdname = 'James Bond';

Note that the 'where' clause is optional. It is also possible to include a SELECT statement. In this example it is used to return values to which the updated columns will be set. In the following example, James Bond's row is updated, setting his depot number to the one for

Islington.

```
update busdriver
set dno =
   (select dno
   from depot
   where dname ='Islington')
where dname = 'James Bond';
```

Removing data in a table – delete

The DELETE is used to remove rows from a table. For example, to delete James Bond's record:

```
delete from busdriver
where bdname = 'James Bond';
```

We can also remove a number of rows at a time. For example, to delete all bus drivers who work at the Islington depot:

```
delete from busdriver
where dno in
   (select dno
   from depot
   where dname ='Islington');
```

Again this example includes a select statement. It returns the dno for the Islington depot. We will see in the next section how powerful this statement is.

3.4   Data manipulation – the select statement

SQL data manipulation and relational algebra (RA)

We have seen in chapter 1 that the manipulative part of the relational model consists of a set of operators known collectively as relational algebra. The eight relational algebra operations originally defined by Codd are listed below. If you have forgotten the details, go over the relational algebra operations in chapter 1.

Set operators:	UNION
	INTERSECTION
	DIFFERENCE
	DIVIDE

The special relational operators:	RESTRICT
	PROJECT
	JOIN
	Cartesian PRODUCT

Each operator takes one or more relations as its input and produces a new relation as output.

Implementing RA operations in SQL

As we have seen, relational algebra (RA) is used as the basis for other, higher-level data manipulation languages including SQL and is also used as a measure to compare high-level relational languages (such as SQL) to test if the language is relationally complete – i.e. to check if the query language is as powerful as the algebra. We now look (in this chapter and the following chapter) at how these operations have been implemented in SQL. The RA operations all take one or more relations and generate a new relation from this. In SQL this is achieved with different forms of the SELECT statement.

The select statement

The select statement is used to query data in the database. A simplified general form of the select statement is given below:

```
SELECT [DISTINCT | ALL] <*| output columns >
    FROM <input tables>
[WHERE <search condition> ]
[GROUP BY <grouping columns>  [HAVING condition] ]
[{UNION | UNION ALL | INTERSECT | MINUS} SELECT command ]
[ORDER BY <ordering columns>  [ASC | DESC]
```

where standard symbols are used: [ ] means optional; | indicates choice of alternatives and < > indicates one or more. The following table describes the purpose of a number of the clauses in the select statement.

Select clause	Purpose
SELECT [DISTINCT] <output columns >	Specifies columns in output
FROM <input tables>	Specifies tables used in query
WHERE <complex condition>	eliminates unwanted rows
GROUP BY <grouping columns>	groups rows
HAVING condition	eliminates unwanted groups
ORDER BY <ordering columns>	sorts rows

Some simple examples of SELECT statements are given below:

1. **select** bdname
   from busdriver;

2. **select** *
   from busdriver
   where bdname = 'Peter Piper';

All select statement will have the two clauses: 'select' and 'from'. The 'from' clause specifies the table or tables to be used (Busdriver in both examples). The 'select' clause specifies the columns, which will appear in the output – bdname in the first example. In the second example an asterisk (*) is used in place of a column name or names. This causes all columns or attributes of the specified table to be output.

Implementing RA restriction

Restriction generates the output from those rows that satisfy a condition, e.g. list details of bus drivers who have passed their PVC driving test after 09-jan-2000.

BDNO	BDNAME	BDSALARY	PVCDATE	DNO
001	Jane Brown	1800	09-FEB-85	101
006	Sally Smith	1750	09-MAR-96	
007	James Bond	1500	09-JAN-99	102
008	Maggie May	2200	09-JAN-00	102
009	Jack Jones	1400	09-AUG-01	101
010	Peter Piper	3500	09-JUN-04	104
011	John Peel	2000	09-FEB-05	102

In SQL a **search condition** is included in the WHERE clause to restrict the output

```
select *
from busdriver
where pvctestdate > '09-jan-2000';
```

Implementing RA projection

Projection outputs a subset of the attributes of all rows, e.g. list registration numbers with models.

REG_NO	MODEL	TNO	DNO	CNO
A123ABC	Routemaster	1	101	113
D678FGH	Volvo 8700	2	101	114
D345GGG	Volvo 8500	1	101	112
H259IJK	Daf SB220	3	102	114
P200IJK	Mercedes 709D	2	102	110
P300RTY	Mercedes Citaro	4	102	111
R678FDS	Daf SB220	1		110

In SQL the desired attributes are listed in the SELECT clause.

```
select reg_no,model
from bus;
```

The following example illustrates the two relational algebra operations of restriction and projection, i.e. it lists the number and salary of bus driver Peter Piper.

```
select bdno, bdsalary
from busdriver
where bdname = 'Peter Piper';
```

Calculated values

Arithmetic expressions can be used in both the select clause and the where clauses. So, for example, if we wanted to display the annual salary of the cleaners based at depot 101:

```
select cname, csalary *12
from cleaner
where dno='101';
```

This gives the following output based on our sample data (see Appendix).

CNAME	CSALARY*12
John	30600
Jean	30000

Note that the data is displayed as above but the data in the database remains unchanged.

Naming query columns

Notice that the column heading in the above example is the expression itself. We are able to change the heading for any attribute to make it more readable:

```
select cname, csalary *12   "annual salary"
from cleaner
where dno='101';
```

giving a result this time of

CNAME	annual salary
John	30600
Jean	30000

Distinct and ALL

The keyword 'distinct' is used in the select clause to suppress unwanted duplicate rows. So, for example, to list the bus drivers' numbers of those who have done training since 09-feb-2006 :

> **select distinct** bdno
> **from** training
> **where** trainingdate >'09-feb-2006' ;

This gives the following output from our sample data. Note that if 'distinct' is omitted the default is ALL and in this case all 11 rows would be output with a number of duplicated rows.

BDNO
008
011
007
009

Retrieving from a list of values using IN

If we wish to search for values in a given list, we can use the IN predicate. The example below is to list the names of bus drivers who belong to depots who have the depot numbers 101 or 102. Note that NOT IN is also allowed.

> **select** bdname
> **from** busdriver
> **where** dno **in** ('101','102')

Querying over a range of values

When we wish to test whether a value falls within certain range, we use the keyword BETWEEN. For example, to find names of bus drivers who earn >=2000 and <=300:

> **select** bdname, bdsalary
> **from** busdriver
> **where** bdsalary **between** 2000 and 3000

BDNAME	BDSALARY
Maggie May	2200
John Peel	2000

Searching for partial matches

The LIKE keyword is used for pattern matching, that is, it allows us to search for items when we only know part of a character string value. LIKE is used along with the symbol '%' and '_':

- % means 'zero or more characters'
- _ (underscore) which means exactly one character.

The following two queries are used to find bus details of type Mercedes and cleaners names with exactly four characters beginning with J and ending in N.

```
select *
from bus
where model like 'Mercedes%';

select cname
from    cleaner
where cname like 'J__N';
```

Testing for null values in a table

IS NULL and IS NOT NULL are used to test for the presence or absence of a null value in a field. From chapter one you may recall that null values are used when, either the value of a field is unknown at the time when the record was entered, or not applicable to that field for that particular record. So, for example, we might want to find all bus drivers who have not been assigned to a depot. In this case we could assume the information was not known when the row was inserted.

```
select bdname
from busdriver
where dno is null;
```

BDNAME
Sally Smith

Extending the WHERE clause using AND, OR

The general form of the select clause which we saw above can now be given in more detail:

```
SELECT [DISTINCT | ALL] <*| output columns >
FROM <input tables>
[WHERE < search  condition1> <, AND/OR search condition1>]
```

SQL provides a number of operators and keywords in the search condition. We have already seen examples of the normal comparison operators =, <, > and so on. We have also seen IN, BETWEEN, LIKE and IS NULL. Each of these can be combined with NOT. We can also combine the search conditions with the logical operators AND and OR.

For example, to find bus drivers who earn less than 1750 and have a PCV date of later than 09-jan-1999:

select *
from busdriver
where bdsalary < 1750
and pvcdate >'09-jan-1999';

BDNO	BDNAME	BDSALARY	PVCDATE	DNO
009	Jack Jones	1400	09-AUG-01	101

Alternatively to find bus drivers who earn less than 1750 or have a PCV date of later than 09-jan-1999:

select *
from busdriver
where bdsalary < 1750
or pvcdate >'09-jan-1999';

BDNO	BDNAME	BDSALARY	PVCDATE	DNO
007	James Bond	1500	09-JAN-99	102
008	Maggie May	2200	09-JAN-00	102
009	Jack Jones	1400	09-AUG-01	101
010	Peter Piper	3500	09 JUN 04	104
011	John Peel	2000	09-FEB-05	102

Aggregate functions

SQL provides a wide range of predefined functions to perform manipulation of data. There are four types of functions: arithmetic, date, character and aggregate. Examples of **arithmetic** are *sqrt* (square root), *round* (used for rounding numbers) and *least* (for returning the smallest value in a list). Examples of **date** functions are *sysdate* (current date) and *months_between* (returns the number of months between two dates). **Character** functions include *length* (returns the length of a string) and *lower* (converts a string to all lowercase characters).

We shall examine **aggregate functions** here. This type of function is applied to sets of rows in a table and returns a summary value – always one. For example, in the bus driver's table we might want to find the minimum and maximum salary, the average salary, the total salary bill and the count of all the bus drivers.

For this type of query, SQL has provided the following aggregate functions:

Function	Meaning	Example
Min(expression)	Returns the lowest value of a specified column	min(salary)
max(expression)	Returns the highest value of a specified column	max(salary)
avg(expression)	Returns the average of the values of a specified column. It will ignore null values	avg(salary)
sum(expression)	Returns the sum of the values of a specified column	sum(salary)
count(expression) or COUNT(*)	Returns the number of rows in the specified table (i.e. only the number of rows in which the expression is not null). COUNT(*) counts all rows	Examples: count (*) count (bdno)

The following example is to find the oldest and latest training dates for bus driver 007.

```
select min(trainingdate), max(trainingdate)
from training
where bdno='007';
```

MIN(TRAININGDATE)	MAX(TRAININGDATE)
09-FEB-06	09-MAR-06

Product

In SQL, if you specify more that one table in a select clause you automatically get the product of the tables. For example:

```
select *
from bus, cleaner
```

This query will give every combination of bus and cleaner in the database, whether the cleaner is connected to that bus or not. Note that it is unusual for a query to require the use of product. All further examples and exercises will not include the use of product. Note that a common SQL error is to perform a product where a join was intended.

Natural join

Joining tables involves linking two (or more) tables together by combining rows that are related to each other in some way. A special case is the **natural join** where the link is through some shared characteristic, usually (but not necessarily) a foreign key. To get the natural join of bus and cleaner you would need to specify the join condition for the rows to be paired:

```
select *
from    bus, cleaner
where bus.cno = cleaner.cno;
```

So the join of the two tables gives:

REG_NO	MODEL	TNO	DNO	CNO	CNO	CNAME	CSALARY	DNO
A123ABC	Routemaster	1	101	113	113	Vince	2800	102
D678FGH	Volvo 8700	2	101	114	114	Jay	3000	102
D345GGG	Volvo 8500	1	101	112	112	Betty	2400	102
H259IJK	Daf SB220	3	102	114	114	Jay	3000	102
P200IJK	Mercedes 709D	2	102	110	110	John	2550	101
P300RTY	Mercedes Citaro	4	102	111	111	Jean	2500	101
R678FDS	Daf SB220	1		110	110	John	2550	101

In our example, we list all buses and also information about the cleaners who look after each bus.

Using an alias in a multi-table join

The above query can also be done using aliases. An alias is an abbreviation for a table name, such as 'b' for the bus table. In this case, 'b' is used anywhere in the query to replace the table name 'bus', apart from the table named in the 'from' clause.

```
select *
from    bus b, cleaner c
where b.cno = c.cno;
```

For all subsequent examples involving multi-table joins, aliases will be used. We shall see later that aliases are required for naming tables when there is the possibility of ambiguity.

Inner joins

The previous example, besides being a natural join is also an example of an **inner join**. An inner join retrieves data only from those rows where the join condition is met. The example below shows that rows that do not have a match are lost.

Given the two tables Cleaner and Depot:

```
select * from  cleaner;
```

CNO	CNAME	CSALARY	DNO
110	John	2550	101
111	Jean	2500	101
112	Betty	2400	102
113	Vince	2800	102
114	Jay	3000	102
115	Doug	2000	102
116	Geeta	4000	

select * from depot;

DNO	DNAME	DADDRESS
101	Holloway	Camden Road
102	Hornsey	High Road
104	Islington	Upper Street

The inner join of these tables gives the cleaners and the depots at which each cleaner is based, but only for those cleaners who are actually based at a depot. Cleaners who have not been assigned to a depot are not output.

select *
from cleaner c, depot d
where c.dno=d.dno;

gives a result of 6 rows rather than 7, which might have been expected:

CNO	CNAME	CSALARY	DNO	DNO	DNAME	DADDRESS
110	John	2550	101	101	Holloway	Camden Road
111	Jean	2500	101	101	Holloway	Camden Road
112	Betty	2400	102	102	Hornsey	High Road
113	Vince	2800	102	102	Hornsey	High Road
114	Jay	3000	102	102	Hornsey	High Road
115	Doug	2000	102	102	Hornsey	High Road

Cleaner '116 Geeta', who is not based at a depot, is not output. Note that we have used aliases in our example 'cleaner c, depot d'.

Outer joins

Unmatched rows can be included in the output using an outer join. This is specified by appending the symbol (+) to the name of the primary key or the foreign key in the join condition.

So to find the cleaners and the depots at which they are based, and also include those cleaners who have not been assigned to a depot:

select *
from cleaner c, depot d
where c.dno=d.dno(+);

which outputs 7 rows including Geeta's:

CNO	CNAME	CSALARY	DNO	DNO	DNAME	DADDRESS
110	John	2550	101	101	Holloway	Camden Road
111	Jean	2500	101	101	Holloway	Camden Road
112	Betty	2400	102	102	Hornsey	High Road
113	Vince	2800	102	102	Hornsey	High Road
114	Jay	3000	102	102	Hornsey	High Road
115	Doug	2000	102	102	Hornsey	High Road
116	Geeta	4000				

This is an example of a left outer join which keeps every tuple in the left-hand relation in the result. Here the symbol (+) appears on the right with the table (Depot) which has the deficient entry. A right outer join would show non-matching rows from the right-hand table.

Group by

Rows of data can be grouped in a table using the GROUP BY clause. This is particularly useful for when you wish to get the aggregate properties of values in the group. For example, to count the number of bus drivers who are based at each depot:

> **select** dno, count(bdno)
> **from** busdriver
> **group by** dno;

DNO	COUNT(BDNO)
101	2
	1
102	3
104	1

Notice that bus drivers who are not assigned to a depot are also included in the output. In the next example, multiple tables are specified (bustype, bus and depot) and the 'group by' clause includes more than one column. The query is to list, for each depot, the types of buses based at the depot and a count of models of that type.

> **select** d.dname, tdescript, count(model)
> **from** bustype bt, bus b, depot d
> **where** bt.tno=b.tno
> **and** d.dno=b.dno
> **group** by d.dname, tdescript;

DNAME	TDESCRIPT	COUNT(MODEL)
Holloway	doubledecker	2
Hornsey	midibus	1
Hornsey	bendy-bus	1
Holloway	metrobus	1
Hornsey	metrobus	1

In the above example we have created a new relation when we joined the three tables together – i.e. the depots with their buses and the bus types of each bus. Within the table we have grouped the depots together (using depot name) and within each depot we have grouped the models together (by description) and counted these models.

The example above assumes that depot names and type descriptions are unique. Often this is not the case with names. For example, if we wanted to group the bus drivers by driver name, then the names may well not be unique. If there is a possibility that data items in columns are not unique, then the primary key of the table should be included in the 'group by' clause, for example:

Group by bdno, bdname

Note that a common error when using the group by clause is:

ORA-00979: not a GROUP BY expression

This is when you are trying to output values in the attribute list (columns) which are not single valued in the group. For example:

```
select  dno, bdsalary, count(bdno)
from busdriver
group by dno;
```

The above query would produce an error message. This is because there are a number of bus driver salaries for each depot, and therefore bdsalary is not single-valued for the group.

Group by having

The having clause can be included with group by and is used to eliminate unwanted groups. So, for example, to count the number of buses looked after by cleaners, excluding cleaners who look after less than 2 buses:

```
select  cname, count(reg_no) as buses
from bus b, cleaner c
where b.cno=c.cno
group by c.cno,cname
having count(reg_no)>1;
```

CNAME	BUSES
Jay	2
John	2

Sorting data

To sort data in a table (or joined tables) we use the ORDER BY clause. You can specify one or more colums as the sort key. For example, to sort the data in the Bustype table, ordered by type description:

> **select** *
> **from** bustype
> **order by** tdescript;

TNO	TDESCRIPT
4	bendy-bus
1	doubledecker
2	metrobus
3	midibus
5	open top

By default, ORDER BY sorts in ascending order. To sort in descending order, the reserved word DESC is provided:

> **order by** tdescript **desc;**

SQL also allows a sort within a sort. For example, list details of buses ordered by registration number within depot where the buses are based:

> **select** dno, reg_no, model
> **from** bus
> **order by** dno, reg_no;

DNO	REG_NO	MODEL
101	A123ABC	Routemaster
101	D345GGG	Volvo 8500
101	D678FGH	Volvo 8700
102	H259IJK	Daf SB220
102	P200IJK	Mercedes 709D
102	P300RTY	Mercedes Citaro
	R678FDS	Daf SB220

It sorts the bus table using the first attribute in the ORDER BY list (dno) and then uses the second attribute (reg_no) to sort the registration numbers within each depot grouping.

3.5 Summary

This chapter introduced the student to the query language SQL and we discussed its importance to database applications. Students gained knowledge of SQL data definition statements and to the data manipulation statement, select. We focused on understanding how the relational algebra operators project, restrict, product and join are implemented in SQL using the select statement.

3.6 Review questions

 Review question 3.1 Explain the purpose of the integrity constraint, in the SQL create table statement, relating to primary keys.

 Review question 3.2 Explain the purpose of the integrity constraint, in the SQL create table statement, relating to foreign keys.

Review question 3.3 How can we test if SQL is relationally complete?

Review question 3.4 How are the relational algebra commands 'restriction' and 'projection' implemented in SQL? Give example SQL queries to illustrate these.

Review question 3.5 A programmer wrote the following code. Give the English meaning of the code (from a user point of view). Now rewrite this code using aliases for table names.

```
select busdriver.bdno, bdname, dname
from busdriver, depot
where busdriver.dno= depot.dno
and bdname='James Bond';
```

Review question 3.6 A programmer wrote the following code to list the buses that cleaner Vince is responsible for. Comment on the code.

```
select reg_no, model
from bus, cleaner
where cname='Vince';
```

 Review question 3.7 What are aggregate functions? Describe the aggregate functions that SQL has provided.

 Review question 3.8 What is the difference between an inner and outer join? How is the outer join implemented in Oracle's SQL?

Review question 3.9 Explain how the GROUP BY clause works. What restrictions exist on the contents of a select-list (i.e. first line of Select statement) which appear in the same query as a GROUP BY clause?

 Review question 3.10 What is the difference between the WHERE and the HAVING clause?

 Review question 3.11 The following is part of a larger entity-relationship model for a hospital. This subsystem concerns doctors who work at the hospital and the diagnoses that they make. It is assumed that the Patient entity exists with primary key patient_no, but it is not shown here. Each time a diagnosis (such as 'Broken Limb' or 'Multiple Sclerosis') is made on a patient, this is recorded showing the date and the doctor who carried out the procedure. The diagnosis is expressed as a code number called an SDC number (standard diagnostic category). The hospital keeps lists of diagnoses, together with estimates of the cost of treating a patient with this condition and the number of days of hospitalisation required:

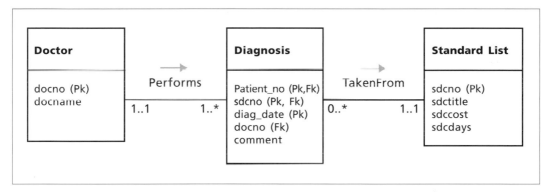

Give the English meaning of the following SQL command:

```
select doctor.docname, sdc.sdctitle, count(*),
    sum(sdc.sdccost), sum(sdc.sdcdays)
from doctor d, diagnosis dg, standard_list sdc
where d.docno = dg.docno
and   dg.sdcno = sdc.sdcno
group by d.docno, d.docname, sdc.sdcno, sdc.sdctitle
having sum(sdc.sdccost) > 1000;
```

 Review question 3.12 What is the difference between the GROUP BY and the ORDER BY clauses?

 Review question 3.13 In SQL can I just ask for the first three rows in a table?

3.7 Answers to review questions

Answer to review question 3.1   SQL includes in the create table statement the optional clause:

> constraint constraint_name primary key(pk_no)

which specifies the primary key. This is used to ensure entity integrity.

The entity integrity rule states that no attribute which forms part of the primary key of a relation can accept null values. This is achieved in SQL by stating the primary key in the clause as above and by defining the key attribute 'pk_no' as NOT NULL.

Answer to review question 3.2   SQL includes in the create table statement the optional clause:

> constraint constraint_name foreign key(fK_no) references table_name(pk_no)

The constraint states the foreign key (fK_no) in a table, and the referenced table's primary key [table_name(pk_no)]. It is used to ensure referential integrity. This rule states that the database must not contain any unmatched foreign key values.

Answer to review question 3.3   If the complete set of relational algebra operators can be implemented then it is relationally complete.

Answer to review question 3.4   Restriction: in the 'where' clause of a select statement (e.g. where cname='Bill').

> Projection: in the 'select' clause of a Select statement (e.g. select dno, dname).

Answer to review question 3.5   This requires us to list driver number, name and depot where James Bond is based. Code with aliases:

```
select bd.bdno, bdname, dname
from busdriver bd, depot d
where bd.dno= d.dno
and bdname='James Bond';
```

Answer to review question 3.6   The code is incorrect – it does not list the buses that cleaner Vince is responsible for. To do this we would need to include the join condition:

> and bus.cno=cleaner.cno;

The code, as given, illustrates relational algebra product, where the result is every bus and cleaner whether the cleaner is associated with the bus or not.

Answer to review question 3.7   Aggregate functions are functions which are applied to sets of rows in a table. They return a single value. For this type of query, SQL has provided the aggregate functions min, max, avg, sum and count.

Answer to review question 3.8   An inner join retrieves data only from those rows where the join condition is met; unmatched rows are ignored. With an outer join, unmatched rows are included as well as matched rows. In Oracle it is specified by appending the symbol (+) in the join condition clause, either with the primary key or the foreign key: on the opposite table for which we want to include all the rows.

Answer to review question 3.9   A GROUP BY clause groups the data from the selected tables and returns groups of rows. It produces a single summary row for each group, so that for example aggregates (e.g. avg, min, max) of the grouped data can be retrieved.

Restrictions: each item in the select-list must be single-valued per group. The words GROUP BY are followed by one or more data items, specifying the categories into which the data is to be grouped.

Answer to review question 3.10 The HAVING keyword is used to filter groups out of the results set of a query, in the same way that the WHERE clause is used to filter rows. The HAVING clause is optional, and must always follow and relate to a GROUP BY clause, in the same way that the WHERE clause is optional, and must always relate to a SELECT statement.

Answer to review question 3.11 Give the name of the doctor, the title of the diagnosis, the number of times the doctor made the diagnosis, the total estimated cost and total estimated admission days for each doctor for each standard diagnosis, where that doctor has made diagnoses for that standard diagnoses with a total estimated cost greater than £1000.

Answer to review question 3.12 GROUP BY and ORDER BY perform similar functions However, there is one major difference in that the GROUP BY is specifically designed to group identically defined data. On the other hand, the function of ORDER BY is to sort the data into a particular order.

Answer to review question 3.13 This is not possible because, in relational databases, rows are inserted in no particular order. You can only request rows using valid SQL features, such as ORDER BY.

CHAPTER 4

Further SQL

OVERVIEW

In this chapter we again focus on SQL, introducing the student to some additional features. In the previous chapter we looked at the relational algebra operations project, restrict, product and join, and how these are implemented in SQL. We will examine the implementation of some of the other relational algebra operators, namely **union**, **intersection**, **difference** and **divide**. For the latter, the EXISTS and NOT EXISTS SQL constructs will be introduced.

We also look further at joins: we examine **self-joined tables** and **non-equi joins**, where we join tables on the basis of an operation other than equality. SQL often has more than one alternative for performing a query and sometimes **subqueries** can be used instead of joins. Subqueries are important in their own right and we will look at the two types of subqueries – **non-correlated** and **correlated subqueries**. Other features of SQL will be explained and investigated, i.e. **views** and running SQL **queries interactively**.

| **Learning outcomes** | On completion of this chapter, you should be able to: |

- Understand how the relational algebra operators union, intersection, difference and divide are implemented in SQL

- Understand features of SQL including self-joins, non-equi joins, subqueries, correlated subqueries, set comparison operators, existential qualification and views.

Note that the example queries later in this chapter have been executed in Oracle10g using the Bus Depots' database which was given in section 2.2, chapter 2. You will find details of the sample data used in the appendix. You should refer to the entity relationship diagram and the appendix to assist in your understanding of each query execution code.

4.1 Recursive relationships and self-joins

In chapter 1 we looked at recursive relationships, where an entity occurrence can relate to other occurrences of the same entity. The bus drivers' database does not contain any obvious recursive relationships; we could identify the following, for example:

Figure 4.1: Recursive relationship examples

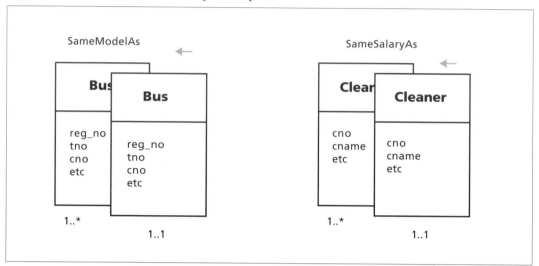

SQL allows you to join the same table together by using aliases. As we saw in the previous chapter, an alias is an alternative name for each table.

So for the query 'Find any buses which are the same model as bus H259IJK' then the SQL is:

```
select b2.*
from bus b1, bus b2
where b1.reg_no = 'H259IJK'
and b1.model =b2.model;
```

which outputs:

REG_NO	MODEL	TNO	DNO	CNO
H259IJK	Daf SB220	3	102	114
R678FDS	Daf SB220	1		110

You can think of the table Bus b1 and b2 as two copies of the same table, one with each alias name. Table b1 is used to search for 'H259IJK's record. Table b2 is used to find those records with the same model as b1 (i.e. 'H259IJK'). The tables have been joined in the usual way with a join condition. Notice that in the select clause (the first line of the statement) you need to specify which table the output should come from – in this case b2. Note that to omit H259IJK from the final output we add the line:

```
and b2.reg_no <>'H259IJK';
```

Another example illustrating a self join

Suppose we want to list the names of cleaners who are responsible for any bus types that cleaner Betty is responsible for.

This uses the Bus and Cleaner tables thus:

Figure 4.2: ResponsibleFor example

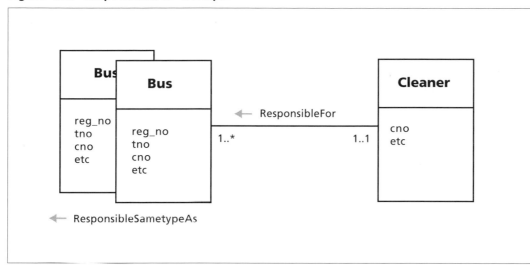

The ResponsibleFor relationship shows which rows are related to Betty's – i.e. Betty's buses. The ResponsibleSameTypeAs relationship finds all rows linked to those bus types. The ResponsibleFor relationship is used again to find who is linked to these bus types.

In SQL:

```
select c2.cname
from   bus b1, bus b2,
    cleaner c1, cleaner c2
where c1.cname = 'Betty'
and c1.cno =b1.cno
and b1.tno=b2.tno
and b2.cno=c2.cno
and c2.cname<>'Betty';
```

CNAME
John
Vince

Here the alias 'c1' is used to identify Betty's record in the Cleaner table. This row, or rows, is then joined to bus (b1) to find the bus types for which Betty is responsible. These rows are joined using the recursive relationship – ResponsibleSameTypeAs – to all rows for the same bus types in Bus (alias b2). The rows in b2 are joined to a second copy of Cleaner c2. Lastly, Betty is eliminated from the output.

4.2 Subqueries

Subqueries using IN

In addition to joining tables together using a join condition, SQL provides an additional way of handling queries involving multiple tables – i.e. using subqueries. In a subquery, a Select statement (the inner select) can be embedded inside the WHERE clause of a main Select query (the outer select). To understand how a subquery is evaluated, consider the following example, to find cleaners who have been allocated to a bus:

> **Select** cname
> **From** cleaner
> Where cno in
>   **(Select** cno
>   **from** bus);

CNAME
John
Jean
Betty
Vince
Jay

In a subquery the inner select executes first and the result is passed to the outer select. So in the example, 'select cno from bus' is evaluated and the result, i.e. all the cleaner numbers in the bus table is passed to the outer select, so that the cleaner names for these cleaners can be output.

Note that the operator IN is used where the subquery returns a set of items in a column (zero or more). Other subquery operators are ANY and ALL. Another comparison operator EXISTS is discussed later in the chapter. In the examples we have considered above, the subquery is embedded in the 'where' clause. Note that it is also possible to include subqueries in the 'select' and 'from' clauses.

Subqueries using NOT IN

The keyword NOT can be used with the IN operator – this specifies that all rows are retrieved (from the table(s) in the outer select) except for those rows that are returned by the inner select. The following example finds those cleaners who have not been allocated to a bus:

> **Select** cname
> **From** cleaner
> Where cno not in
>   **(Select** cno
>   **from** bus);

CNAME
Doug
Geeta

Subqueries that return a single value

Where the inner select returns a single value, the comparison operator '=' can be used. For example, to find any cleaners by name, whose earnings are exactly equal to the average cleaner's salary:

```
Select cname
From cleaner
Where csalary =
    (Select avg(csalary)
      from cleaner);
```

This example query will produce no rows. Note that other operators such as >, >= can also be used in subqueries instead of =.

Nested subqueries

Subqueries can be created to multiple levels. However, subqueries take longer to execute than joins, so deep levels of subqueries are not recommended. An example of a nested subquery is given, to find names of bus drivers who are trained to drive bendy-buses.

```
Select bdname
From busdriver
Where bdno in
    (Select bdno
      from training
      where tno in
          (Select tno
            from bustype
            where tdescript = 'bendy-bus'));
```

BDNAME
Maggie May
John Peel
Jack Jones

4.3 The non-equi join

So far we have looked at equi-joins, i.e. we have joined tables on the basis of equality between common attributes. The non-equi join, which must be used carefully, is a join based on any valid comparison operator, such as <>, > ,=<. It is equivalent to taking the product of two relations and then performing the appropriate restriction on the result. Examples may involve recursive relationships, e.g. Which cleaners have a lower salary than cleaner Betty?

In SQL:

```
Select c1.cname
From cleaner c1, cleaner c2
Where c2.cname = 'Betty'
And c1.csalary < c2.csalary;
```

CNAME
Doug

Subqueries and the non-equi join

Note that a **common SQL error** is to use a non-equi join where only a subquery will give the correct results. So, for example, if it is required to find the bus drivers who are not qualified to drive bus type 2, a student might write the query as follows:

```
Select distinct bdname
From busdriver bd, training t
Where tno = '2'
And bd.bdno <> t.bdno;
```

BDNAME
Maggie May
Jack Jones
Jane Brown
Sally Smith
Peter Piper
James Bond
John Peel

The result here is all the bus drivers, which is not what the student expected. What the student has, in fact, done is to consider each bus driver in turn and compared this record with each one in the training table. Those bus driver names are printed where there is a record in the training tables with type '2' that has a different bus driver number. All drivers fall into this category so the names of all bus drivers will be output. The correct solution is to use a subquery with NOT IN.

```
Select bdname
From busdriver
Where bdno not in
    (select bdno
    from training
    where tno = '2');
```

BDNAME
Jack Jones
Peter Piper

As illustrated by the foregoing example we cannot use a non-equi join in place of NOT IN, i.e. NOT IN does not have the same relationship to negative joins as IN does to the equi-join. NOT IN looks for no matches while the non-equi join forms a product of the tables (i.e. every combination) and then eliminates those rows in the join condition.

4.4 Correlated subqueries

A correlated subquery is one where information from the outer select statement is referenced in the subquery. The subquery is executed differently from the non-correlated subqueries we saw earlier. Then it was executed from the bottom up. With correlated subqueries, on the other hand, the outer select is executed first and provides the values, one at a time, for the evaluation of the inner subquery.

Steps to execute a correlated subquery

1. The outer query fetches a row.
2. The inner query is executed, using the value from the row fetched in 1.
3. Data from the row fetched in 1. will be selected and output depending on the values returned by the execution of the inner query.
4. Repeat until no rows (outer query).

Example of correlated subquery

We can use a correlated subquery, for example, to find cleaners who earn less than the average salary for their depot:

```
select cname
from cleaner c1
where csalary <
    (select  avg(csalary)
    from cleaner c2
    where c1.dno =c2.dno);
```

CNAME
Jean
Betty
Doug

We can see that this is a correlated subquery, since we have used an attribute (c1.dno) in the 'where' clause of the inner select. The table c1 was, however, specified in the outer select. Note that the alias is necessary only to avoid ambiguity in column names.

4.5 Set operators

It is useful sometimes to combine information of a similar type from more than one table. We can use the normal relational algebra set operations of union, intersection and difference to do this. For example, if we had two bus drivers' tables: one of current drivers; the other of drivers who have left the company:

- The union of the two tables would be everyone in both tables (people who had left the company or people who are currently employed)

- The intersection of the two tables would be only those people who were in both tables (people who had left the company and were now employed again)

- The difference of the two tables would be one of two alternatives: everyone in the current bus drivers' tables but not people who had left the company and were now re-employed; everyone in the 'old' bus drivers' table but not anyone who was now re-employed.

When using these set operators, the two tables involved must have the same structure – that is, the same number of columns of a compatible type. It is said that the two tables are union compatible. Oracle uses the set operators UNION, INTERSECT and MINUS to perform these operations.

Union of tables

As an example, we might want to find all those bus drivers who are based at the Holloway depot, or those drivers who are qualified to drive a bus of type 'midibus', or both:

```
select  bdname
from busdriver bd, depot d
where bd.dno = d.dno
and dname = 'Holloway'
union
select  bdname
from busdriver bd, training t, bustype bt
where bd.bdno = t.bdno
and t.tno = bt.tno
and tdescript = 'midibus';
```

BDNAME
Jack Jones
James Bond
Jane Brown
John Peel
Maggie May

Intersection of tables

In this example, we find all those bus drivers who are based at the Holloway depot, and are qualified to drive a bus of type 'midibus':

```
select  bdname
from busdriver bd, depot d
where bd.dno = d.dno
and dname = 'Holloway'
```

intersect
select   bdname
from busdriver bd, training t, bustype bt
where bd.bdno = t.bdno
and t.tno = bt.tno
and tdescript = 'midibus';

BDNAME
Jack Jones

Difference of tables

In this example, we find all those bus drivers who are based at the Holloway depot, but are not qualified to drive a bus of type 'midibus':

select   bdname
from busdriver bd, depot d
where bd.dno = d.dno
and dname = 'Holloway'
minus
select   bdname
from busdriver bd, training t, bustype bt
where bd.bdno = t.bdno
and t.tno = bt.tno
and tdescript = 'midibus';

gives the output:

BDNAME
Jane Brown

Alternatively, we could find all those bus drivers who are qualified to drive a bus of type 'midibus', but are not based at the Holloway depot:

select   bdname
from busdriver bd, training t, bustype bt
where bd.bdno = t.bdno
and t.tno = bt.tno
and tdescript = 'midibus'
minus
select   bdname
from busdriver bd, depot d
where bd.dno = d.dno
and dname = 'Holloway';

BDNAME
James Bond
John Peel
Maggie May

4.6 Existential qualification

Exists

A particular case of a correlated query is one that includes the Boolean qualifier 'exists'.

The EXISTS keyword is used for what is called the 'existence test' – to test for the existence or non-existence of data that meets the criteria of the subquery.

For example, find the names of cleaners who are responsible for at least one bus:

```
select cname
from cleaner c
where exists
  (select *
  from bus b
  where c.cno = b.cno);
```

CNAME
John
Jean
Betty
Vince
Jay

'Exists' tests for the presence or absence of 'the empty set' of rows returned by the subquery. If the subquery returns at least one row, then the subquery evaluates to true. If no rows are returned, the subquery evaluates to false. In this example, the subquery is evaluated in turn for each row in the cleaner table. The first cleaner is John with cno = '110'. The subquery checks to see if there are any rows in the bus table where the cno is 110. In this case the empty set is not present and 'true' is returned. Cleaner John is therefore included in the output. The process is repeated for each of the cleaners' names. Only with the last iterations, with cleaners Doug and Geeta, will 'false' be returned and the cleaner be excluded.

Not exists

Similarly, 'not exists' tests for the presence or absence of 'the empty set' of rows returned by the subquery. In this case, if the subquery returns at least one row, then the subquery evaluates to false. If no rows are returned, the subquery evaluates to true. For example:

```
select cname
from cleaner c
where not exists
  (select *
  from bus b
  where c.cno = b.cno);
```

CNAME
Doug
Geeta

In this example, the subquery is evaluated in turn for each row in the cleaner table. The first cleaner is John with cno = '110'. The subquery checks to see if there are any rows in the bus table where the cno is 110. In this case the empty set is not present and 'false' is returned. Cleaner John is therefore not included in the output. The process is repeated for each of the cleaners' names. Only with the last two iterations, with cleaner Doug and Geeta, where the empty set is present will 'true' be returned and the cleaner be included.

In the above examples where the operators EXISTS and NOT EXISTS have been used, these queries could have been formulated using subqueries (IN and NOT IN) instead. Another alternative, in the first example only (i.e. EXISTS), a join condition could have been used instead. In fact, it is usually always possible to perform the queries using alternative and simpler methods. There is one case where the use of EXISTS is mandatory – relational algebra divide.

Relational algebra division

We saw the relational algebra operation division in chapter 1. Divide takes two relations: one binary, one unary and builds a relation consisting of all values of one attribute of the binary relation that match (in the other attribute) all values in the unary relation.

Figure 4.1: Examples of divide

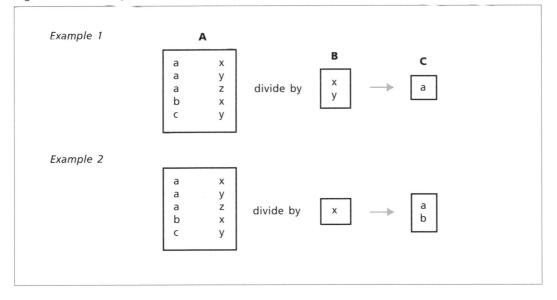

The division operation allows us to compare two relations to see if one is a subset of the other. This is what we would need to do to answer questions such as:

Find routes which allow buses of every type

or

Which bus drivers can drive all the buses based at the Holloway depot?

Double negative existential qualification

The double negative existential qualification is an SQL construct that allows us to directly compare two sets, as opposed to the set comparison operators such as IN, which allows us to compare a scalar [single] value with a set/relation. For example, if we wanted to find the names of bus drivers who could operate on every route:

```
select bdname
from busdriver bd
where not exists
    (select *
    from route r
    where not exists
        (select *
        from ability a
        where bd.bdno = a.bdno
        and a.rno = r.rno));
```

The result, in this case, is 'no rows selected' as there is no driver in the database who operates every route.

Figure 4.2: Many-to-many relationship example

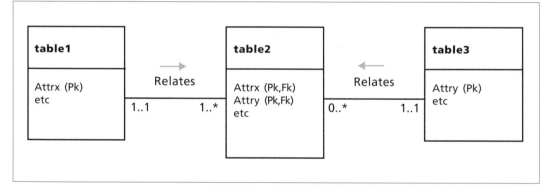

Given the many-to-many relationship, the following template can be used for relational algebra type queries:

```
SELECT attributes
FROM   table1
WHERE NOT EXISTS
    (SELECT *
    FROM   table3
    WHERE NOT EXISTS
        (SELECT *
        FROM table2
        WHERE table1.attrx = table2.attrx
        AND table2.attry = table3.attry));
```

In more complicated relational algebra type queries which involve more tables, then it will be necessary to join tables together, possibly within a VIEW (discussed in a later section), or within the nested subqueries to achieve the correct result.

4.7 Interactive queries

A very useful facility is provided to enable users to run the same query again, entering a different value of a parameter to a WHERE or HAVING clause. This is done by prefixing the column specification for which different values are to be supplied by the '&' sign. For example, we can easily find the number of buses of type 2. It is also possible to find the number of buses of any type by running the same query, in each case entering the value of the bus type number interactively.

> **select Count(reg_no)as buscount**
> **from bus**
> **where tno = &tno;**

produced the following execution:

> Enter value for typeno: 1
> old   3: where tno = &tno
> new 3: where tno = 1

BUSCOUNT
3

Thus it can avoid the need to recode in order to vary the values of interactively specified parameters.

4.8 SQL views

The permanent tables in the database are called the **base tables**. A view is derived from the base tables using any desired restriction, projection or join operations. It allows you to view the data that only concerns you, and to create tables tailored to particular requirements. The data that is output when a view is executed is not what is actually stored when a view is created. It is a **virtual table**, which means it does not actually exist as a table in the database: only the view definition is stored. Views are dynamic – each time the view is used it is re-created from the base tables.

Views are used for a number of reasons:

- To enforce security by hiding data from certain users
- To simplify complex queries by providing intermediate answers which are dynamically updated and can be reused as input
- As input to utilities such as report generators.

You should consider using views in the examples and courseworks – particularly when you have a complex query and you can produce an intermediate answer by first of all creating a view.

Creating views in SQL
Views are created using the CREATE VIEW statement. The syntax of this statement is very similar to that for creating tables using a SELECT. For example, to create a view showing

the cleaner numbers and registration numbers of buses for which the cleaners are responsible:

```
create view CleanersAndTheirBuses
as select c.cno, reg_no
from cleaner c, bus b
where c.cno=b.cno;
```

To examine the structure of the view CleanersAndTheirBuses, we can use the describe command just as for table objects:

```
describe CleanersAndTheirBuses;
```

Name	Null?	Type
CNO	NOT NULL	VARCHAR2(5)
REG_NO	NOT NULL	VARCHAR2(10)

To see the data in the view, we can issue a SELECT statement just as if the view CleanersAndTheirBuses is a table:

```
select *
from CleanersAndTheirBuses;
```

CNO	REG_NO
113	A123ABC
114	D678FGH
112	D345GGG
114	H259IJK
110	P200IJK
111	P300RTY
110	R678FDS

4.9 Summary

In this chapter we discussed in more detail the SQL query language. We introduced some advanced features of SQL including self-joins, subqueries, correlated queries, the EXISTS operator and views. We continued our discussion of how the relational algebra operators are implemented in SQL, namely union, intersection, difference and divide.

4.10 Review questions

Review question 4.1 Examine the following query involving a self-join. Give the English meaning of the query. What is the purpose of each of the tables?

```
Select   b2.reg_no
From   bus b1, bus b2,
        depot d1, depot d2
Where b1.reg_no= 'P200IJK'
And   b1.dno=d1.dno
And   d1.daddress=d2.daddress
And   d2.dno=b2.dno;
```

Review question 4.2 Examine the following query involving a self-join. Rewrite the question using nested selects (subqueries) instead.

```
Select   b2.reg_no
From   bus b1, bus b2,
        depot d1, depot d2
Where b1.reg_no= 'P200IJK'
And   b1.dno=d1.dno
And   d1.daddress=d2.daddress
And   d2.dno=b2.dno;
```

Review question 4.3 State whether you think the pair of SQL statements below are equivalent:

```
select distinct c.cno, cname      select cno, cname
from cleaner c, bus b             from cleaner
where c.cno = b.cno               where cno in
and model like 'Daf%';              (select cno
                                     from bus
                                     where model like 'Daf%');
```

Explain your answer.

Review question 4.4 State whether you think the pair of SQL statements below are equivalent:

```
select distinct c.cno, cname      select cno, cname
from cleaner c, bus b             from cleaner
where c.cno <> b.cno              where cno not in
and model like 'Daf%';              (select cno
                                     from bus
                                     where model like 'Daf%');
```

Explain your answer.

Review question 4.5 The following entity-relationship model concerns patients who have been admitted to hospital and given various treatments. For each patient's admission, the date admitted is held, plus the doctor who authorised the admission. Each time a patient is treated this is recorded, along with the doctor who authorised the treatment and the date.

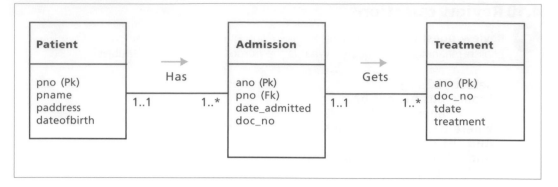

Give the English meaning of the following SQL command:

```
select p.pname
from patient p, admission a
where p.pno = a.pno
and not exists
    (select * from treatment t
    where t.ano = a.ano
    and   t.docno = a.docno);
```

 Review question 4.6 Given the following entity-relationship model concerning patients who have been admitted to various hospitals:

Patient		Admission		Hospital
pno (Pk) pname paddress dateofbirth	Has → 1..1 1..*	ano hno date_admitted	← Gets 1..* 1..1	hno (Pk) hname

describe what the following statement does and outline how it achieves it:

```
select pname
from patient
where not exists
    (select * from hospital
    where not exists
        (select *
        from admission
        where patient.pno = admission.pno
        and hospital.  hno = admission.hno));
```

Review question 4.7 An SQL programmer wanted to find (as in review question 4.6) the names of patients who have been admitted to every hospital. He did this by using the COUNT function to count the total number of hospitals each patient had been admitted to and then comparing this with the total number of hospitals in the database, i.e.:

> **select** distinct pname, count (hno)
> **from** patient p, admission a
> **where** p.pno = a.pno
> **group** by pname,hno
> **having** count(hno) =
>   (**select** count(hno)
>   **from** hospital);

Is this a valid way of tackling this query?

Review question 4.8 Explain the purpose of views in SQL. Give an example in SQL of a view, again using the sample database. You should create a view, and then illustrate how it might be used.

4.11 Answers to review questions

Answer to review question 4.1 List the buses by registration number which are based at the same address as the bus with registration number 'P200IJK'.

Table Bus b1 is to find the bus with registration number 'P200IJK'. Table Depot d1 is used to find the depot where this bus is based with its location. Table Depot g2 is used to find depots at the same location. Finally table Bus b2 is used to find the registration numbers of buses based at these depots.

Answer to review question 4.2

> **Select** reg_no
> **From** bus
> **Where** dno **in**
>   (**select** dno
>   **from** depot
>   **where** daddress in
>   (**select** daddress
>   **from** depot
>   **Where** dno in
>   (**select** dno
>   **from** bus
>   **where** reg_no= 'P200IJK')));

Both queries give output:

REG_NO
H259IJK
P200IJK
P300RTY

Answer to review question 4.3   The statements are equivalent.

The first query is the natural join of the two tables, so only includes rows from each table that have a match on the other. The result is to identify those cleaners who are responsible for buses of model Daf.

The second query does the same thing more directly, searching for a cleaner identifier in the list of cleaners who are responsible for buses of model Daf.

Answer to review question 4.4   The statements are not equivalent.

The first query does NOT make sense. It asks for the number and name of any cleaner such that there is a different cleaner that is responsible for buses of model Daf. Since two different cleaners have buses for which they are responsible, then this is true for all cleaners, so the result will be the numbers and names of all cleaners.

The second query is 'sensible' SQL. For each cleaner, a check is made to see if that cleaner is responsible for buses of model Daf, and if the cleaner is not, then that cleaner (no. and name) is included in the result, i.e.: lists all those cleaners not responsible for buses of model Daf.

Answer to review question 4.5   Give the name of each patient who was never treated during an admission by the doctor who admitted him/her on that occasion.

Answer to review question 4.6   This gives the names of patients who have been admitted to every hospital.

It can be thought of as looping for each hospital within each patient. The inner loop returns a row if there is any hospital where there is no admission row for that patient at that hospital (not exists true). If any row has been assembled by the end of the cycle, the outer not exists is false so the patient is eliminated.

Answer to review question 4.7   Under most circumstances it will give the correct answer. If there is incorrect data in the database, it may give misleading results. The relational algebra solution is a better solution, as it checks for the existence for each patient's admission to each hospital.

Answer to review question 4.8   Views are used for a number of reasons:

- To enforce security by hiding data from certain users

- To simplify complex queries by providing intermediate answers which are dynamically updated and can be reused as input

- As input to utilities such as report generators.

```
create view HollowayBuses
as   select reg_no, model, d.dno
     from bus b, depot d
     where b.dno = d.dno
     and dname = 'Holloway';
```

This creates a view of registration numbers, models and cleaner no. for buses based at Holloway. The view name is then incorporated into a select-statement in the normal way. For example:

```
Select distinct cname
from HollowayBuses h, cleaner c
where h.dno = c.dno
```

This gives the names of cleaners who look after buses based at the Holloway depot.

CHAPTER 5

PL/SQL

OVERVIEW

Following on from the previous topic, this chapter introduces you to **PL/SQL**, Oracle's procedural language. The syntax and constructs will be looked at through several illustrative examples. In particular, **stored procedures** and **database triggers** will be examined. These features have been made available in a number of DBMSs including Oracle and are used for storing and applying logic at the database level rather than at application level. They provide those DBMSs with greater flexibility and power in dealing with complexities in many demanding business applications. The chapter starts off with a summary of the main features of Oracle, which is the most widely used database management system.

| **Learning outcomes** | On completion of this chapter, you should be able to: |

- Understand how SQL has been extended procedurally into PL/SQL

- Explain how stored procedures can be used to implement processing logic at the database level

- Describe the use of database triggers in providing an automatic response to the occurrence of specific database events.

Note that the example programs found later in this chapter have been executed in Oracle10, using the Bus Depots' Database which was given in section 2.2 of chapter 2. You will find details of the sample data used in the appendix. You should refer to the entity-relationship diagram and the appendix to assist in your understanding of each program's execution.

5.1 Introduction

We begin with an examination of the database management system, Oracle. In 1979, a company called Relational Software, Inc. released the first commercially available implementation of SQL. This company later became the Oracle Corporation. Oracle version 2, which incorporated a reasonably complete implementation of SQL, was the first of many versions to come over the years. There was no 'version 1' – the company thought potential customers would be likely to purchase a second version rather than an initial release. This was the first of many versions to come over the years, each adding new technologies and improved features, with the most recent being Oracle10g.

Oracle is now available in many of today's popular computing environments, in particular Windows, UNIX and Linux. Oracle Corporation has expanded far beyond being just about database systems. Like its competitors, it has expanded into related business areas, notably eCommerce, data casting over the Web, and even mobile telephone technology.

The latest versions of Oracle (with each new version being a superset of the previous one) are as follows:

- **Oracle8 – Object Oracle**

  Released in 1997, this version included features for supporting the Internet, network computing and new types of information. Oracle8 included support for object-oriented development and new multimedia applications

- **Oracle8i – Internet Oracle**

  Oracle8i was introduced in 1998. It was associated with the Internet (hence the 'i'), because its new features were designed to support Internet-based activities and applications. Oracle8i consists of a family of products varying from single-user products through to Oracle8i Enterprise Edition, which is intended for a large number of users with large databases.

- **Oracle9i – 'Unbreakable' Oracle**

  In 2001, Oracle9 further extended the product, including features to improve performance and manageability of the data warehouse. This version also contains a powerful facility for storing and accessing XML documents.

- **Oracle10g – Grid Computing**

  Oracle10g was released in 2003. Grids are used to solve large-scale computing problems by connecting the resources of a group of low-cost servers. These servers are connected by a network (e.g. the Internet). Oracle maintains that Oracle Grid can run applications faster than the fastest mainframe. If a server fails, unlike the mainframe, the Oracle Grid keeps running.

These versions include the procedural language PL/SQL which we will study in the rest of the chapter.

5.2 Example PL/SQL blocks

PL/SQL stands for **procedural language SQL** and is Oracle's procedural extension to SQL. PL/SQL, in some ways, is similar to a modern programming language as it includes features such as block structures, variables, constants, control structures (such as 'if' and loops), functions and procedures. PL/SQL is used for the following:

- To add programming logic to the execution of SQL commands (e.g. 'if' statement, 'for' and 'while' loops)
- To trigger database events to occur, such as referential constraints
- To store procedures which enforce business rules and application logic.

Any SQL statement (apart from 'Create Table') can be used in a PL/SQL program without any special pre-processing. PL/SQL can be considered as a superset of SQL. It allows the storage of compiled code in the database, enabling different applications to share functions and procedures. For example, PL/SQL can be used to implement program logic embedded within applications such as those for manipulating forms. In this brief introduction to the language, instead of presenting a formal syntax for PL/SQL, a number of examples are used to illustrate various features of the language.

Program structure – blocks

PL/SQL is grouped into units called **blocks**. Blocks can be **stand alone** or **nested**. A block will take the form:

```
declare
<declarations section>
begin
<executable commands>
exception
<exception handling>
end;
```

Keywords are in bold. The declaration section consists of type, constants, variables etc. Variables are used to temporarily store values. The executable section contains the program statements. When an error occurs, an exception is raised and program control transfers to the exception handling section (optional). There are pre-defined and user-defined errors.

Simple example program

Note: when executing the sample PL/SQL programs, you should type in the command **'set serveroutput on'**. It allows the user to display information to the session's output device (screen). This only needs to be entered once per session. Also don't forget to end the code with '/' to execute the code.

The program in example 5.1 adds two numbers together and displays the sum.

Example 5.1: Simple PLSQL block and execution

```
--pl/sql program to add numbers and print message
declare
  num1 number:= 7;
  num2 number:= 5;
  totnum number;

begin
--main block
  totnum := num1 + num2;
    dbms_output.put_line(' The number is  ' || totnum );

end;


The number is 12
PL/SQL procedure successfully completed.
```

This is an example of an **anonymous block**, i.e. an unnamed block. PL/SQL programs comprise one or more blocks. These blocks can be separate or nested. Besides anonymous blocks there are also procedures and functions which we will look at later in this chapter. Anonymous blocks are declared in an application at the point where they are to be executed. They are passed to the PL/SQL engine for execution at runtime.

In the example, in the declaration section, we have declared three variables num1, num2 and totnum. These variables can hold data of type number. The initial value of any variable, regardless of its type, is NULL. We can assign values to variables, using the ":=" operator. The assignment can occur either immediately after the type of the variable is declared (as in the example), or anywhere in the executable portion of the program.

In the main block, num1 and num2 are added together and the total stored in totnum. 'Dbms_output.put_line' is used in a PL/SQL program to output to the screen. Note that the lines of code starting with two dashes (--) are comments.

Executable commands

Like any other high-level programming language, PL/SQL provides the following:

- The assignment statement (in the example above, 'totnum := num1 + num2')
- The null statement
- Conditional statements (if-then and variants)
- Loops (for, while)
- Procedures and functions.

Example including SQL 'select into' and 'update' statements

The code below relates to our bus depots' database case study. This program increases bus driver Maggie May's salary by 10% if she earns less than 2500. The results of the execution are shown:

Example 5.2: PLSQL block

```
--pl/sql program to update a busdriver salary by 10% if she earns less than 2500
- includes SQL select into, update statements and exceptions handling

declare
   temp_sal  number(6,2);
   minsal    number(6,2) := 2500;
   driver    varchar2(20) := 'Maggie May';

begin
--main block
   select bdsalary into temp_sal
   from busdriver
   where bdname = driver;
   if temp_sal <minsal then
      update busdriver set bdsalary = (temp_sal *1.1)
      where bdname = driver;
      dbms_output.put_line(' Bus driver '|| driver || ' salary updated to ' ||
      temp_sal*1.1 );

   else
      dbms_output.put_line(' Bus driver '|| driver || ' earns' || temp_sal );
   end if;
commit;

exception
   when no_data_found then
      dbms_output.put_line(' Maggie May record not found ');
end;
```

Bus driver Maggie May salary updated to 2420
PL/SQL procedure successfully completed.

The '**select into**' statement is used in the above example. It states where the returned data values, found in the database table, are to be stored. In the above example, the database value of 'bdsalary' is stored in the variable 'temp_sal'. The INTO clause is mandatory for SELECT statements within PL/SQL blocks (which are not within a cursor definition).

Notice the '**if then else**' statement control structure, which is found in many procedural languages. So far, all examples have been processed sequentially. The 'if then else' construct alters the order in which statements are executed depending on certain conditions. The condition 'temp_sal < minsal' tests to see if the Maggie May's salary is less than minsal, which has been set to 2500. If true, her salary is updated by 10%; otherwise a message stating her current salary is output.

Exception handling is also illustrated in this example. Blocks have the ability to trap and handle local error conditions. You may also self-generate explicit exceptions that deal with logic and data errors. Block execution is terminated after an exception handling routine is executed.

Example using a procedure

The example below accepts a driver number '009' as input to a prodedure, and returns the driver's name and driver's depot name.

Example 5.3: PLSQL block with procedure

```
--pl/sql program block to call procedure from main program
declare
bdrno        busdriver.bdno%type := '009' ;
bdrname      busdriver.bdname%type;
depname      depot.dname%type;

status       boolean;

procedure get_drivers_depot(
driverno     in    busdriver.bdno%type,
drivername   out   busdriver.bdname%type,
depotname    out   depot.dname%type,
status       out   Boolean) is
begin
  select bdname, dname
  into drivername, depotname
  from busdriver b, depot d
  where b.bdno = driverno
  and b.dno = d.dno;
  status := true;
  exception
  when no_data_found then
  status := false;
end;

begin
--main block
  get_drivers_depot (bdrno,bdrname,depname,status);
  if (status) then
    dbms_output.put_line(' Bus driver   ' || bdrno || ' ' || bdrname || ' works at '
|| depname );
  else
    dbms_output.put_line (' Bus driver   ' || bdrno || ' not  found');
  end if;
end;
/
```

The following SQLPLUS session illustrates the execution:

```
set serveroutput on

Bus driver 009 Jack Jones works at Holloway
PL/SQL procedure successfully completed.
```

This example includes a procedure. A procedure is a type of **subprogram.** Subprograms are named PL/SQL blocks that can take parameters and are one of two types: procedures or functions. A procedure is used to perform an action. A function is similar to a procedure, except that a function *must* compute and return a single value.

In the foregoing program, the procedure is called get_drivers_depot and is specified in the declare section. The table below has been drawn to show how the different sets of data names relate to one another. Different names have been used for the 2 sets of variables to aid understanding of the purpose of the various variables. Two variables can, in fact, have the same name, provided that they are defined in different blocks. Variables names should be different from the names of attributes in the table.

Description	Database attribute name	Main program variables	Procedure variables (parameters)
Bus driver number	bdno	bdrno	driverno
Bus driver name	bdname	bdrname	drivername
Depot name	dname	depname	depotname

Also in the declaration sections, the variables are declared with their types. For example, Boolean (true or false) is the type for status, and busdriver.bdno%type is the type for bdrno. The latter is called an **anchored data type** – the type for bdrno is determined by looking up the bdno in the busdriver table (varchar2).

The main block calls the procedure get_drivers_depot passing the bus driver's number bdrno = '009'. In the procedure, notice the SQL select statement. If the driver is found, 'status' is returned as true, and the details will be printed, otherwise it is false and an error message will be printed.

5.3 PL/SQL cursors

Almost any SQL statement can be used in a PL/SQL statement, including **update, delete** and **insert**. However, a **select into** statement (as in the example above) cannot be used to return more than one row. When more than one row is required, PL/SQL provides **cursors**. This allows rows of a query result to be accessed one row at a time. The cursor can be thought of as a pointer, which points to a particular row of a query result.

A cursor must be declared. It is opened, used and then closed when no longer required (using the **open**, **fetch into** and **close** statements). The **fetch** statement, when executed, puts the 'current' row pointed at by the cursor into a record or variable list. Information from a cursor that is being processed can be obtained by using **cursor attributes**. An example, in the following sample code, is **%found** which returns true if a record was successfully fetched from the cursor. Another example is **rowcount** which returns the total number of rows returned so far.

PL/SQL cursor example

This example lists all the drivers by name with their depot.

Example 5.4: PLSQL cursor

```
--pl/sql program to list all drivers and their depots, using a cursor
declare
cursor    drivercursor is
  select bdno,bdname,dname
  from busdriver b, depot d
  where b.dno = d.dno;
  drivercursor_rec  drivercursor%rowtype;

begin
  open drivercursor;
  fetch drivercursor into drivercursor_rec;
  while drivercursor%found loop
      dbms_output.put_line( drivercursor_rec.bdno || '  ' ||
drivercursor_rec.bdname|| '  ' || drivercursor_rec.dname ||' depot '   );
      fetch drivercursor into drivercursor_rec;
  end loop;
  close drivercursor;
end;
/
```

Output from running the code within SQLPLUS is as follows:

```
SQL> set serveroutput on
001 Jane Brown Holloway depot
007 James Bond Hornsey depot
008 Maggie May Hornsey depot
009 Jack Jones Holloway depot
010 Peter Piper Islington depot
011 John Peel Hornsey depot
PL/SQL procedure successfully completed.
```

Notice the 'while' loop above. There are three kinds of loops in PL/SQL:

- **Loop** – the loop body is executed repeatedly until an exit statement
- **For loop** – the loop body is executed a specific number of times
- **While loop** – the loop body executes as long as a condition is true.

In the example, the first record is fetched into the drivercursor_rec variable and then the while loop is performed while '%found' returns true. If there are no records returned, then the while loop will not be executed.

5.4 PL/SQL stored procedures and functions

Stored procedures

The procedure that we looked at in an earlier example was declared and called from within the PL/SQL program. It is possible to store procedure and function definitions **in the database**, and to have them invoked from various environments that have access to the database. This allows code that enforces business rules to be moved from the application to the database. Some of the most important advantages of using stored procedures are summarised as follows:

- The code can be stored once for use by different applications. Since the procedural code is stored within the database and is fairly static, applications may benefit from the reuse of the same queries within the database
- The use of stored procedures can make the application code more consistent and easier to maintain. This principle is similar to the good practice in general programming, in which common functionality should be coded separately as procedures or functions
- Because the processing of complex business rules may be performed within the database, significant performance improvement can be obtained in a networked client/server environment.

Stored functions

In Oracle, a procedure is implemented to perform certain operations when called upon by other application programs. Depending on the operations, it may not return any value, or it might return one or more values via corresponding variables when its execution finishes. Unlike procedures, a **function** always returns a value to the caller as a result of completing its operations. It is also worth mentioning that a function may be invoked by code within a procedure, and a procedure may be called from within a function. Again, we use an example to illustrate how to create a function. This stored function takes as input a bus registration number, and returns the type (description) of that bus:

Example 5.5: Stored function

```
--pl/sql stored function to return the bus type for a given bus
create function get_bus_description(bus_reg in bus.reg_no%type)
   return bustype. tdescript%type as
typedesc bustype. tdescript%type;
begin
   select tdescript
   into typedesc
   from bus b, bustype bt
   where b.tno=bt.tno
   and reg_no = bus_reg;
   return (typedesc);
end;
/
Function created.
```

The stored function is created within SQLPLUS in the same way that a table or view is created. The **create function** clause defines the function's name (e.g. 'get_bus_description') as well as input variables. The keyword defines an input variable, together with its data type (in this case, the type is the same as the reg_no in the Bus relation, i.e. varchar2). The **return** keyword specifies the data type of the function's return value, which can be any valid PL/SQL data type. Every function must have a return clause, because the function must, by definition, return a value to the calling environment.

The function can now be called from a number of environments such as an SQL statement, another stored procedure or function, or a database trigger (see later section in this chapter). The following is a call made to the function 'get_bus_description' within an SQL query:

select reg_no, get_bus_description(reg_no)
from bus
where dno = '101';

REG_NO	GET_BUS_DESCRIPTION(REG_NO)
A123ABC	doubledecker
D678FGH	metrobus
D345GGG	doubledecker

5.5 Database triggers

What is a trigger?

A trigger defines an action the database should take when a modification is made to the database. They are associated with a single table within the database, and are specific to an Update, Insert or Delete operation, or a combination of these, against rows in the table. The database stores triggers in the same way that it stores normal data. The execution of triggers is transparent to the user. They are automatically executed whenever a specified event occurs and a condition is satisfied. They may be used to:

- Maintain database integrity
- Enforce complex business rules
- Audit changes to data.

Examples of how triggers are used include:

- To enforce referential integrity. For example, when a cascading delete is required if a 'Bus driver' record is deleted with all the 'Training' details linked to that driver
- When a bus driver's PVC (Passenger Carrying Vehicle) driving test date is earlier than a certain date, a trigger could create a training record automatically to indicate that certain training is due
- To recalculate ongoing tallies. For example, year-to-date information relating to bus drivers' salaries.

Triggers can be used to supplement database integrity constraints. However, they should not be used to replace the constraints. When enforcing business rules in an application, the declarative constraints available with the DBMS (e.g. Oracle) should be used. Triggers should then be created to enforce rules that cannot be coded through declarative constraints. The reason for this is that the enforcement of the declarative constraints is more efficient than the execution of triggers.

Triggers in Oracle

In Oracle, an SQL trigger automatically executes a PL/SQL block (the trigger action) when a triggering event (Insert, Update or Delete) occurs on a table. We say that the trigger is **fired** when the triggering event occurs.

To design a trigger, we need to specify the following:

- When the trigger is to be executed
- The actions which need to be taken when the trigger executes.

Example trigger

Instead of presenting a formal syntax for creating triggers, a number of examples are used to illustrate how different types of triggers are created. An example of a trigger is given below. It enforces the constraint that a cleaner cannot be responsible for more than four buses.

Example 5.6: Trigger example

```
--pl/sql trigger  to enforce constraint cleaner cannot be responsible for
--more than four buses.

create or replace trigger overworked
before insert or update on bus
for each row
declare
   maxnum  number;
   ex exception;

begin
   select count(*) into maxnum
   from bus
   where cno = :new.cno;
   if maxnum < 4 then
      dbms_output.put_line('Row added to bus table successful');
   else
      raise ex;
   end if;

   exception
   when ex then
      raise_application_error(-20000, 'Cleaner'||:new.cno|| 'already
         responsible for 4 buses');
end;
/
Trigger created.
```

In our example, the trigger will fire **before** (timing) any **insert or update** (event) operation on the Bus table. Timing could also be **after**, and event could also be **delete**. **For each row** means that this is a **row trigger** which is fired once for each row that is affected by the triggering event.

The last part of a trigger definition is the **begin/end** block containing PL/SQL code. It specifies what action will be taken after the trigger is invoked. In this block we use the RAISE_APPLICATION_ERROR procedure (system provided) to generate an error message and stop the execution of any Insert or Update on Bus operation which may result in a cleaner being responsible for more than four buses. In RAISE_APPLICATION_ERROR, the number '–20000' is a user-defined error number for the condition (the number must be between –20000 and –20999), and the text in single quotes is the error message to be displayed on the screen.

The special variables 'new' and 'old' are used to refer to new and old rows respectively. **Note** that in the trigger body, 'new' and 'old' must be preceded by a colon ':' (except in the 'when' clause, where a preceding colon is not used, as in the next example).

Trigger execution

A program block which inserts new values into the Bus table is created for testing the trigger. The following SQLPLUS session illustrates the execution to test the trigger 'overworked':

```
insert into bus values ( 'S123ABC','Daf','1','101', '114');

1 row created.

insert into bus values ( 'T123ABC','Daf','1','101', '114');

1 row created.

insert into bus values ('T124ABC','Daf','1','101', '114');

ERROR at line 1:
ORA-20000: Cleaner114already
responsible for 4 buses
ORA-06512: at "PATRICIA.OVERWORKED", line 17
ORA-04088: error during execution of trigger 'PATRICIA.OVERWORKED'
```

Row-level and statement-level triggers

Database triggers are classified as follows:

- **Row-level triggers** include the clause FOR EACH ROW in the CREATE TRIGGER statement. They fire once for each row affected by the SQL statement. The example above is a row-level trigger, with the 'for each row' statement defining it as such. They are the most common type of triggers. These triggers execute once for each row operated upon by a SQL statement affects and can access the original (old) and new column values processed by the SQL statement. For example, if an 'Update' statement updates 100 rows in the bus drivers' table, the row-level trigger for that table would be executed 100 times

- **Statement-level triggers** are the default trigger and do not include the clause 'for each row' in the 'Create Trigger' statement. A statement-level trigger fires only once for each triggering statement. They do not have access to the column values of each row that the trigger affects. For example, if an UPDATE statement updates 100 rows in the bus drivers' table, the statement-level trigger of that table would only be executed once.

Row-level triggers are typically used when you need to know the column values of a row to implement a business rule as in the trigger example above. Statement-level triggers are used to process information about the SQL statement that caused the trigger to fire and may be used to enforce additional security measures on a table.

The 'when' option in row-level triggers

For row-level triggers, there is another optional clause which can be used to further specify the conditions that must be met for the trigger to fire. The 'when' clause is used to specify the exact condition for the trigger to fire. The condition can be a complex Boolean expression connected by AND/OR logical operators. For the trigger to fire, the condition must be evaluated to true. If it is evaluated to false or does not evaluate because of NULL values, the trigger will not fire. For example, if we want to take some action when a cleaner is moved to the Holloway depot, we can define a trigger as follows:

Example 5.7: Trigger illustrating 'when' option

```
--pl/sql row-level trigger  with when option
create or replace trigger Holloway_depot_trigger
after update of dno on cleaner
for each row
when (new.dno = '110')
begin
dbms_output.put_line('warning message – new cleaner at Holloway depot');
end;
/
Trigger created.
```

Here the condition to be met is "new.dno= '110' ". So if the new record used to update the cleaner table has a depot number of '110', i.e. it evaluates to true, then the message will be printed.

Triggers and referential integrity

In example 5.6, we saw how a trigger could be used to maintain a business rule (i.e. that cleaners were responsible for no more than four buses). We now look at examples of how triggers can be used to maintain referential integrity. In chapter 3 in the introduction to SQL you learned that the foreign key constraint in the Create Table statement is often used for ensuring the referential integrity among parent and child tables. However, the foreign key constraint can only enforce standard integrity rules: i.e.:

• The foreign key column in the child table cannot reference unmatched rows in the parent table

• If the Delete Cascade option is chosen, then all matching rows in other tables are deleted (child rows) as well as the target row (parent row)

• If the Delete Cascade option is not chosen, a row in the parent table that is being referenced via a foreign key column cannot be deleted.

When non-standard referential integrity rules have to be specified as well, then **triggers are created**. For example:

• Set the foreign key column to NULL for updates and deletes

• Cascade updates – this means update all matching rows in other tables referenced by foreign keys as well as the target rows

• Set a default value to the foreign key column on updates and deletes. Such a default value might be a code number such as '999'.

Note that if we are implementing non-standard referential integrity constraints then the foreign key constraint must not be declared in the 'create table' statement. This is because the standard foreign key constraint will override the trigger and the trigger will therefore not work.

In this section, we are going to see two examples of using triggers to implement the Delete Cascade rule and the Update Cascade rule. The two tables we will use to illustrate this are Depot and Bus:

Depot(dno, dname, daddress)
Bus(reg_no, model, ...dno,.....)

We know that dno in Bus is a foreign key linking to Depot. To create the trigger to cascade deletes see the following example.

Example 5.8: Trigger cascade deletes

```
--pl/sql trigger  to demonstrate cascade deletes
create trigger cascade_deletes_depot_bus
before delete on depot
for each row
begin
delete from bus
where bus.dno=:old.dno;
end;
/
Trigger created.
```

It can be seen from the above example that, before the parent row is deleted from the Depot table, all the child rows in the Bus table are deleted. This maintains the referential integrity. (In the PL/SQL code, ':old.dno' represents the dno of the row in the Depot table, which is to be deleted.)

To create the trigger to cascade updates:

Example 5.9: Trigger cascade updates

```
--pl/sql trigger  to demonstrate cascade updates
create trigger cascade_updates_depot_bus
after update of dno on depot
for each row
begin
update bus
set bus.dno = :new.dno
where bus.dno = :old.dno;
end;
/

Trigger created.
```

Again it can be seen from example 5.9, that after the parent row is updated in the Depot table, all the child rows in the Bus table are updated accordingly. This maintains referential integrity.

Listing triggers and removing triggers

It is sometimes useful to list the triggers that you have created for a table. Make sure the table name is in upper case.

```
select trigger_name
from user_triggers
where table_name = 'BUS';
```

TRIGGER_NAME
OVERWORKED

Existing triggers can be deleted via the 'Drop Trigger' command. For example, the 'overworked' trigger is removed from the Bus table in the following way:

```
drop trigger overworked;
```

5.6 Summary

The main focus of this chapter is to provide an understanding of how SQL has been extended procedurally into PL/SQL. The chapter introduced the student to the PLSQL block and explained how stored procedures and functions can be used to implement processing logic at the database level. Finally, the chapter described the use of database triggers in providing an automatic response to the occurrence of specific database events.

5.7 Review questions

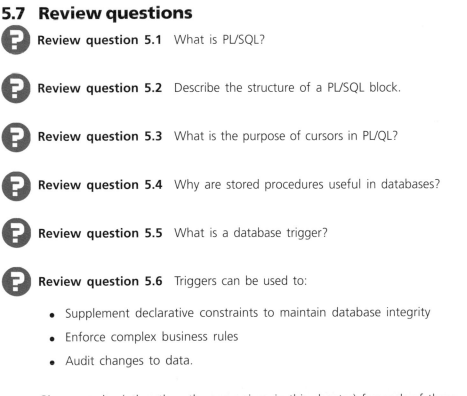

Review question 5.1 What is PL/SQL?

Review question 5.2 Describe the structure of a PL/SQL block.

Review question 5.3 What is the purpose of cursors in PL/QL?

Review question 5.4 Why are stored procedures useful in databases?

Review question 5.5 What is a database trigger?

Review question 5.6 Triggers can be used to:

- Supplement declarative constraints to maintain database integrity
- Enforce complex business rules
- Audit changes to data.

Give examples (other than the ones given in this chapter) for each of these.

Review question 5.7 Should triggers be used to replace declarative constraints and, if so, why?

 Review question 5.8 When and how do we use triggers to maintain referential integrity?

5.8 Answers to review questions

Answer to review question 5.1 PL/SQL is an extension to SQL. It includes high-level programming features such as block structure, variables, constants, types, assignment statement, conditions, loops, procedures and functions.

Answer to review question 5.2 PL/SQL is grouped into units called blocks. Blocks can be stand alone or nested. A block is divided into three parts. The declaration section consists of types, constants, variables, exception and cursor declarations. At the end of this section, subprograms (procedures and functions), if any, are declared. The executable commands section contains the program statements. The exception section is for exception handling.

It has the following structure:

```
declare
<declarations section>
begin
<executable commands>
exception
<exception handling>
end;
```

Answer to review question 5.3 In PL/SQL a 'Select into' statement can be used if the query returns one – and only one – row. Cursors are provided when more than one row is returned. This allows rows of a query result to be accessed one row at a time. The cursor acts as a pointer to a particular row of a query result.

Answer to review question 5.4 Stored procedures, containing SQL or PL/SQL statements, allow one to move code that enforces business rules from the application to the database. As a result, the code can be stored once for use by different applications. Also the use of stored procedures can make the application code more consistent and easier to maintain. This principle is similar to the good practice in general programming, in which common functionality should be coded separately as procedures or functions.

Some of the most important advantages of using stored procedures are summarised as follows:

- The code can be stored once for use by different applications. Since the procedural code is stored within the database and is fairly static, applications may benefit from the reuse of the same queries within the database

- The use of stored procedures can make the application code more consistent and easier to maintain. This principle is similar to the good practice in general programming, in which common functionality should be coded separately as procedures or functions

- Because the processing of complex business rules may be performed within the database, significant performance improvement can be obtained in a networked client/server environment.

Answer to review question 5.5   A trigger defines an action the database should take when some database-related event occurs. They are associated with a single table within the database and are specific to an Update, Insert or Delete operation or a combination of these against rows in the table. The database stores triggers in the same way that it stores normal data. They are automatically executed whenever a specified event occurs and a condition is satisfied.

Answer to review question 5.6

- For example, integrity of the database can be enforced before an event instead of after. If we wish to disallow overdrafts in a bank database, a trigger could be set up that rolls back a transaction if a balance field goes negative

- A trigger might reject updates to a price greater than 50%

- They can be used to recalculate ongoing tallies – for example, in an employee relation containing salary and department triggers an Insert/Delete/Update of an employee relation can be used to maintain the total salary bill for each department. Note that using triggers is not the only way to maintain summary data and may not be the best way.

Answer to review question 5.7   Because of their flexibility, triggers may supplement database integrity constraints. However, they should not be used to replace them. When enforcing business rules in an application, you should first rely on the declarative constraints available with the DBMS (e.g. in Oracle within the Create Table statement); only use triggers to enforce rules that cannot be coded through declarative constraints. This is because the enforcement of the declarative constraints is more efficient than the execution of user-created triggers.

Answer to review question 5.8   The foreign key constraint is often used for ensuring the referential integrity among parent and child tables. However, the foreign key constraint can only enforce standard integrity rules. When other non-standard rules have to be enforced as well, appropriate triggers need to be created instead of using the foreign key constraint. Some possible non-standard rules are:

- Cascade updates (cascade update means update all related dependent objects as well as the specified object.)

- Set the foreign key column to NULL on updates and deletes

- Set a default value to the foreign key column on updates and deletes.

It must be noted that if triggers are to be used, then for each of the integrity rules (standard and non-standard), one or more triggers may need to be created to perform appropriate actions. Also, the foreign key constraint must not be declared when creating the corresponding tables. Otherwise, the triggers will not work, because the standard foreign key constraint will override the trigger actions.

CHAPTER 6

Query processing and optimisation

OVERVIEW

When users submit queries to a DBMS, they expect a response that is not only correct and consistent for a particular instantiation of the database; but also timely, that is, it is produced in an acceptable period of time. However, queries can be written in a number of different ways, many of them being inefficient. In this chapter we look at the stages of query processing: in particular, we look at **query decomposition** and **optimisation**, where the high-level SQL query is transformed into relational algebra. We examine the **heuristic approach** to query optimisation where transformation rules are used to achieve an efficiently executed query.

Learning outcomes	On completion of this chapter, you should be able to:

- Understand the purpose of query processing and optimisation

- Understand why DBMSs incorporate optimisers

- Describe the stages of query processing and optimisation

- Understand how SQL queries are translated into relational algebra during query decomposition

- Explain how to apply heuristic transformation rules to improve the efficiency of a query.

6.1 Introduction

When a query is submitted to a DBMS, the response should be produced in an acceptable period of time. However, queries can be written in a number of different ways, many of them being inefficient. Therefore, the DBMS should take a query and, before it is run, prepare a version that can be executed efficiently. This process is known as **query optimisation**.

As it is usually impossible to produce an optimal version of a query within a short period of time (due to the underlying intractability of the problem), a fairly efficient version, generated quickly, is acceptable. It is clear that it would not be appropriate to spend thirty minutes optimising a query that only takes two minutes to execute in an unoptimised form! Thus, in reality, we are concerned with the improvement of execution strategy, rather than finding the most efficient version (which is effectively impossible for most queries).

Note that current RDBMS optimisers are complex pieces of software and will vary in design. The optimisers are based on rules, and in this chapter we give a simplified version of a typical execution plan which is not based on particular database management software. The rules are often expressed using a symbolic notation: here we present the relational algebra and the heuristic rules informally.

SQL query example

Consider a simple query using the bus drivers' database: display the route descriptions that bus driver Jack Jones can operate. There are a number of ways to evaluate this simple query and each may be significantly different in terms of execution time and memory used.

This query involves three tables: BusDriver, Dr_Route and Route:

- BusDriver (bdno, bdname, bdsalary, dno)
- Ability (bdno, rno)
- Route (rno, rdesc, dno).

In order to achieve the result, we would need to join these tables together and restrict the answer to Jack Jones. If, for instance, there were three hundred bus drivers, fifty possible routes and thousands of rows in the Ability table, then a join of the three tables would produce a very large intermediate table held in main memory. Rather than start by joining the three tables together, the DBMS optimiser could first restrict the BusDriver table to Jack Jones's, and thus reduce the BusDriver table to one row before joining the result to the other two tables.

We will see that it is not our job to worry about the efficiency of the SQL code that we write: the DBMS considers various alternatives and opts for a good execution strategy. The choice of the strategy, as we have seen in the example, can have a dramatic impact on the execution time.

6.2 Relational algebra

Before examining the topic of query optimisation in detail, we need to look again at **relational algebra**. We saw in chapter 1 that many high-level data manipulation languages are based on either (or both as in the case of SQL) **relational algebra** or **relational calculus**, both of which were defined by EF Codd. They are theoretical languages – formal and non-user-friendly. They illustrate the basic operations required by any data manipulation language such as SQL. The algebra also serves as a convenient basis for optimisation. In this chapter, we introduce a simple syntax for relational algebra.

Relational algebra (RA) operators again

We saw in chapters 1 and 3 how each operator takes one or more relations as its input, and produces a new relation as output. Codd originally defined eight operators. In this chapter, we will restrict our discussion to the special relational operators 'restrict', 'project' and 'join'.

Being a high-level symbolic language, RA expressions can be easily rewritten in equivalent forms.

For example:

((BusDriver JOIN Ability) WHERE rno = '10') [bdname]

is equivalent to:

(BusDriver JOIN (Ability WHERE rno = '10')) [bdname]

The relational algebra above is used to find the names of bus drivers who can operate on route number ten. The syntax in the language is fairly simple, and will be discussed in the next section. Rewriting these expressions serves as the basis for optimisation. We now briefly remind you of the commands and then discuss the syntax.

RESTRICT

Restrict returns a table where the rows satisfy a given condition.

Table BusDriver:

bdno	bdname	bdsalary	dno
001	Jane Brown	1800	101
006	Sally Smith	1750	
007	James Bond	1500	102
008	Maggie May	2200	102

The relational algebra to select depots with dno of '102':

BusDriver where dno = '102'

returns:

bdno	bdname	bdsalary	dno
007	James Bond	1500	102
008	Maggie May	2200	102

PROJECT

Project returns a table consisting of all tuples from the source table with certain selected columns. The relational algebra to display bus driver names and their salaries:

BusDriver[bdname,bdsalary]

returns:

bdname	bdsalary
Jane Brown	1800
Sally Smith	1750
James Bond	1500
Maggie May	2200

JOIN

The operator joins tables, matching them on common columns.

Table BusDriver:

bdno	bdname	bdsalary	dno
001	Jane Brown	1800	101
006	Sally Smith	1750	
007	James Bond	1500	102
008	Maggie May	2200	102

Table Ability:

bdno	rno
001	6
001	7
001	8
007	6
007	10
008	10

The relational algebra to join bus drivers and their routes:

BusDriver JOIN Ability

bdno	bdname	bdsalary	dno	rno
001	Jane Brown	1800	101	6
001	Jane Brown	1800	101	7
001	Jane Brown	1800	101	8
007	James Bond	1500	102	6
007	James Bond	1500	102	10
008	Maggie May	2200	102	10

RA example using the notation

If we examine the earlier example, to find the names of bus drivers who can operate on route number ten:

[((Busdriver JOIN Ability) WHERE rno = '10') [bdname]

This is executed from left to right:

- Firstly there is a **join** on the two tables BusDriver and Ability
- Followed by a **restrict** (rno –'10')
- Finally a **project** of bdname.

Notice the round brackets – using these, the precedence can be altered as one might expect. The square brackets are used for the projection only. The RA is equivalent to:

(Busdriver JOIN (Ability WHERE rno = '10')) [bdname]

In this case the precedence has been altered by the round brackets. This is executed as follows:

- Firstly there is a **restrict** (rno ='10') on the Ability table
- Followed by a **join** on the 2 tables Busdriver and restricted Ability
- Finally a **project** of bdname.

In both cases the output will be identical, but the way that each query has been executed will differ.

6.3 Why do DBMSs incorporate optimisers?

Optimisation is required if a DBMS is to perform a query in a reasonable period of time. The larger a database becomes, the greater the need for an optimiser. As many databases may contain over a million records, even a modest improvement in efficiency would have a dramatic effect on response times. It is one of the strengths of relational databases that query optimisation can be done automatically by a software optimiser included within the DBMS software.

A software optimiser is superior to a human optimiser for the following reasons:

- A software optimiser would have access to a wealth of statistical information not available to programmers (e.g. the cardinality of each domain, the cardinality of each table, and the number of times each different value occurs in each column). This information is kept in the **system catalogue**

- A software optimiser can assess many more different forms of query than a human optimiser would be inclined to do, or capable of doing

- A software optimiser can embody the best optimising practices.

6.4 Query processing and optimising

Phases of query processing

Figure 6.1: Stages in processing an SQL query

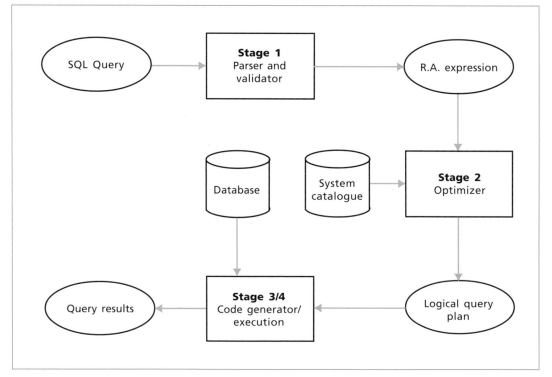

We can see from figure 6.1 that query processing consists of four main phases. In this chapter we concentrate on the first two phases. These phases can be further subdivided.

6.5 Stages 1 and 2: parsing and optimising

Stages 1 and 2 can be divided into several distinct substages including:

1.1. Syntactic and semantic checking.

1.2. Casting the query into some internal representation: the query is converted into a form more suitable for machine manipulation, such as relational algebra.

2.1. Heuristic optimisation: this involves reorganising the query into a more efficient form.

2.2. Systematic optimisation: next the query optimiser must consider how to retrieve the information physically from the database. It must, therefore, generate a query plan using access routines for the various operations. There may be a variety of access routines that can perform the same activity – for example, a join can be evaluated using either nested loop (used for small relations) or sort merge (for large relations), each with its own cost function.

2.3. Selection of the cheapest plan: having generated several access plans, the systemic optimiser would then choose the cheapest.

This is then coded for execution at the appropriate time to retrieve the required data from the database. We will now look at the first three substages above in more detail.

Stage 1.1: Syntactic and semantic checking

A query is expressed in a high-level query language (SQL) and parsed to check if it is **syntactically** correct (i.e. obeys the rules of SQL grammar). The query is then validated to see if it is **semantically** correct (i.e. verified to see that the attributes, tables, views and other objects actually exist in the database).

Syntactic checking example

Assume the relation:

BusDriver (bdno varchar2(5), bdname varchar2(50), ...)

and query:

```
select d_no
from BusDriver
where d_no = 07;
```

Why would this query be rejected? The query is rejected on two (syntax) grounds:

- d_no is not defined for the BusDriver relation (it should be bdno)
- Comparison = '07' is incompatible with the type for bdno, which is variable character string.

Semantic checking example

Assume the relation:

BusDriver (bdno, bdname, bdsalary, dno)
Depot(dno, dname, daddress)

And the query:

```
select bdno, bdname
from BusDriver,  Depot
where bdsalary >5000 and dname = 'Hornsey'
and BusDriver.dno = Depot.dno
and bdsalary < 2000;
```

Why is the query incorrect? The query is incorrect on semantic grounds:

- We cannot have a salary that is both greater than 5000 and less than 2000.

Stage 1.2: *Casting the query into some internal representation*

The query is converted into a form more suitable for machine manipulation. This form should be rich enough to be capable of representing all possible queries in a DBMS query language and should be neutral (i.e. it should not prejudice any subsequent choices in the optimisation process). In relational data models, the form is based on relational algebra or relational calculus. This chapter assumes the use of relational algebra, which is usually manipulated in the form of a parse tree (also called a relational algebra tree).

Parse tree example

Given tables Cleaner and Bus:

```
Cleaner (cno, cname, csalary, dno)
Bus (reg_no, model, tno, dno, cno)
```

Our query is to 'Get names of Cleaners who are responsible for bus 'H259IJK' '. In SQL we might write it as:

```
select cname
from Cleaner c, Bus b
where c.cno = b.cno
and reg_no='H259IJK';
```

In relational algebra:

```
((CLEANER JOIN BUS) WHERE reg_no='H259IJK') [cname]
```

As a parse tree:

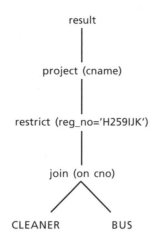

Note that the tree is inverted:

- The bottom level (the leaves) contains the relations in the query
- The middle layer contains relational algebra operations to be performed on the relations or results of previous operations
- The top level (the root) is a single operation that produces the final result.

When viewing the tree, you should understand that it is executed from the bottom right hand side. When creating your own trees in the various exercises in this chapter, you should draw them starting from the bottom right-hand side.

Stage 2.1: Heuristic optimisation (converting to a more efficient form)

Heuristic optimisation depends on the syntax and not the semantics of the database. It is based only on the general qualities of the relational algebra expressions, and involves substituting relational algebra with more efficient expressions, using **equivalence-preserving transformation rules**. This results in more efficient evaluation. It may include the reordering of expressions, or the removing of redundant or useless operations.

The equivalence-preserving transformation rules are not independent of each other. Given a particular expression to transform, the application of one rule might generate an expression that is susceptible to transformation, after the application of another equivalence rule. The optimiser applies transformation rules until it finally results in an acceptable version of the query. There are many equivalence rules. Here we present a set of **heuristics** (rules of thumb) that are known to produce more efficient queries.

Heuristics used to optimise queries

The **first principle of heuristic optimisation** is to minimise disk input/output and processing by reducing the size of intermediate tables in a query. The earlier the tables appear in the processing, then on balance, the greater is the advantage in reducing their size. This is an important principle. Firstly, it means that processing time is reduced.

Secondly, it may be possible to process a small table in main memory, whereas large tables may be too big to fit into main memory and would require expensive reading and writing to secondary memory. Therefore, the operations that tend to reduce the size of tables (e.g. select, project) are performed before operations that could produce large tables (e.g. union, Cartesian product).

The **second principle of heuristic optimisation** bears more directly on the amount of computation involved. It is sometimes possible to reduce the complexity of queries by rewriting them in a simpler form.

The **third principle of heuristic optimisation** is that it is sometimes possible to rewrite expressions in a form, which although not simpler, is less computationally demanding.

We will now look at examples of rules that fall into each of these categories.

Rules that tend to reduce the size of intermediate tables

These are the rules of thumb that tend to reduce the size of intermediate tables and that we are going to use in our examples:

- Perform restriction as early as possible
- Rearrange leaf nodes so that the leaf with the most restrictive restriction operates first
- Perform projection as early as possible.

Query optimisation example

The tables used to demonstrate heuristic processing are:

Table name	Attributes		
STUDENT	Std_No	Std_Name	
REGISTRATION	Std_No	Course_No	Date
COURSE	Course_No	Course_Name	Instructor

Our example query is 'List the registration numbers and names of students registered on the database course'. In SQL we might write it as:

```
select Std_No, Std_Name
from student s, registration r, course c
where s.Std_No = r.Std_No
and r.Course_No = c.Course_No
and Course_name = 'Database';
```

Converting from SQL to relational algebra, we have the following:

```
((COURSE JOIN (REGISTRATION JOIN STUDENT))
WHERE Course_name = 'Database') [Std_No, Std_Name]
```

As a parse tree:

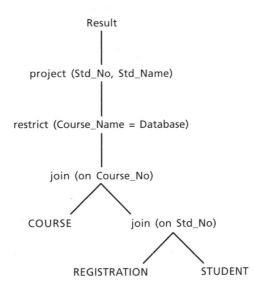

In this case we have joined the REGISTRATION to STUDENT as the first join, followed by joining the result of this to COURSE.

Rule 1: Perform restriction as early as possible

This rule reduces the cardinality (number of tuples) of the resulting relation, and therefore reduces subsequent processing time. For example, if a restriction is performed before a join, then this reduces the size of the input to the join, as it reduces the amount of data to be scanned in performing that join. It also reduces the size of the output, which could make a difference, keeping the output in main memory and not having to spill it out onto disk.

Therefore, the restriction operator is pushed as far down the parse tree as possible. At intermediate nodes, the operators are pushed down the appropriate branches. In this case it is not applicable to pass restriction down the STUDENT branch, as STUDENT does not contain the Course_Name attribute. This reasoning does not apply to the other branch.

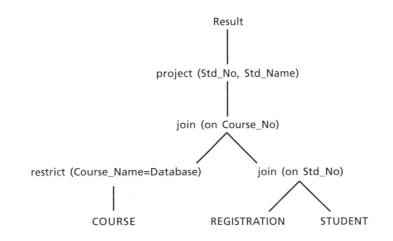

Rule 2: Rearrange leaf nodes so that the most restrictive restriction operates first

Our previous rule **'Perform restriction as early as possible'** pushed 'restrict Course_name = Database' down the tree just above the COURSE leaf. This means the restriction will only occur after REGISTRATION has been joined to STUDENT. Remember that execution occurs from the bottom right of the tree to the top. If there are thousands of student records, then the intermediate joined table will be huge. So, instead of the above arrangement, a better option is to first rearrange leaf nodes so that the leaf with the most restrictive restriction operates first, that is, restrict the COURSE table to 'database' tuples only, before performing joins. Therefore the tree above is transformed to:

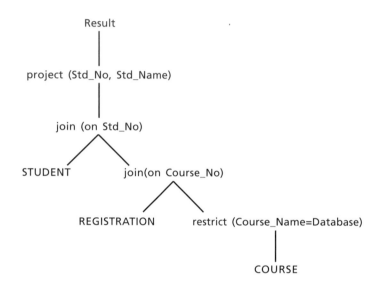

Rule 3: Perform projection as early as possible

Under certain conditions projection may be commuted with a Cartesian product (or join). However, a projection cannot be simply moved down the tree. When a projection is preceded by a join, it is possible to push the projection down before the join. As the projection is pushed down the tree it will acquire new attributes, therefore the original projection must be performed after the join. Unless the cardinalities of the intermediate relations are reduced, the usefulness of pushing a projection down before a join is questionable.

Our example query as before is 'List the numbers and names of students registered on the Database course'. With this rule we take each attribute, one by one, in the original projection. This simplified algorithm will try to push the attribute down the tree as far as possible. It will not always produce the most optimum version of the query. We begin by considering the first attribute Std_No.

Expressed in relational algebra:

(STUDENT JOIN (REGISTRATION JOIN (COURSE WHERE Course_name = 'Database')))
[Std_No, Std_Name]

As a parse tree:

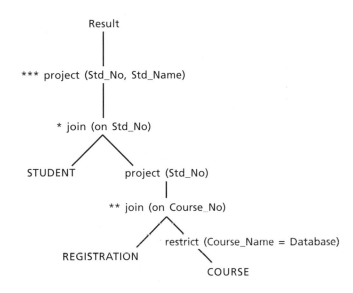

Here, we have pushed the attribute Std_No down the tree before the join (*). Remember that the tree is executed from the leaves (at the bottom of the tree) to the root (at the top of the tree) as shown in the following diagram.

In order to push the projection further down the tree, the projection has to acquire a new attribute Course_No so that the join at (**) is to be performed. The original projection (***) is still performed after the join. Here we have succeeded in reducing the cardinalities of the intermediate relations attributes, such as registration date, which is no longer needed and has not been included in the join.

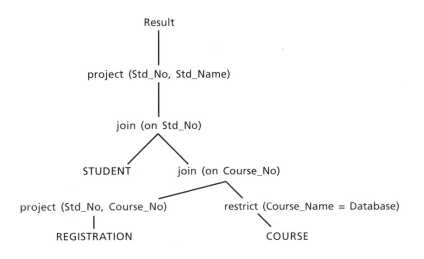

Our projection project (Std_No, Course_No) has been pushed down the tree as far as possible. Note that, with this rule of thumb, projections of more than one attribute are moved as a whole and are not split into sub-projections. We now consider pushing the next attribute in our original projection, Std_Name, as far down the tree as possible:

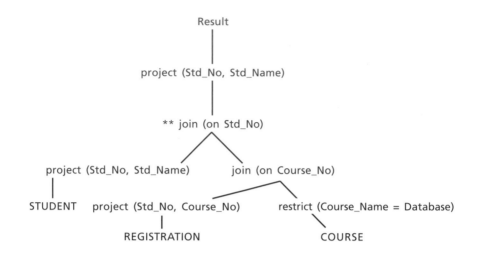

Note that as the projection 'project (Std_Name)' is pushed down the tree, it acquires a new attribute (Std_No) in order that the Join can take place at **. Expressed back in relational algebra form:

> (STUDENT [Std_No, Std_Name] JOIN ((REGISTRATION[Std_No, Course_No]) JOIN (COURSE WHERE Course_name = 'Database')))[Std_No, Std_Name]

We have thus succeeded in reducing the size of the intermediate tables created during the execution of the query.

Additional rule: Performing restrict before project by commuting (exchanging) restrict with project

An additional rule for reducing the size of intermediate tables is to perform restrict before project by commuting (exchanging) restrict with project. An operator is said to be **commutative** if 'a operator b' is equal to 'b operator a' (e.g. 3 + 2 = 2 + 3).

If the restriction condition c involves only the attributes A...An in the projection list, then the two operations can be commuted, for example:

> ((GRADE [Std_No, Course_No]) where Std_No = 123)

can be commuted to:

> (GRADE where Std_No = 123) [Std_No, Course_No]

Thus, the restriction is performed before the projection, and the size of the intermediate tables are reduced.

Rules that tend to directly reduce the amount of computation involved: part I

The following rules make expressions simpler:

- Combine a cascade of restrictions into one restriction
- Combine a cascade of projections into one projection.

Combine a cascade of restrictions into one restriction

Example query

Get the full details of courses with course number COMP353 where the instructor is Smith. Expressed in relational algebra:

((Course where instructor = 'Smith') where Course = 'COMP353')

can be converted to:

COURSE WHERE instructor = 'Smith' AND Course_No = 'COMP353'

Combine a cascade of projections into one projection

((COURSE [Course_Name, Instructor]) [Course_Name])

can be converted to

COURSE [Course_Name]

In fact, in a sequence of projections, all but the last can be ignored.

Rules that tend to directly reduce the amount of computation involved: part II

The following rule involves rewriting the query in a less computationally demanding form:

- Any restriction condition is converted into conjunctive normal form.

For example:

where P OR (Q AND R)

can be rewritten as:

where (P OR Q) AND (P OR R)

This transformation is desirable as it reduces computation: if P is false, then the former version will usually involve more work. Consider the truth tables:

P	Q	P AND Q	P OR Q
T	T	T	T
T	F	F	T
F	T	F	T
F	F	F	F

Conjunctive normal form is desirable for the following reason. A condition that is in conjunctive normal form evaluates to true only if every conjunct evaluates to true, equivalently. It evaluates to false if any conjunct evaluates to false. Thus, if a conjunct of statements has an equal chance of being true or false, on average for a true result, all conjuncts must be evaluated; for a false result only half need to be evaluated. This emphasis on efficient evaluation of false conditions is preferable, if the majority of tuples that are to be tested are likely to evaluate to false, which is the case for most queries submitted to a database.

In a parallel processing system, moreover, it might be possible to evaluate all the conjuncts simultaneously, each one on a different processor, and terminate the entire evaluation as soon as any one of them returns a false. A statement in **disjunctive normal form**, on the other hand, evaluates to false only if all disjuncts are false, and true if at least one conjunct is true. This is less efficient if the majority of tuples that are to be tested are likely to evaluate to false.

Activity 6.1

Query optimisation exercise

Given the following database where patients are assigned to a ward and may have operations given by one surgeon:

Table	Attrib 1	Attrib 2	Attrib 3	Attrib 4
Ward	wardno	wardname		
Patient	patno	patname	wardno	pataddress
Surgeon	surgno	surgname		
Operation	opno	patno	surgno	opdate

a. Write the following query in SQL (in an inefficient form). Display patient numbers and surgeon names for operations which have taken place since the 1st March 2001, for patients in the Alexandra Ward.

b. Now convert the query into relational algebra form.

c. Draw a parse tree for the expression you have produced.

d. Use heuristic rules, which reduce the size of intermediate tables, to transform the relational algebra query into a more efficient form. At every step indicate the rule you are applying.

6.6 Summary

In this chapter, students were introduced to query possessing. The focus was particularly on the first stages of query processing – parsing and optimisation. A simple syntax for relational algebra operators – restrict, project and join – was introduced. It was shown how a query could be converted into this form and how heuristic transformation rules can be applied to improve the efficiency of a query.

6.7 Review questions

 Review question 6.1 Given the following database:

Table	Attrib 1	Attrib 2	Attrib 3	Attrib 4
Supplier	sno	sname	city	status
Part	pno	pname	description	
Shipment	sno	pno	quantity	

    a. Write the following query in SQL – display part names for part supplied by suppliers who are located in Manchester.

    b. Now convert the query into relational algebra form.

    c. Try doing questions a) and b) again but this time reorder the statements in your clause.

 Review question 6.2 Why is a software query optimiser superior to a human optimiser?

 Review question 6.3 Explain why database management systems incorporate optimisers.

Review question 6.4 What is heuristic optimisation?

Review question 6.5 Given the following database as in review question 6.1:

Table	Attrib 1	Attrib 2	Attrib 3	Attrib 4
Supplier	sno	sname	city	status
Part	pno	pname	description	
Shipment	sno	pno	quantity	

and the following RA expression, to display part numbers and part names for parts supplied by suppliers who are located in Manchester:

((Supplier Join (Shipment Join Part)) where city = 'Manchester') [pno, pname]

Draw a parse tree for this.

 Review question 6.6   Now apply heuristic rules to the parse tree in review question 6.5, which reduce the size of intermediate tables to transform the relational algebra query into a more efficient form. The first rule is to 'perform restriction as early as possible'.

 Review question 6.7   Now continue with the optimisation example, by taking the parse tree in review question 6.6 and using the rule, if necessary, to rearrange the leaf nodes so that the leaf with the most restrictive restriction operates first.

 Review question 6.8   Now continue with the optimisation example, by taking the parse tree in review question 6.7, and use the rule, if necessary, to 'perform projection as early as possible'. Consider only the first attribute to be projected, 'pno'.

 Review question 6.9   Take the parse tree in review question 6.8, and transform it back into algebraic form.

 Review question 6.10 Give examples of heuristic rules which reduce the size of intermediate tables.

 Review question 6.11 Give examples of heuristic rules that tend to directly reduce the amount of computation involved.

6.8 Answers to review questions

Answer to review question 6.1

a. Select pname

   from part p, shipment sp, supplier s

   where p.pno = sp.pno

   and sp.sno = s.sno

   and city ='Manchester';

b.

((Supplier Join (Shipment Join Part)) where city = 'Manchester') [pname]

In the solution above, note that Shipment and Part are joined first (inner bracket); followed by Supplier; next, city has been restricted to Manchester after the join.

Alternatively:

c. Select pname

from part p, shipment sp, supplier s

where city ='Manchester'

and s.pno = sp.pno

and sp.sno = p.sno

((Supplier where city = 'Manchester' Join Shipment) Join Part) [pname]

In this solution, the Supplier table is restricted; followed by a join to Shipment; followed by a join to Part.

Answer to review question 6.2   A software optimiser is superior to a human optimiser because:

- A software optimiser would have access to a huge amount of statistical information kept in the system catalogue and not available to programmers (e.g. the cardinality of each domain, the cardinality of each table, and the number of times each different value occurs in each column)

- A software optimiser can assess many more different forms of query than a human optimiser would be inclined, or capable of doing

- A software optimiser can embody the best optimising practices.

Answer to review question 6.3   Optimisation is required if a DBMS is to perform a query in a reasonable period of time. Queries can be written in different ways, many of them inefficient. It is the job of the optimiser in the DBMS to take a query and transform it into a version that can be executed efficiently. The larger a database becomes, the greater the need for an optimiser. As many databases may contain over a million records, even a modest improvement in efficiency would have a dramatic effect on response times.

Answer to review question 6.4   Heuristic optimisation involves substituting relational algebra expressions with more efficient expressions, using equivalence-preserving transformation rules. This results in more efficient evaluation and may include the reordering of expressions, or removing of redundant or useless operations. The transformation rules are not independent of each other: given a particular expression to transform, the application of one rule might generate an expression that is susceptible to transformation after the application of another rule. The optimiser applies transformation rules until it finally results in an acceptable version of the query.

Answer to review question 6.5   In this example, assume we have started the process with the following tree:

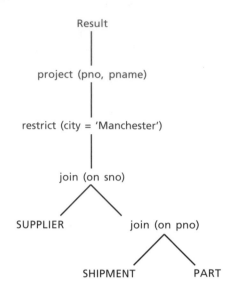

Answer to review question 6.6   Perform restriction as early as possible; therefore, push the restriction operator as far down the tree as possible:

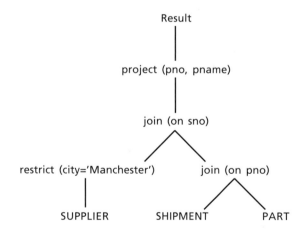

Answer to review question 6.7   In the example, SUPPLIER is the only table to be restricted, so we exchange PART and SUPPLIER. Remember that the tree is executed from the bottom right-hand side, so the first join is now a join from SUPPLIER to SHIPMENT:

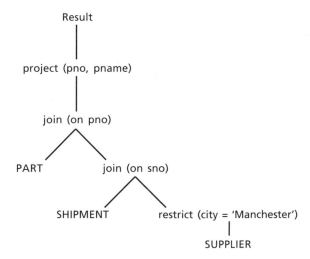

Answer to review question 6.8

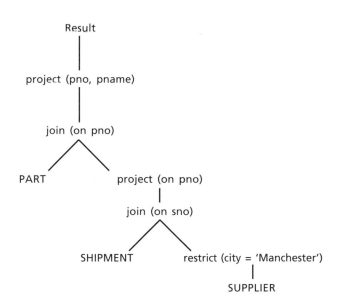

Remember that a project cannot be simply moved down the tree. When a projection is preceded by a join, it is possible to push the projection down before the join. As the projection is pushed down the tree it will acquire new attributes, therefore the original projection must be performed after the join.

Here, we have pushed the attribute pno down the tree before the join. In order to push the projection further down the tree, the projection has to acquire a new attribute sno, so that the join (on sno) can be performed. The original projection (pno, pname) is still performed after the join.

Here, we have succeeded in reducing the cardinalities of the intermediate relations:

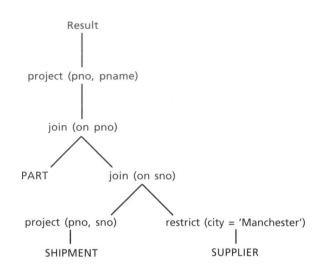

Answer to review question 6.9

(PART JOIN (SHIPMENT [pno, sno]JOIN (SUPPLIER WHERE city = 'Manchester'))) [pno, pname]

Answer to review question 6.10 Example rules:

- Perform selection as early as possible

- Rearrange leaf nodes if necessary so that the leaf with the most restrictive selection (restriction) operates first

- Perform projection as early as possible – under certain conditions projection may be commuted with a Cartesian product or join. However, a projection cannot be simply moved down the tree. When a projection is preceded by a join, it is possible to push the projection down, before the join, but the projection acquires new attributes. Therefore, the original projection must be performed after the join. This is worthwhile only if the cardinalities of the intermediate relations are reduced

- Performing restrict before project by commuting (exchanging) restrict with project.

Answer to review question 6.11 The following rules make expressions simpler:

- Combine a cascade of selections into one selection

- Combine a cascade of projections into one projection.

The following rule involves rewriting the query in a less computationally demanding form:

- Any restriction condition is converted into conjunctive normal form.

6.9 Feedback on activity

Activity 6.1: Query optimisation exercise

a. We have deliberately started with an inefficiently written query – the SQL is written with the restriction last. Note that the user need not worry about the efficiency of the SQL code as it is the job of the DBMS optimiser to transform the query.

Select patno, surgname
from surgeon s, operaton o, patient p, ward w
where p.wardno = w.wardno
and p.patno = o.patno
and o.surgno = s.surgno
and wardname = 'Alexandra'
and opdate > '01-03-2001';

b.
((SURGEON JOIN (OPERATION JOIN (PATIENT JOIN WARD))) WHERE wardnmame = 'Alexandra' AND date > '01-03-2001') [patno, surgname]

c.

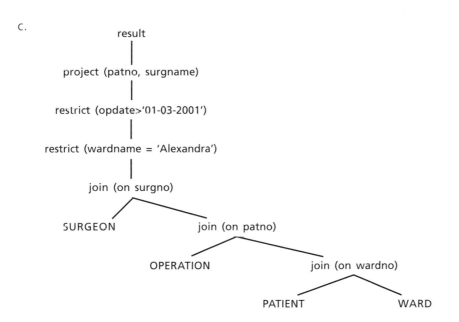

d. Rules to reduce the size of intermediate tables:

Perform selection (restriction) as early as possible: therefore, push the restrict operator as far down the tree as possible.

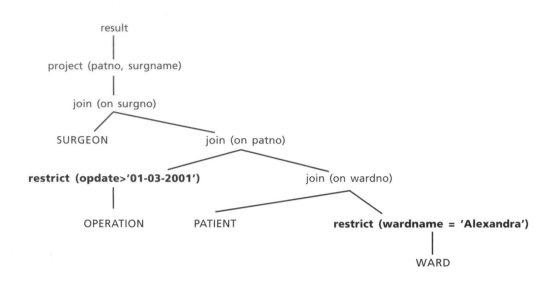

Rearrange the leaves of the tree so that the leaf node with the most restrictive restriction is executed first: Consider the rule to increase optimisation by rearranging the leaves of the tree so that the leaf node with the most restrictive restriction processes is executed first. In this example there are two restrictions which affect two different tables (Operation and Ward). During execution the optimiser can work out which restriction is more restrictive by looking up data in the system catalogue. In the above solution we will assume that we have already obeyed the rule by joining a restricted WARD table first of all.

Perform projection as early as possible: when a projection is preceded by a join, it is possible to push the projection down before the join. As the projection is pushed down the tree, it will acquire new attributes, therefore the original projection must be performed after the join.

Here, we have pushed the attribute patno down the tree, before the join on SURGEON. The original projection is still performed after the join in order that we can output the two required attributes (patno, surgname).

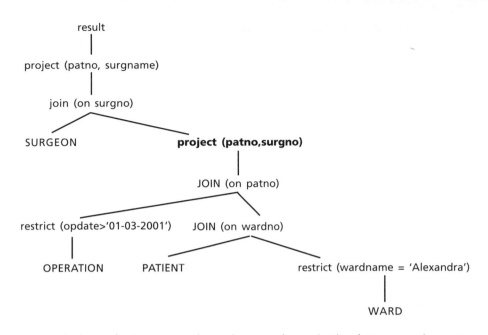

In order to push the projection patno down the tree, the projection has to acquire a new attribute 'surgno' so that the join with SURGEON can be performed.

Our projection 'project (patno, surgno)' is now pushed down the tree as far as possible. Note that with this rule of thumb, projections of more than one attribute are moved as a whole, and are not split into sub-projections. Here, we have succeeded in reducing the cardinalities of the intermediate relations – attributes such as 'opdate' are no longer needed and have not been included in the join.

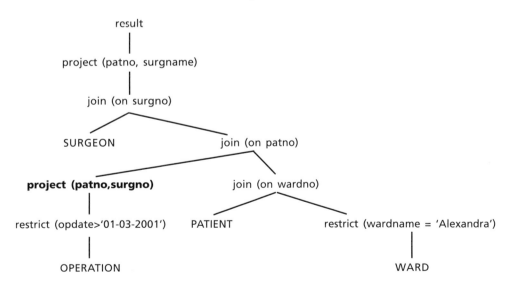

Transformed query expressed in algebraic form:

(SURGEON JOIN ((OPERATION where opdate > '01-03-2001' [patno, surgno])
JOIN (PATIENT JOIN (WARD where wardname = 'Alexandra')))) [patno, surgname]

Consider any additional transformation which might be introduced to further restrict intermediate tables, for example performing project (surgname) as early as possible.

CHAPTER 7

Object-oriented and object-relational models

OVERVIEW

Object-oriented (OO) concepts are influencing the development of information systems in general and database systems in particular. Many relational DBMS vendors are now offering OO features and the ISO SQL standard SQL3, released in 1999, has added features to support object-oriented data management. At the same time there is often confusion as to what object-oriented actually means and, unlike the relational model, there is no internationally agreed standard for the critical elements underlying OO database systems. Nevertheless, there is a consensus emerging as to the key elements of an OO data model. This chapter attempts to examine some of these elements.

After introducing the basic concepts of relational databases and entity-relationship modelling in the previous chapter, we now discuss **object-oriented data models** and **OO database systems**. Relational data models and systems have been very successful for the development of databases used by traditional business applications. We saw in the previous chapter that there are certain shortcomings in relational databases when we need to design databases for more complex applications. Some examples of these advanced database systems are now described and their requirements are examined. These new applications were the major motivation for OO databases. We will also examine those elements of the object-oriented programming model that object-oriented database systems provide for and study some issues associated with OODBMSs. This chapter sets the scene for the next one, which examines a methodology for object-oriented database conceptual design.

Following on from the description of the object-oriented database model and the review of entity-relationship modelling in chapter 1, we now describe a methodology for object-oriented database conceptual design. We examine how an entity-relational schema can be mapped to the object-oriented schema. Finally, we look at how relational database vendors, such as Oracle, have recognised the need for additional data modelling features and have incorporated many OO elements in their products. Specifically, we examine the extensions to the relational model and the features which characterise those products generally known as object-relational DBMSs.

7.1 Introduction

In chapter 1 we looked at the disadvantages of relational databases systems. In this chapter we will see that relational database systems cannot meet the more demanding requirements of applications whose needs are quite different from those of traditional business database applications such as order processing and stock control. These new applications are often termed **advanced database applications**. Among the applications that have proved difficult to support within the relational environment are those involved in the storage and manipulation of design data. Examples of such applications include computer-aided design (CAD), computer-aided manufacture (CAM), geographic information systems (GISs), databases to support CASE tools and image processing applications.

These new applications were the major motivation for the development of object-oriented databases. Another reason for their creation is the increasing use of OO programming languages in developing software applications. Traditional databases (i.e. relational) are more difficult to use when embedded in OO languages such as C++ or Java. In this chapter, we will look at the **components** which make up an **object-oriented database system** and examine those elements of the object-oriented programming model that object-oriented database systems provide for, in addition to the traditional DBMS functionality. Traditionally, database management and software engineering have emphasised different approaches: database management has been concerned with the static aspects of storing information; software engineering has been concerned with the more dynamic aspects of the software. With the adoption of many of the concepts of software engineering and, in particular, object-oriented programming, the two disciplines have come together.

From chapter 1 you may recall that data modelling is concerned with the design of the data content and structure of the database. So far we have looked at the more traditional approach of the entity-relationship model. As with any data modelling activity, object-oriented data modelling gives us a formal model of an organisation. The process is very similar, but OO design requires the schema to include both a description of the object data structure and constraints, and the object behaviour. The easiest way to begin to build an object model is to use some of the methods already developed for entity-relationship modelling and extended entity-relationship modelling. The latter includes generalisation and specialisation and refers to abstraction mechanisms which enable more complex applications to be represented in semantic models.

Relational database vendors such as Oracle have recognised the need for additional data modelling features and have incorporated many OO features in their products. We next examine the extension to the relational model and the features which characterise those products generally known as object-relational DBMSs.

7.2 Advanced database applications

Among the applications that have proved difficult to support within the relational environment are those involved in the storage and manipulation of design data. Design data is often complex, variable in length, and may be highly interrelated. Its structure may evolve rapidly over time, though previous versions may have to be maintained and may involve longer-duration transactions. Examples of applications that have proved difficult to implement in relational systems include computer-aided design (CAD), computer-aided manufacture (CAM), geographic information systems (GISs), databases to support CASE tools, digital publishing, office information systems (OISs) and multimedia systems.

Geographic information systems

Geographic information systems (GISs) provide the functions and tools needed to store, analyse, and display spatial information. Spatial data covers multidimensional points, lines, polygons, cubes and other geometrical objects. A spatial object is characterised by its location and boundary.

The key components of GIS software are:

- Tools for entering and manipulating spatial data such as geographic information like addresses or political boundaries
- A database management system (DBMS)
- Tools that create intelligent digital maps you can analyse, query for more information, or print for presentation
- An easy-to-use graphical user interface (GUI).

Computer-aided design

Two other applications which involve spatial data are CAD and CAM (computer-aided manufacture). These were the major motivation for object-oriented databases. A CAD database stores data relating to mechanical and electrical design for buildings, cars, integrated circuits etc. Designs of this type have some common characteristics:

- Data have many types, each with a small number of instances
- Designs may be very large, with maybe millions of parts and often there will be interdependent subsystem designs
- They evolve through time
- Updates are far-reaching – one change may effect a large number of design objects

- Various versions of designs must be maintained, with many staff working on these versions at the same time. There needs to be version control and the final product must be consistent and coordinated.

Consider, for example, a CAD database for an electronic circuit. A circuit uses many parts which are of different types. Each part may refer to other parts, and some of these parts may also be connected to one another. Each part of a type will have the same properties. The design of the circuit may change over time and updates may affect many of the interconnected parts.

7.3   Object-oriented systems overview

Object orientation has its roots in the SIMULA language (late '60s), which incorporated some OO concept such as objects and classes. In the '70s, SMALLTALK was developed which in addition incorporated concepts such as inheritance. Later the programming language C was extended to incorporate OO concepts and C++ came into being. More recently, Java, suitable for sharing programs across the World Wide Web, has been widely adopted.

Many object-oriented databases have their origin in OO programming languages. An **object** used by such languages is similar to (but not the same as) a program variable and exists only during program execution. The important difference between OO programming languages and more traditional programming languages is that the software should be constructed from reusable components. **Object-oriented database management systems** (OODBMSs) have incorporated the features of the OO programming model. Also an OO database extends the existence of objects so they are stored permanently – in other words, OO databases store **persistent data**. In contrast to OO programming languages' variables, OODBMs data is stored on secondary storage and can be shared by many programs and applications.

With relational and previous generation databases the concentration was on the static aspects of the information system – that is, only the structure of the data, and the data itself was stored in the database. The dynamic aspects of the software (the actual programs) were stored separately. An object has two components:

- **State** (value)
- **Behaviour** (operations).

Thus, in an object-oriented database system, both the data and the processes acting on the data are incorporated.

7.4   Alternative strategies for developing an OODBMS

There are a number of approaches to developing an OODBMS (Khoshafian and Abnous, 1990). Most approaches do not start from scratch but extend existing data models/ languages. For example:

- Extend an existing OO programming language (such as C++ or Java) with database capabilities. This is exactly the approach taken by the OODBMS Gemstone

- Embed OO database language constructs in a conventional host language. This was the approach taken by the OODBMS O2, which provides embedded extensions in C. Relational databases have a similar approach when SQL is imbedded in a host language
- Extend an existing language (such as SQL) with OO capabilities. This approach has been taken by both RDBMSs and OODBMSs. Later in this chapter we will also look Object-Relational Oracle which supports some object-oriented features. Also Versant and other vendors provide a version of Object SQL (OQL) the object database standard query language.

7.5   Object-oriented components and concepts

OODBMSs combine the following:

- **Many of the features of the OO programming model**
  Note that there is no common OO programming model to use as a point of reference, no formal foundation for the concepts described, and, as yet, no standard for object-oriented models. Each OODBMS provides its own interpretation of base functionality. In the next section we will examine some of the common features including classes, objects and attributes, inheritance, methods and object identity
- **Traditional DBMS facilities**
  DBMSs traditionally provide support for persistence, sharing, querying, transaction and concurrency control, recovery, security, integrity and scalability. These are the facilities that are usually available in a DBMS.

In this chapter we concentrate on the first component above (i.e. those common elements in OO programming models). We will consider the second component (traditional DBMS facilities) in other chapters in this module, for example when we look at transaction and concurrency control and query processing.

Objects, classes and attributes (instance variables)

- **Objects:** an object is similar to the idea of an entity occurrence in entity-relationship modelling but there is an important difference. An entity models only the state (the structure of the data). However, an object encapsulates both data and functions into a self-contained package. Thus, objects that have the same structure and behaviour can be grouped together to form a **class**. An example of an object might be an instance of the class SalesPerson
- **Classes:** these are blueprints for defining a set of similar objects (i.e. an object is an instance of a class). The structure and behaviour (defined as we will see by attributes and methods respectively) are defined once for the class rather than separately for each object. Each instance has its own value(s) for each attribute, but shares the same attribute names and methods with other instances of the class
- **Attributes:** the current state of an object is described by one or more attributes (also called instance variables). There are various classifications of attributes (e.g. simple, complex and reference) – we will examine these in detail next.

Example attributes for bus driver instance

Name	John
Date of birth	19/01/63
Address	......
Salary	35000
Bus Types	type1, type3, type4

Note that Name and Salary in the above example are simple attributes, as they cannot be broken down further and contain primitive types (e.g. integers or literals). Date of birth, Bus Types and, possibly, Address are complex attributes. Bus Types is also a reference attribute because it contains a value (or collection of values in this case) which are themselves objects.

Methods and messages

Methods: these are fragments of program code or procedures which are used to carry out operations relevant to the object in question. They are internal to each object and may alter an object's private state. By state is meant here the values of the data items of the object in question. Examples of methods for Bus Driver are AddNewBusType and GiveRise.

Methods are activated by **messages** passed between objects. A message may be viewed as a request from one object (the sender) to another object (the receiver) asking the second object to execute one of its methods. If object A in the database wants object B to do something, it sends B a message. The success or failure of the requested operation may be conveyed back from object B to object A, via a further message. In general, each object has a set of messages that it can receive and a set of replies it can send. An object does not need to know anything about the other objects that it interacts with, other than what messages can be sent to them. The internal workings are thus encapsulated into the definition for each object.

Example of a method

```
method void Update_salary (float increment)
    {    salary = salary + increment;
    {
```

In this example a method consists of two parts: a name, and a body. The body performs the behaviour associated with the method name and consists of a block of code that carries out the required functionality. For example, the method Update_salary has code, which takes the input parameter increment and adds it to the instance variable salary to produce an updated salary. The name of the method, known as the message, is Update_salary. The keyword 'void' denotes that Update_salary does not return a value.

Example of method execution

```
BusDriver.Update_salary(1000)
```

In the above example: execute Update_salary method on a BusDriver object and pass the method, an increment of 1000 is given.

Example of the class BusDriver

The structural component of a class is implemented as **instance variables** (the attributes). For the class BusDriver these are *Name, Salary, Depot, BusTypes...* The behavioural component is defined by the **methods** of the class BusDriver including the operator Update_Salary which has as an argument (or parameter) the increment (incr) to be allocated to the driver. Thus methods can (among other things) be used to change the object's state by modifying its attribute values.

Figure 7.1: The private and public components of a class

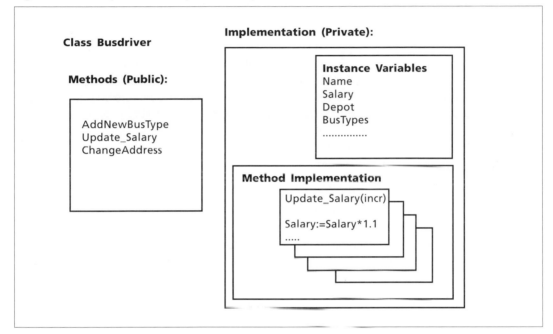

In figure 7.1, all instances (objects) of the class BusDriver will always have these variables and methods, and a single code base implements the operator which is always invoked when an instance (e.g. John Smith) is sent the message. For instance, John's internal representation consists of his description (name, salary etc) and the bus types he has had training to drive. Some of the values that describe John might also describe other objects: for example, John shares his depot with his co-worker Jim, so the depot is a shared value. The aggregation of the full set of these values captures the state of John as an instance of BusDriver. In relational DBMS terms these instances would represent rows in at least one table. Although the values of the variables in the internal representation vary for each instance of a class (i.e. they may be in different states), all instances will be of the same class.

Encapsulation and information hiding

Encapsulation means the packaging together of both the data structure and the methods that are used to manipulate the object. The term implies that the internal structure and methods are packaged in such a way that other objects cannot see them. Classes distinguish between the public interface and the private internal implementation and components. The private internal representation is not available to other objects. The public interface is composed of the methods 'understood' by that object. The only way that an object can be manipulated or accessed is through the public interface, with the attributes on the inside protected from the outside by the methods. This concealing of the internal structure, with its inherent complexity, is known as **information hiding**.

In database systems, encapsulation and information hiding ensure that application programmers have access only to the interface part, and thus they provide a form of **logical data independence** – we can change the internal implementation of a class without changing any of the applications using that class. Encapsulation allows the internal details of an object to be changed without affecting the external details. These concepts simplify the construction and maintenance of database applications through modularisation. An object is a 'black box' that can be constructed and modified independently of the rest of the system, provided the public interface is not changed.

Example class definition

The class definition is like a template which defines the set of data items and methods available to all instances of that class of object. Some object database systems also allow the definition of database constraints within class definitions, but this feature will be ignored here. For example, consider the object type Book as might exist in a library database. Information to be held on a book includes its title, date of publication, publisher and author. Typical operations on a book might be:

- Take a book out on loan
- Reserve a book for taking out on loan when available
- A Boolean function which returns true if the book is currently on loan and false otherwise.

These operations will be implemented as methods of class 'book'. The class 'book' may be defined by the following structure:

Example of class book defined by structure

```
class book
    properties
        title:                  string;
        date_of_Publication:    date;
        published_by:           publisher;
        written_by:             author;
    operations
        create () -> book;
        loan (book, borrower, date_due);
        reserve (book, borrower, date_reserved);
        on_loan (book) -> Boolean;
end book;
```

The notation used in the class definition will be explained later in this chapter. An important point to note here is that data abstraction, as provided by the class mechanism, allows one to define properties of classes in terms of other classes. Thus we see from the above example that the properties published_by and written_by are defined in terms of the classes 'publisher' and 'author' respectively. This will also be explained more fully later in this chapter.

Class definitions for author and publisher

Outline class definitions for author and publisher could be as follows:

```
class    author
         properties
               surname:           string;
               initials:          string;
               nationality:       country;
               year_of_birth:     integer;
               year_of_death:     integer;
         operations
               create () -> author;
end author.

class    publisher
         properties
               name:          string;
               location:      city;
         operations
               create () -> publisher;
end publisher.
```

Inheritance

Inheritance allows one class to be defined as a special case of a more general class. These special cases are known as **subclasses**, and the more general cases are known as **superclasses**. By default, a subclass inherits all the properties (both state and behaviour) of its superclass, and it also defines its own unique properties. However, as we shall see shortly (in the section on overloading and overriding), a subclass can redefine inherited methods. If class B is a subclass of class A, then if class B inherits the characteristics of class A, every instance of B is automatically an instance of A. However, the reverse is not true.

Example of inheritance hierarchy

Consider the hierarchy of people illustrated in figure 7.2.

Figure 7.2: Classes and the inheritance hierarchy

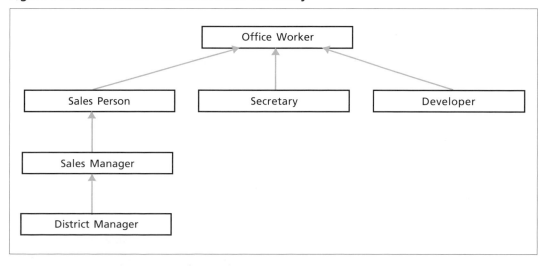

In figure 7.2, Secretaries and Sales Persons are Office Workers, Sales Managers further specialise Sales Persons, and District Managers specialise Sales Managers. The classes Developer, Secretary, and Sales Person are subclasses of Office Worker. The class Office Worker is a superclass of Developer, Secretary, and Sales Person.

The advantages of inheritance

All OODBMSs provide inheritance of some sort. The main advantages of inheritance are:

- **Reusability:** through the inheritance mechanism, the characteristics of an object can be made available to other objects. Depending on the system, this may involve both state (data) and behaviour (methods) of objects

- **Extensibility:** another aspect of the mechanism is that it provides a natural way for applications or systems to evolve. As new features, data, or program code are added, these can be defined in terms of new objects. These inherit the already tested characteristics of the earlier part of the system. This will include both the behaviour (operations, methods etc) and the representation (instance variables, attributes etc) from existing classes.

Object identity

OIDs

An OO database system provides a unique identity for each independent object stored in the database. This identity is implemented via a unique system-generated object identifier (OID). The use of primary keys (as used in relational databases) is not a satisfactory means for identifying objects in databases. For a database table storing 'office worker', for example, the identifier key might be an employee name (lastname, firstname). The use of primary keys from home relations as foreign keys in referencing relations has intrinsic problems. These lead to drawbacks such as:

- The need to use inefficient joins to retrieve object data

- A primary key is only unique within a relation, but not across an entire system

- A primary key is generally chosen from the attributes of a relation, making it dependent upon object state. If a candidate (potential) key is subject to change, identity has to be simulated by unique identifiers, such as the employee number, but as these are not under system control there is no guarantee of protection against violations of identity.

In the case of the OID, its value is not visible to the external user, but is used internally by the system to identify each object uniquely. The OID is unique to that object. Each identifier can be associated with one, and only one, object. Also, the OID is invariant, in the sense that it cannot be altered during its lifetime. The OID will not be reused by another object, even after an object has been removed. An important advantage is that objects can use it to contain or refer to other objects.

An OODBMS must have some mechanism for generating OIDs. It is not usually the physical address of the OID but, more often, a long integer is used which maps to the physical address. It is therefore independent of the values of any of its attributes (that is, its 'state'). An object identity is permanent, whereas the state of an object (the values of its instance variables) can change arbitrarily; thus, an office worker's address can change, but the identity remains the same. Object-oriented systems that support this strong built-in identity also allow the object to undergo structural modifications (i.e. change its class) without any changes in its identity. Another consequence of this independence is that two objects could have the same state but would have different identities.

Object identity advantages

Object identity offers several advantages in OODBMSs:

- They are efficient: OIDs require little storage within a complex object
- As they cannot be modified by the user, the system can ensure entity and referential integrity more easily, and users do not need to maintain referential integrity
- They help locate objects quickly, as the OIDs point to an actual address or to a location within a table that gives the address of the referenced object
- They do not depend upon the data contained in the object in any way. This allows the value of every attribute of an object to change, but for the object to remain the same object with the same OID.

Complex objects

Conventional relational databases allow a fixed number of types for their attributes (e.g. reals, integers, strings, and dates). Many advanced DB applications include data which have many types. Modern systems must be able to handle freeform text, photographs, audio, video etc. Data (e.g. designs in a CAD system) may be very large, with many interdependent subsystems. Fixed structure (horizontal and vertical homogeneity) of the relational model is too restrictive for many objects that have a complex structure.
OO systems offer a rich collection of types in addition to the basic ones. Importantly, these additional types include other objects.

7.6 The object-oriented database system manifesto

The OODB manifesto (Atkinson et al, 1989) proposed thirteen mandatory features for an object-oriented DBMS. It is still generally agreed that an OODBMS should support these features. Eight of these apply to OO concepts; the rest to features one would expect to find in any DBMS. The features are listed below in no particular order:

- OODBMSs should allow **complex objects:** we will see next that OO systems offer a rich collection of types, in addition to the basic ones, such as integers and strings. Importantly, these additional types include other objects
- **Encapsulation** must be supported: the state and behaviour of an object are encapsulated, that is, not visible outside of the object. This is achieved by ensuring that programmers have access only to the interface specification of methods. It means that the internal details can be changed without affecting the applications that use it
- **Classes** must be supported: the blueprint for creating objects; defines static and dynamic properties of an object (attributes and methods); organised in a hierarchy of classes
- The DML must be **computationally complete:** the DML should be a general purpose programming language (not the case with SQL2), otherwise there will be impedance mismatch problems
- **Data persistence** must be supported: data must persist after the application that created it has terminated
- **Large databases** must be supported: OODBMSs (as well as conventional DBMSs) have indexes, buffers etc to manage secondary storage – these are transparent to the user

- **Concurrent users** should be supported
- An efficient, application-independent ad hoc **query language** should be supported
- Classes must be able to **inherit from their ancestors:** a subclass will inherit attributes and methods from its superclass – this can greatly reduce redundancy
- **Recovery mechanisms** should exist
- **Dynamic binding** must be supported: methods are not linked to their associated code until an application is invoked. This is known as dynamic binding. When dynamic binding occurs, the systems binds message selectors to their methods at run time instead of at compile time
- The set of **data types must be extensible:** the user should be able to build new types from the set of predefined types and these should be indistinguishable in usage from system-defined types
- **Object identity** must be supported: all objects must have a unique identity which is independent of its attribute value – this means fast and efficient locating of objects.

7.7 Comparison of OODBMSs and RDBMSs

In the past few years, object-oriented (OO) concepts have been applied to many areas of computer science and this has led to the widespread use of object-oriented programming languages such as C++ and Java. However, OO database systems have been relatively slow to be adopted. We have seen that relational data models and systems have been very successful for the development of databases used by traditional business applications. Also, OO techniques are sometimes favoured in database applications because the OO model is semantically much richer than earlier data models, thus a database based on the OO model is more capable of storing data that accurately reflects 'real world' information.

We saw previously, that there are certain shortcomings to relational databases when we need to design databases for advanced database systems. In activity 7.1 we again look at these shortcomings and consider how the OO model has overcome these disadvantages.

Activity 7.1

Comparing the relational model and OO model

Examine the following tables:

Weaknesses of RDBMSs:

- Poor representation of 'real world' entities
- Semantic overloading
- Poor support for integrity and enterprise constraints
- Homogeneous data structure
- Limited operations
- Difficulty handling recursive queries
- Impedance mismatch.

Advantages of OODBMSs:

- Enriched modelling capabilities
- Extensibility
- Removal of impedance mismatch
- More expressive query language
- Support for schema evolution
- Support for long-duration transactions
- Applicablility to advanced database applications
- Improved performance.

Examine the **weaknesses of RDBMSs** above. If you have forgotten the details, look at chapter 1. Also examine the **advantages of OOBDMSs** above, which have been discussed throughout this chapter. Now produce a grid with two columns. On the left-hand side, list the shortcomings of the relational approach and on the right-hand side, explain how the OO approach might overcome these problems.

7.8 Object-oriented data modelling

Object-oriented data modelling gives us a formal model of an organisation, in a similar way as the entity-relationship model did. In the entity-relationship model the schema includes both a description of the object data structure and constraints. OO design requires these, but in addition the object behaviour is identified and mapped to a set of methods that are unique for each class. In this section we will show how the **extended entity-relationship model** (EER) can be amended to complete the design of the data structure part of the OO model. 'Behaviour modelling', a technique that identifies and documents the behaviour of each class in the model, is not covered in this section.

The extended entity-relationship model is, as the name suggests, an extension of the entity-relationship model. Two of the most important extensions are relevant to the OO approach. These are **specialisation** and **generalisation**. The process of forming a superclass is referred to as generalisation and the process of forming a subclass is known as specialisation. We now discuss these in more detail.

Specialisation

Most existing object-oriented systems allow developers to extend an application by specialising existing components (in most cases, classes) of their applications. Software extensions are achieved by creating subclasses of existing classes.

Figure 7.3: Specialisation

Specialisation is illustrated in figure 7.3, in which the class with the shaded background is an 'older' existing class, and the classes with a white background are created by inheriting structure and behaviour from existing classes. Therefore, specialisation is a **top-down approach** to software development. We start with a general class hierarchy (the top-level superclasses) and extend it by the creation of subclasses (the classes that are the leaves, or at the bottom of the hierarchy). Specialising an existing class can be achieved by adding instance variables, restricting existing instance variables, adding methods, overriding existing methods, and so on.

Generalisation

Generalisation is the complement of specialisation. It uses a **bottom-up approach** by creating classes that are generalisations (or superclasses) of existing subclasses. This is illustrated in figure 7.4. Here, the new class (which is at the top of the hierarchy), is created by extracting common structures, including instance variables and methods of existing, more specialised classes, from existing classes (which are at the bottom of the hierarchy).

Figure 7.4: Generalisation

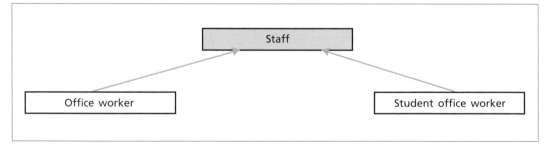

As an example of generalisation, assume that we have two existing classes, 'lecturer' and 'student'.

Lecturer has the following attributes:

Name
TelephoneNumber
Address
Salary
EmployeeNumber
WorksFor

Student has the following attributes:

Name
StudentNumber
Address
TelephoneNumber
Advisor

These existing classes have a common structure and behaviour. In order to abstract this common structure and behaviour, we need to generalise the two classes in class 'UniversityMember' with attributes:

Name
TelephoneNumber
Address

Once UniversityMember is created, it can be used as a superclass of other classes that could be constructed by specialising UniversityMember.

UML inheritance hierarchy diagram

Inheritance, as we saw earlier in this chapter, is relevant to the object-oriented model. The UML (unified modelling language) notation was introduced in chapter 1 for entity-relationship diagrams. We now show how inheritance is included in the diagram, i.e. by using the open arrow to indicate inheritance. The diagram is similar to the entity-relationship diagram, but in this case each rectangle denotes a superclass or subclass that includes entity name, attribute names and methods. An example is given in figure 7.5.

Figure 7.5: Inheritance hierarchy diagram example

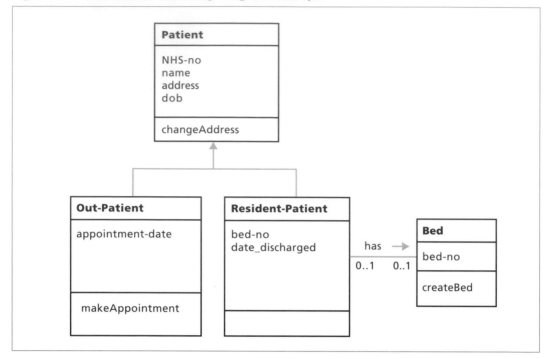

Here each subclass (Out-Patient, Resident-Patient) participates in different relationships – an outpatient is not assigned to a bed, whereas all other patients are. Also, each entity subclass may have different attributes (e.g. Resident-Patient may have 'date-discharged' as an attribute; Out-Patient might have 'appointment-date').

Representing relationships

Here we examine the way that relationships are represented in OODBMSs. The representation of relationships is one of the most fundamental ways in which data models differ. Before we look at this representation, it is useful to explore how types are created and several relevant varieties of variables: reference, collection and derived attributes.

Creating types

Creating types in an OODBMS is far more flexible than is the case for relational databases. In the relational model, there is only one category of type that a user may create – the table. The definitions of a table's attributes (columns) are the type definition, and the rows of a table are instances of the type. An important restriction on the table is that attributes of the table must be the system-defined literal types. User-defined types cannot be used as attribute types. Hence, for example, an attribute may not have another table as an attribute. OODBMSs typically allow more flexibility in the types of attribute values permitted: object attributes may have complex values, such as sets or references to other objects. Like the attributes of relational records, attributes (instance variables) of OODBMS objects have names, and they are generally referenced by a 'dot' notation. For example, the revision attribute of a document d may be referenced as d.revision. Attributes that contain literal values are called simple attributes. There are three kinds of complex attributes: **references**, **collections** and **procedures**.

Reference attributes

Reference attributes, or associations, are used to represent relationships between objects. They take on values that are objects, that is, references to entities. For example, referring to a document tracking application, we might define two classes, Document and Chapter. Instead of using a foreign key as in the relational model, we could define a 'Document' reference attribute of 'Chapter' to indicate to which document a chapter belongs:

Example 7.1

```
classChapter
    properties
        title:      string;
        number:   Number;
        doc:       Document;
```

Note that methods (operations) are not included in the examples in this section.

Collection attributes

The second kind of complex attribute is one that represents a collection of objects or literals. The ODMG object model specifies five built-in collections subtypes including **set** (unordered collection/no duplicates), **bag** (unordered collection/duplicates allowed) and **list** (ordered collection/ duplicates allowed). As in example 7.2, we can define two collection-valued attributes of the 'Document' object type in our example database:

Example 7.2

```
classDocument
    properties
        title:       string;
        revision:   date;
        keywords:  SET [string]
        chaps:      LIST [Chapter];
```

The first collection, 'keywords', is a set of keyword strings (i.e. literals) associated with the document, perhaps used to look up documents associatively by subject matter. The second collection, 'chaps', is a list of chapter objects (i.e. an object) for this document. Note that we chose to make the keywords a set, since there is no particular reason to order them, but we chose to make the chapters a list, rather than sorting by a chapter number when retrieving them. It is important to note that relational first normal form does not permit collection-valued attributes (as this would constitute a repeating group); in contrast, most of the OODBMSs we discuss do allow collections. Thus, we diverge in an important way from the relational model on this point: sets and lists of objects are important concepts in the data model.

Representing binary relationships

Relationships are represented in an object-oriented data model using the complex attributes described in the previous section: references and collections of references. The representation used depends on both the multiplicity and the degree of the relationship. Binary relationships can be represented as follows:

Example 7.3

```
class Document
    properties
        title:      string;
        revision:   date;
        chaps:      LIST [Chapter] <-> doc;
        authors:    LIST[Person] <-> pubs;
        index:      Index <-> for;

    class Chapter
    properties
        title:      string;
        number:     Number;
        doc:        Document <-> chaps;

    class Index
    properties
        entries:    Number;
        for:        Document <-> index;

    class Person
    properties
        name:       string;
        pubs:       LIST [Document] <-> authors;
```

Example 7.3 shows how binary one-to-one, one-to-many and many-to-many relationships may be represented. In all these cases the relationship is manifested as a new attribute of an object that references the associated object, and a new attribute of the associated object that provides a 'back reference', using the '<->' symbol.

Names of attributes

Names must be given to the new attributes used to represent relationships, analogous to the names given to attributes representing relationships in the relational model. For example, in the class examples above, the relationship between documents and chapters is represented by the 'chaps' attribute of the document objects, and by the 'doc' attribute of the chapter objects.

Inverse attributes

Note that the syntax of the class examples specifies both the doc attribute and the inverse attribute (the chaps attribute of document objects), using a double arrow: doc: Document <-> chaps. Conversely, the inverse attribute is defined with a similar syntax in the Document declaration: chaps: LIST[Chapter] <-> doc. The inverse attribute pairs must be kept consistent. For example, if we add another chapter to a document by setting the chapter's doc attribute, the OODBMS must add the chapter to the document's chaps list. If a chapter is moved to another document, then both attributes must likewise be updated. The problem of synchronising inverse attributes is a form of referential integrity (i.e. maintaining the correctness of references when an object is deleted or a relationship is changed).

Creating an object-oriented schema from an entity-relationship model

We now outline a simplified methodology for converting an entity-relationship schema to an object-oriented schema. We will use an example concerning internal candidates for job interviews within an organisation.

The entity-relationship model

The following is a relational schema for part of a database concerning personnel who are applying for internal promotion within a company. Interviews are held for a number of jobs; candidates can take part in more than one interview. Some employees are asked to be members of the interview panel, so that a number of employees will interview a particular candidate for a particular job.

CANDIDATE (cno: Number, cname: char12, deptno:Number, ctel:Number, present-position: char20)

PANEL-MEMBER (pmno: Number, pmname: char12, deptno: Number, pmtel:Number, last-sat-on-panel: date)

JOB (jobno: Number, jobtitle: char20, start-salary: money, deptno: Number)

INTERVIEW (intno: Number, jobno: Number, cno:Number, intdate: date)

PANEL (intno: Number, pmno: Number)

DEPARTMENT (deptno: Number, deptname: char12, depthead: char20)

Given the above relational schema, we will construct an equivalent object-oriented database schema. For this exercise we will ignore methods. Note that all primary keys are underlined, and attributes with the same name have attribute values that are pooled from the same domain.

The entity-relationship diagram

It is helpful to start by drawing an entity-relationship model for the above. Note the assumptions that have been made about optional/mandatory relationships.

Figure 7.6: Entity-relationship model

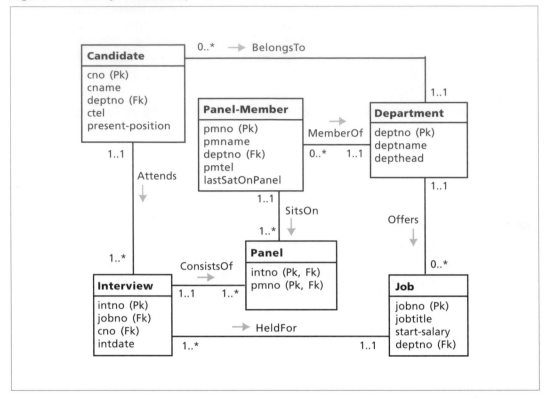

A simplified methodology

1. Using the generalisation process, we examine the relations in figure 7.6 with their attributes in order to see if any superclasses can be created from these entities. Observe that 'name', 'department number' and 'telephone number' are in both the Candidate and Panel-Member relations. Thus we create a superclass which we name Employee. Note that the subclasses Candidate and Panel-Member inherit the attributes (and methods) of the superclass Employee.

2. Next we create classes for all entities. An exception to this is any 'link entities' that had previously been created from the decomposition of many-to-many relationships (in the example Panel and Interview entities). Notice that Panel has no non-key attributes. In our example the Panel disappears, with both the Interview and Panel-Member classes having references to each other. Interview has attributes in its own right. Later we will look at incorporating Interview as a structure in one of the classes to which it relates.

3. Next we consider the properties or attributes of each class. In this simplified methodology we will consider only reference and collection attributes: derived attributes are not included. Looking at reference attributes, then all foreign keys in the entity-relationship model will become reference attributes in the object model. Thus the class Employee includes an attribute 'dept' which references the Department class. This means that an object Employee will 'include' all attributes and methods for its department as well as the attributes Pname and Ptel.

4. The next step is to consider one-to-many and many-to-many relationships in our entity-relationship model. Entities involved in such relationships may include collection attributes. For two entities, which are associated by a many-to-many relationship, then each class will

have an additional collection entity. So both Panel-Member and Interview will have new collection entities 'pminterviews' and 'ipanel-members' respectively.

5. For all one-to-many relationships in the entity-relationship model, where one X entity occurrence corresponds to many Y entities, a new collection entity will be included in the X entity (class). For example the 'Cinterviews' collection attribute will be included in the Candidate class to incorporate the set of interviews which each candidate will be attending.

The object-oriented schema

```
class    EMPLOYEE
         properties
              pname:              char12
              dept:               department
              ptel:               Number;

class    CANDIDATE inherits EMPLOYEE
         properties
              cand_no:            Number
              present_position:   char20
              cinterviews:        set [interview];

class    PANEL-MEMBER inherits EMPLOYEE
         properties
              pmno:               Number
              last-sat-on-panel:  date
              pminterviews:       set [interview];

class    JOB
         properties
              jobno:              Number
              jobtitle:           char20
              start-salary:       money
              jobdept:            department
              jinterviews:        set [interview];

class    INTERVIEW
         properties
              intno:              Number
              intdate:            date
              ijob:               job
              cand:               candidate
              ipanel-members:     set [panel-member];

class    DEPARTMENT
         properties
              deptno:             integer
              deptname:           char12
              depthead:           employee
              deptmembers:        set [employee]
              availablejobs:      set [job];
```

Note that the state of the classes are considered only (methods have been left out). Also we ignore inverse attributes and the back reference symbol <->.

An entity-relationship diagram for the OO schema – the inheritance hierarchy diagram

We can now draw an inheritance hierarchy diagram based on our object-oriented schema. Attributes have been omitted for simplicity.

Figure 7.7: Inheritance hierarchy diagram

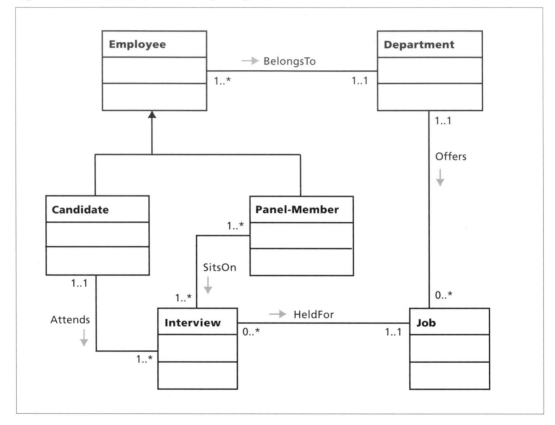

An alternative solution – structured complex objects

As mentioned earlier, INTERVIEW, like PANEL, is part of a decomposed many-to-many relationship but this time has its own non-key attributes (intdate). An alternative to the previous solution is to incorporate the attribute 'interviews' as a **structure** within one of the classes (for example, JOB).

Thus:

```
class   EMPLOYEE
        properties
            pname:              char12
            dept:               department
            ptel:               Number;

class   CANDIDATE inherit EMPLOYEE
        properties
            cand_no:            Number
            present_position:   char20;
```

```
class    PANEL-MEMBER inherit EMPLOYEE
         properties
                 pmno:              Number
                 last-sat-on-panel: date;

class    JOB
         properties
                 jobno:             Number
                 jobtitle:          char20
                 start-salary:      money
                 jobdept:           department
                 interviews:        set  [intdate:  date
                                        cand:     candidate]
                                        panel:    set [panel-member]

class    DEPARTMENT
         properties
                 deptno:            integer
                 deptname:          char12
                 depthead:          Person
                 deptmembers:       set [person]
                 availablejobs:     set [job]
```

In our example, retaining the INTERVIEW class is perhaps a better option but in many cases the use of structures provides a means of modelling complex and interrelated objects.

Referential integrity

You may remember that the referential integrity of a relational database will not be violated if a foreign key in one table matches a primary key in its 'parent' table, or be wholly null. For example, in the Candidates' entity-relational model, a 'deptno' (department number) in the Candidate entity must match a 'deptno' in the Department entity or else be null. In the object-oriented model there are several ways of dealing with referential integrity, and different techniques have been implemented by different vendors. They vary on the amount of control the user has in explicitly deleting objects.

The ODMG (Object Data Management Group) object model suggests the following:

Allow the user to delete and modify objects and relationships when no longer required. Here the system takes care of referential integrity. If we have a relationship from department to candidate and from candidate to department, when a Department object is deleted it is easy for the system to adjust the reference in the Candidate object (for example by setting the reference to NULL).

Comparison of relationships in relational and OO databases

Consider the most obvious differences between the relational and the object-oriented representation of relationships:

- References are represented using primary keys instead of OIDs in the relational model, although all the models use references as the basis to represent relationships
- Relationship (or link) tables are approximately equivalent to the intermediate objects introduced to represent relationships in an object-oriented model. However, in the relational model, far more are required to satisfy relational normalisation (e.g. when representing many-to-many binary relationships)

- The object-oriented models 'package' all the relationships in which an object type participates as attributes associated with the object. In our previous example, all the relationships for a Department object are shown in the object definition. In the relational model, it is necessary to examine the entire schema to determine which tables have foreign keys involving an entity table such as the employee table
- Object-oriented models allow manual ordering of relationships using lists
- The access syntax and semantics are quite different.

Problems with the OO model

One of the key arguments against OO databases is that databases are usually not designed to solve specific problems, but we need to be able to use them to solve many different problems – some not always apparent at the design stage of the database. It is for this reason that OO technology and its use of encapsulation can often limit its flexibility. Indeed, the ability to perform ad hoc queries can be made quite difficult, although some vendors do provide a query language to facilitate this.

The use of the same language for both database operations and system operations can provide many advantages, including that of reducing impedance mismatch (the difference in level between set-at-a-time and record-at-a-time processing). CJ Date (2000), however, does not agree that this is best achieved by making the database language record-at-a-time; he even goes as far as to say that 'record-at-a-time is a throwback to the days of pre-relational systems such as IMS and IDMS'. Instead, he proposes that set-at-a-time facilities be added to programming languages. Nonetheless, it could be argued that one of the advantages of pre-relational systems was their speed. However, the procedural nature of OO languages can still lead to serious difficulties when it comes to optimisation.

Another problem associated with pure OO databases is that a large proportion of organisations do not currently deal with the complex data types for which OO technology is ideally suited, and therefore they do not require complex data processing. It is rather like using a sledgehammer to crack a nut. For these companies there is little incentive to move towards object technology, when relational databases and online analytical processing tools will be sufficient to satisfy their data processing requirements.

7.9 Oracle and the object-relational model

Perhaps the best hope for the immediate future of database objects is the **object-relational model**. A recent development, stimulated by the advent of the object-oriented model, the object-relational model aims to address some of the problems of pure OO technology such as the poor support for ad hoc query languages, and open database technology, and provide better support for existing relational products, by extending the relational model to incorporate the key features of object-orientation. The object-relational model also provides scope for those using existing relational databases to migrate towards the incorporation of objects, and this perhaps is its key strength, in that it provides a path for the vast number of existing relational database users gradually to migrate to an object database platform, while maintaining the support of their relational vendor.

A major addition to the relational model is the introduction of a stronger type system to enable the use of complex data types, which still allow the relational model to be preserved. Several large database suppliers including IBM, Informix and Oracle, have embraced the object-relational model as the way forward. Here we look at some of the object-relational features of Oracle.

Object-relational features in Oracle

Many of the object-oriented features that appear in the ISO SQL standard SQL3 (1999) have been incorporated into Oracle. We shall examine the facilities originally incorporated in Oracle 8 and subsequent versions – these provide a good example of how one of the major database vendors is seeking to increase the level of object support within the DBMS, while still maintaining support for the relational model. Oracle support for OO constructs includes:

- **Abstract data types or object types** – this is discussed further in this section
- **Collection types or collectors** – sets of elements which are treated as a single row. Oracle currently supports array types and nested table – discussed further in this section
- **Object tables** – these are used to store objects while providing a relational view of the attributes of the object – discussed further in this section
- **Object view** – these provide a virtual object table view of data stored in a regular relational table. They allow data to be accessed or viewed as if they were object-oriented tables, even if the data is really stored in relational format
- **Methods** – written in PL/SQL, Java or C.

Note that methods are omitted in the following examples.

Abstract data types

Abstract data types (ADTs) are data types that consist of one or more subtypes. These are provided to enable users to define complex data types – structures consisting of a number of different elements, each of which uses one of the base data types provided within the Oracle product. For example, an abstract data type could be created to store addresses. Such a data type might consist of three separate subtypes such as varchar or number. From the time of its creation, an ADT can be referred to when creating tables in which the ADT is to be used.

The address ADT would be established with the 'create type' definition:

```
CREATE TYPE ADDRESS_TYPE  AS OBJECT
(STREET         VARCHAR2(30),
CITY            VARCHAR2(30),
COUNTRY         VARCHAR2(30));
```

ADTs can be **nested** (their definitions can make use of other ADTs). For example, if we wished to set up an ADT to describe customers, we could make use of the address ADT above as follows:

```
CREATE TYPE CUSTOMER_TYPE  AS OBJECT
(CUST_NO        NUMBER(6),
NAME            VARCHAR2(50),
BIRTHDATE       DATE,
GENDER          CHAR,
ADDRESS         ADDRESS_TYPE);
```

The advantages of ADTs are that they provide a standard mechanism for defining complex data types within an application, and facilitate reuse of complex data definitions.

Object tables

These are tables created within Oracle 8 (and subsequent versions) which have column values that are based on ADTs. Therefore, if we create a table which makes use of the customer and address ADTs described in the previous example, the table will be an object table. The code to create such a table would be as follows:

```
CREATE TABLE CUSTOMER OF CUSTOMER_TYPE;
```

Note that this CREATE TABLE statement looks rather different to those encountered in chapter 3 on SQL data definition language (DDL). It is very brief, because it makes use of the previous work we have done in establishing the customer and address ADTs. It is extremely important to bear in mind the distinction between object tables and ADTs:

- **ADTs** are the building blocks on which object tables can be created. ADTs themselves cannot be queried, in the same way that the built-in data types in Oracle such as number and varchar2 cannot be queried. ADTs simply provide the structure which will be used when objects are inserted into an object table

- **Object tables** are the elements that are queried, and these are established using a combination of base data types such as varchar2, date, number and any relevant ADTs as required.

Nested tables

A nested table is a 'table within a table'. It is a collection of rows, represented as a column in the main table. For each record in the main table, the nested table may contain multiple rows. This can be considered as a way of storing a one-to-many relationship within one table. For example, if we have a table storing the details of departments, and each department is associated with a number of projects, we can use a nested table to store details about projects within the department table. The project records can be accessed directly through the corresponding row of the department table, without needing to do a join. Note that the nested table mechanism sacrifices first normal form, as we are now storing a repeating group of projects associated with each department record. This may be acceptable, if it is likely to be a frequent requirement to access departments with their associated projects in this way.

For example, we could create a table of pet owners which includes data about the owners' pets. Using a nested table, the information about both owners and pets can be stored.

```
CREATE TYPE PET_TYPE  AS OBJECT
(PET_NO          NUMBER(6),
NAME            VARCHAR2(50),
BIRTHDATE       DATE,
GENDER          CHAR,
BREED           VARCHAR2(30)  );
```

To use this ADT as the basis for a nested table we now need to create a new ADT thus:

```
CREATE TYPE PET_NESTEDTABLE AS TABLE OF PET_TYPE;
```

The **as table** clause tells Oracle that the type created will be the basis of a nested table. We now create a table of pet owners. The second column of this table 'pets' has a type which is a nested table.

```
CREATE TABLE OWNER
(OWNER_NO        NUMBER(6),
 NAME            VARCHAR2(50),
 PETS            PET_NESTEDTABLE)
nested table PETS store as PET_NESTEDTABLE_TAB;
```

Thus, the data in the PETS column will be stored in one table and the data in the other columns (owner_no, name) will be stored in a separate table with pointers between the tables. In the example, the nested table will be stored in PET_NESTEDTABLE_TAB.

Varying arrays

A varying array, **varray**, is a collection of objects, each with the same data type. The size of the array is preset when it is created. The varying array is treated like a column in a main table. Conceptually, it is a nested table, with a preset limit on its number of rows. Varrays also then allow us to store up to a preset number of repeating values in a table. The data type for a varray is determined by whatever the type of data that is to be stored.

A varying array is based on either an ADT or one of Oracle's standard data types. Oracle suggests that if the array you wish to create is based on more than one column it is better to use nested tables instead. In the example we will create a varying array which stores pet names in an owner table. We start by creating a new data type PETNAMES_TYPE:

```
CREATE TYPE PETNAMES_TYPE AS OBJECT
(PETNAME        VARCHAR2(50) );
```

To use this ADT in varying array we will need to decide on the maximum number of pets per owner – assume ten. Now we create the varying array:

```
CREATE TYPE PETNAMES_VA AS VARRAY(10) OF PETNAMES_TYPE
```

Now we create an OWNER table with a varying array of type PETNAMES_TYPE for its PET column:

```
CREATE TABLE OWNER
(OWNER_NO        NUMBER(6),
 NAME            VARCHAR2(50),
 PETS            PETNAMES_VA);
```

Listing types and removing types

It is useful to list the types you have created in your Oracle area.

```
SQL> select type_name
2  from user_types;
```

TYPE_NAME

ADDRESS_TYPE

CUSTOMER_TYPE

......

Existing types can be deleted using the drop type command, for example:

SQL> drop type ADDRESS_TYPE;

But note that you cannot drop a type if a table which you have created depends on it.

Object-oriented data modelling

We have already looked at the case study concerning Middlesex Transport, which is responsible for running a fleet of buses throughout North London. The scenario is given in chapter 2 and the entity-relationship diagram is repeated below.

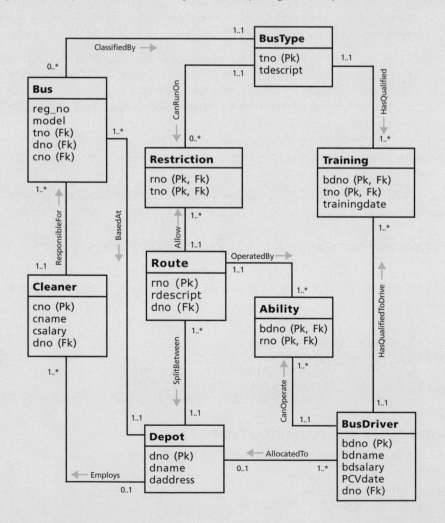

cont...

Remind yourself of the details of the scenario and consider the previous diagram. Now construct an equivalent object-oriented database schema in the form:

```
Class   ClassName
        properties
        name        char12
        address     address
        etc
```

Note: pre-defined types (such as characters and numbers) can be omitted.

Activity 7.3

Further development of objects in Oracle

Visit the website http://Oracle.com and find out about further aspects of object support within the Oracle10g database system. Much of this information is included within white papers. In particular, look for summaries of new features, and a paper on Objects and the Extensibility option.

7.10 Summary

In this chapter, students were introduced to object-oriented and object-relational databases. Object-oriented concepts, which are part of the object-oriented programming model, were first examined and their importance as part of the object-oriented database was emphasised. Students were introduced to a methodology for converting an entity-relationship model to object-oriented. Next the focus was on object-relational databases, and some of Oracle's object-oriented database extensions were studied and practised.

7.11 Review questions

Review question 7.1 Using the template below, fill in the **Relational** column to compare the characteristics of CAD and CAM systems with conventional relational databases.

CAD/CAM	Relational
Data has many types, each with a small number of instances	
Designs may be very large, with maybe millions of parts and often there will be interdependent subsystem designs	
They evolve through time	
Updates far-reaching – one change may effect a large number of design objects	
Various versions of designs must be maintained, with many staff working on these versions at the same time. There needs to be version control and the final product must be consistent and coordinated	

Review question 7.2   Suggest three or four classes that might be needed for the personnel department of a university. Now create two or three instances for each of your university classes.

 Review question 7.3   One approach to developing an OODBMS is to extend an existing OO programming language (such as C++ or Java) with database capabilities. Describe three other approaches.

 Review question 7.4   Describe the difference between methods and messages in object-oriented systems.

 Review question 7.5   What are the advantages of inheritance?

 Review question 7.6   Define each of the following concepts:

1. Object

2. Attribute

3. Object identity

4. Complex object

 Review question 7.7   What are the advantages of OIDs compared with primary keys in relational databases?

Review question 7.8   The OODB Manifesto proposed thirteen mandatory features for an object-oriented DBMS. Eight of these features apply to OO concepts; the rest to features one would expect to find in any DBMS. Can you spot the eight?

Review question 7.9   What is meant by generalisation, and what is its importance to the object-oriented data model?

Review question 7.10 Assume that there are two existing classes, Supplier and Customer, with attributes:

1. Supplier (Sno, company-name, address, telephone-no, contact-person, balance-owing)

2. Customer (Cno, company-name, address, telephone-no, balance-owed)

Use the bottom-up approach of generalisation to create a class or classes from these existing classes.

Review question 7.11 (i) Consider a subset of a hospital information system with the following characteristics:

- Patients can either be resident patients or outpatients
- For both types of patients we will need to hold the name, telephone number, date of birth and the patient's doctor (GP)
- For a resident patient we will need to hold the ward name in which the patient is currently residing, the admission date of the patient, and also information about any operations that the patient has had
- The operation information will include the date and time of the operation, the surgeon (assume one) who carried out the operation, plus the theatre where the operation took place
- For both GPs and surgeons we will hold the name and telephone number; in addition we will hold the surgeon's specialism (e.g. ear, nose and throat) – assume one per surgeon
- For outpatients we will need to hold information about the outpatients' appointments: the appointment date and time.

Draw an entity-relationship diagram for the above case, making any assumptions that you need to make about optional/mandatory relationships. Indicate primary and foreign keys.

 Review question 7.11 (ii) Now construct an equivalent object-oriented database schema including any structured attributes. In this case include the type of the attributes, but only those that are specific to the object-oriented schema.

 Review question 7.11 (iii) Now draw an entity-relationship diagram based on your object-oriented schema in question 7.11 (ii).

 Review question 7.12 (i) Consider an Employee Database. The entities are given below:

> EMPLOYEE (eno: varchar(10), ename: varchar(20), deptno: varchar(10), present-position: varchar(20))

> DEPARTMENT (deptno: varchar(10), deptname: varchar2(20), depthead: varchar2(20))

Write Oracle abstract data type definitions for the Candidate and Department entities and try running these in Oracle SQLPLUS.

 Review question 7.12 (ii) Now create object tables based on these ADTs. State the difference between the object tables and the ADTs.

Review question 7.12 (iii) Suppose that employees are assigned to projects: one project per employee. A project will have a number of employees working on the project. A project includes a project number, description and expected number of days for completion. Create the table for the project (called OTPROJECT) which includes a nested table of employees who work on the project (i.e. use the EMPLOYEE_TYPE type definition created in question 7.12(i) as the basis of a nested table in a project table).

Review question 7.13 Students taking a course can do up to ten assessments. Suggest a table definition for a STUDENT object which holds registration number, name, email address and grades. Include any necessary type statements in your answer.

7.12 Answers to review questions

Answer to review question 7.1

CAD/CAM	Relational
Data has many types, each with a small number of instances	Typically, a database consists of a smallish number of relations (usually tens rather than hundreds) but relations may contain thousands of tuples. For example, consider a database for Middlesex University
Designs may be very large, with maybe millions of parts and often there will be interdependent subsystem designs	Each attribute in a relation is atomic and cannot be broken down further
They evolve through time	Typically, a conventional relational database is relatively static
Updates far-reaching – one change may effect a large number of design objects	Updates to a relational schema only usually effect a small number of other, related relations
Various versions of designs must be maintained, with many staff working on these versions at the same time. There needs to be version control and the final product must be consistent and coordinated	Maintaining versions or the evolution of objects (schema evolution) is not so important for traditional database applications

Answer to review question 7.2 Classes for university personnel department. Your answer should list classes such as the following:

- Employee
- Job
- Department.

Objects that are instances of university personnel system. Your answer should list instances with typical attributes such as the following:

- Class Employee: with name attribute values such as 'Jo Bloggs', 'Jane Smith', 'Nimesh Patel'

- Class Job: with jobFunction attribute values such as manager, cleaner, lecturer, professor, administrator

- Class Department: with departmentTitle attribute values such as 'Computing Science', 'Biology', 'Mechanical Engineering', 'Performing Arts', 'Social Science'.

Answer to review question 7.3

- Embed OO database language constructs in a conventional host language

- Provide OODBMS libraries to an OO programming language

- Extend an existing language (SQL) with OO capabilities.

Answer to review question 7.4   Messages are the means by which objects communicate with one another. Messages are passed between objects in order to convey information, and to request an object to perform a particular function. Methods are fragments of program code that are the part of objects that enable them to perform actions. The details of methods are not visible outside of the object. When a message is received by an object requesting that a particular action be performed, this will be enacted by the object executing one or more of its methods. The result of the action will, in many situations, be conveyed back to the requesting object via a message.

Answer to review question 7.5   The main advantages of inheritance are:

1. **Reusability:** through the inheritance mechanism, the characteristics of an object can be made available to other objects. Depending on the system, this may involve both state (data) and behaviour (methods) of objects.

2. **Extensibility:** another aspect of the mechanism is that it provides a natural means of developing a modelled system. As new features, data or program code are added, these can be defined in terms of new objects, which inherit the already tested characteristics of the earlier part of the system.

Answer to review question 7.6

1. An 'object' is a uniquely identifiable entity, which contains the attributes that describe both the state of a 'real world' object and the actions that are associated with it.

2. An 'attribute' is a property that describes some aspect of an object. Attributes have values, which have a simple or complex structure and are stored within the object.

3. 'Object identity' is a unique identity for each independent object stored in the database. The value of the OID is not visible to the external user but is used internally by the system to identify each object uniquely.

4. A 'complex object' is an object that contains other objects.

Answer to review question 7.7

OODBSs OIDs	RDBSs primary keys
They are efficient: OIDs require little storage within a complex object	Need to use inefficient joins to retrieve data
As the user cannot modify them, the system can ensure entity and referential integrity more easily and users do not need to maintain referential integrity	Can be modified by the user
They help locate objects quickly as the OIDs point to an actual address or to a location within a table that gives the address of the referenced object	Do not relate to the actual address
They do not depend upon the data contained in the object in any way. This allows the value of every attribute of an object to change, but for the object to remain the same object with the same OID	Primary key is one (or more) attribute in the relation and is subject to change – may be subject to integrity violations

Answer to review question 7.8   Eight features which apply to OO concepts:

- OODBMSs should allow complex objects

- Encapsulation must be supported

- Classes must be supported

- The DML must be computationally complete

- Classes must be able to inherit from their ancestors

- Dynamic binding must be supported

- The set of data types must be extensible

- Object identity must be supported.

Answer to review question 7.9   Generalisation involves the identification or abstraction of the common properties of a number of classes into a superclass. With generalisation, all properties of a generalised type (superclass) can be inherited downwards to subclasses of entities. These subclasses may also have some properties pertinent to only that subclass. Also the inheritance of specific properties can be explicitly disallowed. With generalisation, the cardinality of the relationships is always one-to-one.

Inheritance and super-/subclasses are key ideas of OODB systems. Each object in an OODB is an instance of a class, and classes are related to each other via inherited relationships.

Answer to review question 7.10 The new superclass 'Organisation' is created by extracting a common structure (and behaviour) by generalising the two classes in class Organisation with instance variables name, address and telephone-no. Thus we have (note that system types such as characters and numbers have been omitted):

```
class    ORGANIZATION
         properties
         company-name
         address
         telephone-no;

class    Supplier inherits ORGANIZATION
         properties
         Sno
         contact-person
         balance-owing;

class    Customer inherits ORGANIZATION
         properties
         Cno
         balance-owed;
```

Answer to review question 7.11 (i)

Entity-relationship diagram for object-oriented schema:

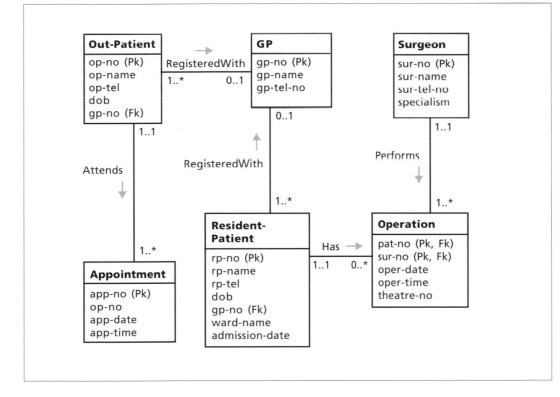

Answer to review question 7.11 (ii)

```
class    PERSON
         properties
         name
         tel;
```

cont...

```
class    PATIENT inherits PERSON
         properties
         patient-number
         dob
         general-practitioner GP;

class    RESIDENT-PATIENT inherits PATIENT
         properties
         ward-name
         admission-date
         pat-operations    set [ surg: surgeon
                                 oper-date
                                 oper-time
                                 theatre-no];

class    OUT-PATIENT inherits PATIENT
         properties
         op-appointment    set [appointment]

class    GP   inherits PERSON
         properties
              gp-no
              patients        set [patient];

class    SURGEON inherits PERSON
         properties
              sur-no
              specialism;

class    APPOINTMENT
              properties
                 out-pat      out-patient
              app-date
              app-time;
```

A number of answers are acceptable. An alternative three-tier hierarchy could be the top tier containing Person, the middle tier Patient and Doctor, and the bottom tier the two types of patients and the two types of doctors. Also Appointment could be included as a structured attribute in the OUTPATIENT class. Operations (pat-operations) have been included in the RESIDENT-PATIENT class to illustrate structured types. Alternatively, they could have been included in the SURGEON class, or retained as class OPERATION.

Answer to review question 7.11 (iii) The following solution assumes the 'alternative' three-tier solution to part (ii) and includes the Operations class.

Object-oriented database schema:

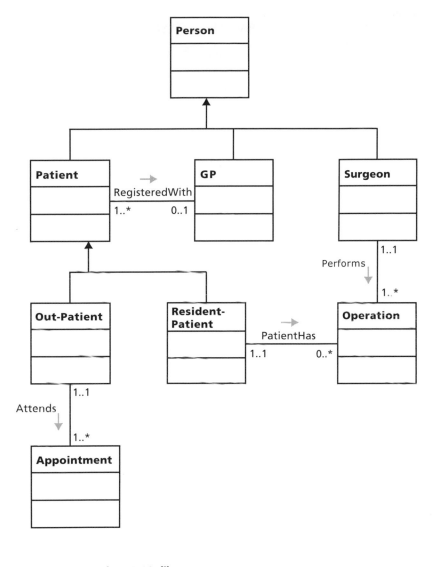

Answer to review question 7.12 (i)

```
CREATE OR REPLACE TYPE DEPARTMENT_TYPE AS OBJECT
   (DEPTNO       VARCHAR2(10),
    DEPTNAME     VARCHAR2(20),
    DEPTHEAD     VARCHAR2(20) );
   /

CREATE OR REPLACE TYPE EMPLOYEE_TYPE AS OBJECT
   (ENO          VARCHAR2(10),
    ENAME        VARCHAR2(20),
    DEPARTMENT   DEPARTMENT_TYPE,
    PRESENT_POS  VARCHAR2(20) );
   /
```

Note use of 'REPLACE' which replaces previous versions of EMPLOYEE_TYPE.

Answer to review question 7.12 (ii)

```
CREATE TABLE EMPLOYEE OF EMPLOYEE_TYPE;
CREATE TABLE DEPARTMENT OF DEPARTMENT_TYPE;
```

ADTs provide the structure which will be used when objects are inserted into an object table. They are the building blocks on which object tables can be created. ADTs cannot be queried, in the same way that the built-in data types in Oracle such as number and varchar2 cannot be queried. Object tables are the elements which are queried, and these are established using a combination of base data types such as varchar2, date, number and any relevant ADTs as required.

Answer to review question 7.12 (iii) Employee type as before:

```
CREATE OR REPLACE TYPE EMPLOYEE_TYPE AS OBJECT
    (ENO            VARCHAR2(10),
    ENAME           VARCHAR2(20),
    DEPARTMENT      DEPARTMENT_TYPE,
    PRESENT_POS     VARCHAR2(20)  );
    /
```

To use this ADT as the basis for a nested table we now need to create a new ADT thus:

CREATE OR REPLACE TYPE EMPLOYEE_NT AS TABLE OF EMPLOYEE_TYPE;

The PROJECT table is now created containing a nested table of type EMPLOYEE_NT:

```
CREATE TABLE PROJECT
    (PROJECT_NO  VARCHAR(6),
    DESCRIPTION  VARCHAR(20),
    DAYS         NUMBER,
    EMPLOYEES    EMPLOYEE_NT)
nested table EMPLOYEES store as EMPLOYEE_NT_TAB;
```

Answer to review question 7.13

```
CREATE TYPE GRADES_TYPE AS OBJECT
    (GRADE         NUMBER );
```

We now create the varying array:

CREATE TYPE GRADES_VA AS VARRAY(10) OF GRADES_TYPE:

Now we create a STUDENT table which includes a varying array of type GRADES_TYPE for its GRADE column:

```
CREATE TABLE STUDENT
    (REGISTRATION_NO  CHAR(10),
    NAME             VARCHAR2(50),
    EMAIL            VARCHAR2(50),
    GRADES           GRADES_VA);
```

7.13 Feedback on activities

Answer 7.1 Your grid should look something like:

Shortcomings of the relational approach	Advantages of OODBMSs
Poor representation of 'real world' entities; only one construct for representing both entities and relationships: the relation (semantic overloading)	Enriched modelling capabilities: both state and behaviour encapsulated. More natural representation of the real world
Homogeneous data structure; all attribute values must be atomic	Objects store the relationship it has with other objects; many-to-many relationships supported. Objects can be formed into complex objects
Poor support for integrity and no support for enterprise constraints	Better support for integrity and enterprise constraints
Limited operations; most DMLs lack computational completeness	More expressive query language. Most OODBMSs provide a DML that is computationally complete
Impedance mismatch – inefficiencies occur when mapping a declarative language such as SQL to procedural language such as C	Removal of impedance mismatch – OO languages are row level (rather than set level)
	Improved performance, although this is arguable
	Extensibility – new types built from existing types
	Reduced redundancy and reusability – forming a superclass involves factoring out common properties of several classes and through this inheritance mechanism the state and behaviour of an object can be made available to other objects.
Schema changes difficult	Support for schema evolution.
Difficulty in modelling complex applications	Applicability to advanced database applications

Answer 7.2 Note that system types such as characters and numbers have been omitted.

```
Class   EMPLOYEE
        properties
            ename
            esalary
            edepot          depot

Class   BUSDRIVER inherit EMPLOYEE
        properties
            bdnno
            ability         set[route]
            training        set[training]
```

cont...

Class   CLEANER inherit EMPLOYEE
      properties
          cno
          cbuses   **set[bus]**

Class   ROUTE
      properties
          rno
          rdescipt
          rdepot   **depot**
          rrestrictions **set[bustype]**
          rability   **set[busdriver]**

Class   BUS
      properties
          reg_no
          model
          btype   **bustype**
          bdepot   **depot**
          bcleaner   **cleaner**

Class   BUSTYPE
      properties
          tno
          tdescript
          brestricions **set[route]**
          btraining   **training**
          bbuses   **set[bus]**

Class   Depot
      properties
          dno
          dname
          address
          droutes   **set[route]**
          demployees **set[employee]**
          dbuses   **set[bus]**

Class   Training
      properties
          tdriver   **busdriver**
          ttype   **bustype**
          trainingdate

CHAPTER 8

Transaction management and concurrency control

OVERVIEW

The purpose of this chapter is to introduce the fundamental technique of **concurrency control**. This provides database systems with the ability to handle many users accessing data simultaneously. Problems arise from the fact that users wish to query and update stored data at the same time. If these operations are not controlled, then the database may become inconsistent. This chapter helps you understand the functionality of database management systems, with special reference to **online transaction processing** (OLTP).

These topics fit closely with the chapter on backup and recovery, so you may want to revisit this chapter later in the course to review the concepts here. It will become clear that there are a number of circumstances where recovery procedures may need to be invoked to salvage previously executed or currently executing transactions.

Learning outcomes	On completion of this chapter, you should be able to:

- Understand the purpose of concurrency control

- Explain what a transaction is, its properties and the reasons for designing databases around transactions

- Analyse the problems of data management in a concurrent environment

- Critically compare the relative strengths of different concurrency control approaches.

8.1 Introduction

This chapter describes the problems that arise from the fact that users wish to query and update stored data at the same time. It examines the **concurrency control techniques** that are used to ensure the non-interference of concurrently executing transactions. Central to the understanding of concurrency control is the concept of the **transaction**. We therefore examine its importance and function. If concurrent operations are not controlled, then the database may become inconsistent. We will be looking at a number of concepts that are technical and unfamiliar. You will be expected to be able to handle these concepts, but not to have any knowledge of the detailed algorithms involved.

We will be examining particular concurrency control problems which occur when multiple transactions, submitted by various users, interfere with one another in a way that produces incorrect results. We will look at ways in which such problems might be addressed, and explore the protocols, or sets of rules, which can be applied to prevent conflict when transactions are executing concurrently. One important set of protocols we will be covering employs the technique of **locking data items** to prevent multiple transactions from accessing the items concurrently. This chapter also looks at the particular problem of **deadlock** and examines ways in which it can be resolved.

8.2 Transactions

What is a transaction?

A transaction is the execution of a program that accesses or changes the content of a database. It may be the entire program, a portion of a program or a single command. It may be distributed (i.e. available on different physical systems or different logical subsystems) and use data concurrently with other transactions.

A transaction has a clear start and finish. The assumption is that it will start its execution on a consistent database, and if it runs to completion then the transaction is said to be **committed** and the database will be in a new consistent state. Once a transaction is committed, the transaction manager knows that the database is (or should be) in a **consistent state** again and all of the updates made by that transaction can now be made permanent. If the changes are made permanent, then the database has reached a **new synchronisation point**.

The other possibility is that the transactions do not commit satisfactorily (i.e. do not reach their end). In this case, the transaction is **aborted** and the incomplete transaction is **rolled back** (the exact way in which this is done will be considered in the backup and recovery chapter) and the database restored to the consistent state it was in before the transaction started. In an SQL database, an entire program or user session is regarded as one transaction; however, the user may explicitly force a commit or rollback using the 'commit' or 'rollback' commands.

Desirable properties of transactions

The acronym ACID indicates the properties of well-formed transactions. Any transaction that violates these principles will cause concurrency problems.

Properties of transactions:

- **Atomicity:** a transaction is an atomic unit of processing; it is either performed in its entirety or not performed at all. A transaction does not partly happen
- **Consistency:** the database state is consistent at the end of a transaction
- **Isolation:** a transaction should not make its updates visible to other transactions until it is committed This property, when enforced strictly, solves the temporary update problem and makes cascading rollbacks of transactions unnecessary
- **Durability:** when a transaction has made a change to the database state and the change is committed, this change is permanent and should be available to all other transactions.

Transaction operations

For recovery purposes, a system always keeps track of when a transaction starts, terminates, and commits or aborts. Hence, the recovery manager keeps track of the following transaction states and operations (these keywords are indicative of many data manipulation languages):

- **BEGIN_TRANSACTION:** this marks the beginning of transaction execution
- **READ or WRITE:** these specify read or write operations on the database items that are executed as part of a transaction
- **END_TRANSACTION:** this specifies that READ and WRITE operations have ended and marks the end limit of transaction execution. However, at this point it may be necessary to check whether the changes introduced by the transaction can be permanently applied to the database (committed) or whether the transaction has to be aborted because it violates concurrency control or for some other reason (rollback)
- **COMMIT_TRANSACTION:** this signals a successful end of the transaction so that any changes (updates) executed by the transaction can be safely committed to the database and will not be undone
- **ROLLBACK:** this signals that the transaction has ended unsuccessfully, so that any changes or effects that the transaction may have applied to the database must be undone.

In addition to the preceding operations, some recovery techniques require additional operations that include the following:

- **UNDO:** similar to rollback, except that it applies to a single operation rather than to a whole transaction
- **REDO:** this specifies that some of a transaction's operations must be redone to ensure that all the operations of a committed transaction have been applied successfully to the database.

Transaction states

This section describes how a transaction moves through its execution states. A transaction goes into an **active state** immediately after it starts execution, where it can issue READ and WRITE operations. When the transaction ends, it moves to the **partially committed state**. At this point, some concurrency control techniques require that certain checks are made to ensure that the transaction did not interfere with other executing transactions. In addition, some recovery protocols are needed, to ensure that a system failure will not result in an inability to record the changes of the transaction permanently. Once both checks are successful, the transaction is said to have reached its **commit point** and enters the **committed state**. Once a transaction enters the committed state, it has concluded its execution successfully.

However, a transaction can go to the **failed state** if one of the checks fails, or if it aborted during its active state. The transaction may then have to be rolled back to undo the effect of its WRITE operations on the database. The **terminated state** corresponds to the transaction leaving the system. Failed or aborted transactions may be restarted later, either automatically, or after being resubmitted as brand-new transactions.

8.3 Read and write operations

From the point of view of interaction with data in a database, the DBMS activities with which we are concerned will be simplified. There are only two activities.

The database item can be read:

    read_item(x)

which reads a database item named x into a program variable x;

and it can be written:

    write_item(x)

which writes the value of a program variable x into the database item named x.

Transaction theory and practice is about ensuring that data is read accurately and written accurately, though, as you will see, there may be compromises to make.

Read and write operations of a transaction

In order to recover successfully, many recovery mechanisms have to make a record of certain operations. These key database access operations are:

read_item(x) – which includes the following steps:

1. Locate disk sector	Compute the address of the disk block that contains item x.
2. Copy item(x)	Read the disk block into a memory buffer (if that disk block is not already in some main memory buffer).
3. Copy item(x)	Copy item x from the buffer to the variable named x.

write_item (x) – which includes the following steps:

1. Locate disk sector   Find the address of the disk block that contains item x.
2. Copy disk block into   Copy that disk block into a buffer in main memory (if that memory
   memory   disk block is not already in some main memory buffer).
3. Copy application   Copy item x from the program variable named x into its
   variable x to item x   correct location in the main memory buffer either
   in main memory   immediately or at some later point in time.
4. Store sector to disk   Store the updated block in the buffer back to disk either
                          immediately or at some later point in time.

In this and subsequent chapters, it is assumed that the read statement 'read(a)', executed by a transaction, has the effect of copying the contents of the field 'a' in the database into the variable 'a' in the transaction. Similarly, a write statement 'write(a)', executed by a transaction, has the effect of copying the variable 'a' in the transaction into the field 'a' in the database.

The database buffer

Note that transactions read and write to a database buffer rather than directly to the disk itself. It is this buffer that transactions read from and write to directly: the buffer in turn reads from and writes to disk. The use of a database buffer dramatically improves processing performance. As we shall see in chapter 9 on recovery, the buffer is not necessarily changed immediately after a program variable is changed. It may not be carried out immediately after a write is issued, but may be deferred while other transaction operations are performed. Usually, the decision is determined by the recovery manager of the DBMS. If the writes are not written directly to the database on disk and transaction failure occurs, then this is a problem that the recovery manager has to solve. For the purposes of this chapter, however, we assume that changes made by an application program are made immediately to the buffer.

8.4 Concurrent access of data

Many computer systems can be used simultaneously by more than one user. This is made possible by **multiprogramming**, a technique that allows the computer to run multiple programs (or transactions) at the same time. If, as is usually the case, only one CPU exists, then only one program can be processed at a time. Therefore, to avoid excessive delays for an individual user, multiprogramming systems give all users equal time slices on the CPU, executing commands from all queued processes for short, interleaved periods.

Due to the speed at which these commands are executed, the impression of concurrent use is given to the users. This process is known as **interleaving**. This uses the CPU efficiently by allowing it to run a portion of another program, when the program currently running on the CPU requires some input or output to secondary storage (such a disk access). An important issue is that more than one application may attempt to access the same data item. As a result, data stored in a multi-user DBMS can be damaged or destroyed. To overcome this problem, **concurrency control techniques** have been developed to protect data from incorrect changes caused by transactions running simultaneously.

Scheduling transactions problems

Scheduling of transactions is under the control of a transaction manager and may involve different users submitting transactions that execute concurrently, for example accessing and updating the same database records. The transaction manager is responsible for interleaving different transactions.

If transactions do not use the same database items, then there are no concurrency problems. However, if transactions do use the same database items, there are various ways in which a transaction, though correct in itself, can nevertheless produce an inconsistent database. This section examines three problems that can occur when concurrent transactions execute in an uncontrolled manner:

- The lost update problem
- The uncommitted dependency problem
- The inconsistent analysis problem.

These problems are described in the following scenarios in which bank accounts undergo credits, debits or money transfers.

The lost update problem

Interleaved use of the same item can be a problem where one update overwrites another. This is known as a **lost update**. Consider the following situation:

In example 8.1, there are two transactions (T1 and T2). These are submitted at approximately the same time. In our bank scenario, there may be an attempt to update a balance field in an account record by two different transactions simultaneously. Suppose that their operations are interleaved by the operating system, as shown in the example.

Example 8.1: Lost update problem

Time	Transaction T1	Transaction T2	Comments
1	read_item(x)		Read operation is performed in transaction T1 at time 1
2	x:=x–40	read_item(x)	At time 2 the value of data item x is modified by T1. A read operation is performed in transaction T2
3	write_item(x)	x:=x+20	At time 3 a write operation is performed in transaction T1. The value of data item x is modified by T2
4		write_item(x)	Write operation is performed in transaction T2 at time 4

Note that transaction operations BEGIN_TRANSACTION, END_TRANSACTION, COMMIT etc have been omitted from the example above (and subsequent examples). The lost update problem occurs when two transactions, which access the same database items, have their operations interleaved in a way that makes the value of some database item incorrect.

The above interleaved operation will lead to an incorrect value for data item x, because at time 2, T2 reads in the original value of x, which is before T1 changes it in the database, and hence the updated value resulting from T1 is lost. For example, if x = 100 at time 1, (i.e. the balance on the account is 100), T1 reduces x by 40 and therefore at time 3, 60 is written to the database. At time 4, T2 writes an updated version of x to the database but this is based on the original value of x. The final result should be x = 100 − 40 + 20 = 80; but in the concurrent operations in our example, it is x = 120 because the update at time 3 by T1 was lost.

The uncommitted dependency problem

An uncommitted dependency problem occurs when a transaction is allowed to retrieve – or worse, update – a record that has been updated by another transaction, but has not yet been committed by that other transaction. This is because, if it has not yet been committed there is always a possibility that it will never be committed, but it will be rolled back instead. In this case the first transaction will have used some data that is now incorrect. Consider the following situation:

Example 8.2: Uncommitted dependency problem

Time	Transaction T1	Transaction T2	Comments
1		read_item(x);	
2		x:=x−20;	
3		write_item(x)	x is temporarily updated
4	read_item(x)		
5		**ROLLBACK**	T2 fails and must change the value of x back to its old value; meanwhile T1 has read the temporary incorrect value of x

At time 3, transaction T2 has updated the value of x. Transaction T1 fetches the result of an uncommitted update at time 4. That update is then undone at time 5. Transaction T1 is therefore operating on a false assumption, namely, that item x has the value at time 3, whereas x has whatever value it has at time 1. As a result, transaction T1 may well produce incorrect output. The rollback of transaction T2 may be due to a system crash, and transaction T1 may already have terminated by that time, in which case the crash would not cause a rollback to be issued for T1.

Consider the following, even more unacceptable, situation:

Example 8.3: The dirty read

Time	Transaction T1	Transaction T2	Comments
1		read_item(x);	
2		x:=x−20;	
3		write_item(x)	x is temporarily updated
4	read_item(x)		
5	x:=x+100;		
6	write_item(x)		
7	**COMMIT**		
8	Read_item(y)	... **ROLLBACK**	T1 depends on uncommitted value and loses an update

In this case, not only does transaction T1 become dependent on an uncommitted change at time 4 but it also loses an update at time 7, because the rollback causes item x to be restored to its value before time 1. This problem is also known as **the dirty read**. Data may be made available to one transaction before completion of the second transaction. If the second transaction does not complete successfully, and the original data is restored, the first transaction may continue with inaccurate data.

The inconsistent analysis problem

The inconsistent analysis problem occurs when a transaction reads several values, but a second transaction updates some of these values during the execution of the first. This is significant, for example if one transaction is calculating an aggregate summary function on a number of records, while other transactions are updating some of these records. The aggregate functions may calculate some values before they are updated, and others after they are updated. Therefore, different summaries (SUMs, and COUNTs for example) may be inconsistent.

Consider the following situation in which a number of Account records have the following values:

ACC1	ACC2	ACC3
40	50	30

If 10 is transferred from ACC 3 to ACC 1, while concurrently calculating the total funds in the three accounts, the following sequence of events may occur:

Example 8.4: Inconsistent analysis problem

Time	Transaction T1	Transaction T2	Comments
0	sum = 0	...	
1	read_item(ACC1)		
2	sum:= sum+ ACC1		
3	read_item (ACC2)		
4	sum:= sum+ACC2		Sum is now 90
5		read_item (ACC3)	
6		read_item (ACC1)	
7		ACC3=ACC3–10	
8		ACC1=ACC1+10	
9		write_item (ACC3)	ACC3 is now 20
10		write_item (ACC1)	ACC1 is now 50
11		COMMIT	
12	read_item (ACC 3)		T1 has value 20 for ACC3
13	sum:= sum+ACC3		Sum Is now 110 which is incorrect!

The two transactions are operating on account (ACC) records: transaction T1 is summing account balances; transaction T2 is transferring an amount 10 from ACC3 to ACC1. The result produced by transaction T1 (110) is obviously incorrect: if T1 were to write that result back into the database, it would leave the database in an inconsistent state. Transaction T1 has seen an inconsistent state of the database, and therefore performed an inconsistent analysis.

Note the difference between this example and the previous one: there is no question in this case of T1 being dependent on an uncommitted change, since T2 commits all its updates before T1 fetches the value in ACC3.

Activity 8.1

Lost update problems

Given the following transactions and assume that x=5 and m=10:

Transaction T1
read_item (x);
x:=x–m;
write_item (x);

Transaction T2
read_item (x);
x:=x+m;
write_item (x);

Generate a schedule of operations that illustrates the lost update problem.

Uncommitted dependency problem

Given the following transactions and assume that x=5, m=10, n=15:

Transaction T1	Transaction T2
read_item (x);	read_item (x);
x:=x−n;	x:=x+m;
write_item (x);	write_item (x);
	ROLLBACK

Generate a schedule of operations that illustrates the uncommitted dependency problem.

Inconsistent analysis problem

Given the following transactions and assume that x=5, y=20, z=30:

Transaction T1	Transaction T2
read_item (x);	sum:=0
read_item(y);	read_item(x);
read_item(z)	sum:=sum+x;
y:=y*z	read_item (y);
write(y)	sum:=sum+y;
x:=x*z	write_item(sum)
write(x)	

Generate a schedule of operations that illustrates the inconsistent analysis problem.

Serial schedules

An obvious way to overcome the problems described earlier is for transactions to be scheduled serially. A schedule S is **serial** if, for every transaction T participating in the schedule, all of the operations of T are executed consecutively in the schedule. In other words, **serial execution of transactions** means transactions are performed one after another without any interleaving of operations. If we have two transactions, A and B, then there are only two possible serial schedules: completing all operations of A then all operations of B, or completing all operations of B then all operations of A. Although in many cases all possible serial schedules will leave databases in identical states, there is no guarantee that this will be the case. Pragmatically, this may be very important. In banking, for example, it matters whether interest for an account is calculated before or after a large deposit. However, as far as the DBMS is concerned, no serial execution will allow the database to be left in an inconsistent state, and every serial execution is considered to be correct even though different results may be produced. In this case, the validity of the sequence of the calculations is the responsibility of the application software, not the DBMS.

Non-serial schedules

The major problem with serial execution is that it is inefficient. Concurrent processing, in which the operations of transactions are interleaved, is far more efficient. These kinds of schedules are termed **non-serial schedules**. However, when operations may be interleaved, there will be many possible orders (or schedules) in which the system can execute the individual operations of the transactions. This is a more flexible approach, but some constraints must be applied if the resulting schedule is to be correct.

Serializable schedules

Intuitively, it is obvious that the schedules shown in the previous examples are 'wrong' in some way. It is also clear that there is a need for a formal definition for the correctness of schedules, as this formal definition can be used to verify the validity of scheduling algorithms. An important area of concurrency control called **serializability theory**, attempts to determine which schedules are correct and which are not, and to develop techniques that only allow correct schedules. If a set of transactions executes concurrently, we say that the schedule is correct if it produces the same results as some serial execution. Such a schedule is called **serializable**. It is essential to guarantee serializability in order to ensure database correctness.

Figure 8.2: Relationship between non-serial and serializable schedules

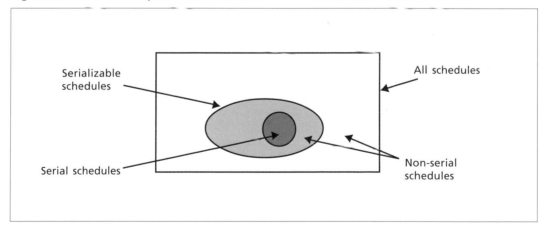

With reference to figure 8.2, the grey areas indicate all serializable schedules, that is, those schedules which produce consistent and correct results. Notice that this includes the darker grey area – serial schedules.

In determining strategies to generate serializable schedules, the following factors are significant:

- If two transactions are only reading a variable, they do not conflict and order is not important
- If two transactions read or write completely separate variables, they do not conflict and order is not important

- If one transaction writes to a variable and another either reads or writes to the same variable, the order of execution is important.

Serializability can be achieved in several ways, but most systems use either **locking** or **time stamping**. Usually, the DBMS has a concurrency control subsystem that is part of the DBMS package, and is not directly controllable by either the users or the DBA. The task of the DBMS is to 'select' an efficient serializable schedule from the huge potential pool of schedules, many of which will be inefficient or incorrect (or both).

8.5 Locking

Aim of locking

One way of providing serializable execution of transactions is by means of a locking mechanism. A **lock** is a variable associated with a data item in the database, and it describes the status of that data item with respect to possible operations that can be applied to the item. The overall aim of locking is to obtain maximum concurrency and minimum delay in processing transactions. The idea of locking is simple: when a transaction needs an assurance that some object it is accessing, typically a database record, will not change in some unpredictable manner while the transaction is not running on the CPU, it acquires a lock on that object. The lock bars access to the object by other transactions. Thus the first transaction can be sure that the object in question will remain in a stable state, as long as the transaction needs it. One important lock is the multiple-mode lock, which can apply an **exclusive** (write) or **shared** (read) lock onto the object to be locked, before the corresponding database read or write operation is performed.

Granularity of locks

Locks have **granularity**: the size of the object locked may vary, it may be the entire database, a whole file, a disk block, a database record, or a field value of a database record. Locks with a large granularity are easy to administer but cause frequent contention for items. Locks with small granularity are difficult to administer (they may involve many more details for the DBMS to keep track of and check) but conflict is less frequent. In examples in this chapter, we are deliberately vague and assume that the granularity is a 'data item'.

Shared locks (S locks)

If a DBMS wishes to read an item, then a **shared lock** is placed onto that item. If a transaction has a shared lock on a database, it can read the item but not update it. If a transaction A holds a shared lock on record R, then a request from transaction B for an S lock on R will be granted (that is, B will now also hold an S lock on R). However, a request from transaction B for an X lock on R will cause B to go into a wait state (and B will wait until A's lock is released).

Exclusive locks (X locks)

If a DBMS wishes to write an item, then an **exclusive lock** is placed onto that item. If a transaction has an exclusive lock on an item, it can both read and update it. To prevent interference from other transactions, only one transaction can hold an exclusive lock on an item at any given time. If a transaction A holds an exclusive lock on record R, then a request from transaction B for a lock of either type on R will cause B to go into a wait state (and B will wait until A's lock is released). This can be summarised in the table 8.1 (if transaction A holds the lock specified along the top of the table, then the matrix indicates whether transaction B can request the types of locks indicated down the left):

Table 8.1: Exclusive and shared locks

	Type of lock that A holds on R **Exclusive lock**	**Shared lock**	**No lock**
Type of lock on R that B requests			
Exclusive lock	N	N	Y
Shared lock	N	Y	Y
No lock	Y	Y	Y

Acquiring and removing locks

Locking is usually achieved by inserting a flag into the field record page, or similar field, to indicate that part of the database is locked. Transaction requests for record locks are normally **implicit** (at least in most modern systems). In addition, a user may specify **explicit** locks. When a transaction successfully retrieves a record, it automatically acquires a **shared lock** on that record. When a transaction successfully updates a record, it automatically acquires an **exclusive lock** on that record. If the transaction already has a shared hold on the record, then the update will promote the shared lock to exclusive level, as long as T is the only transaction with a shared lock on X at the time. Exclusive and shared locks are normally held until the next **synchronisation point:** where all of the updates made by the transaction can now be made permanent, and the database is in a consistent state. However, a transaction can explicitly release locks that it holds prior to termination using the 'Unlock' command.

Use of locking

In the following section, the use of exclusive and shared locks to guarantee serializability will be examined. In the following example, locks are assumed to be implicit and unlocking is not allowed.

Lost update problem

Table 8.2: Deadlock

Time	Transaction T1	Transaction T2	Comments
1	read_item(x) (acquires S lock on x)		Implicit locks are acquired before a read. Read operation is performed in transaction T1 at time 1
2	x:=x−40	read_item(x) (acquires S lock on x)	At time 2 the value of data item x is modified by T1. A read operation is performed in transaction T2
3	write_item(x) (request X lock on x)	x:=x+20	The value of data item x is modified by T2. Also at time 3 a request for an X lock on data item x by T1, but T1 must wait for release of S lock by T2
4	Wait	write_item(x) (request X lock on X)	At time 4 request for an X lock on data item x by T2, but T2 must wait for release of S lock by T1
5	Wait	Wait	Both transactions waiting for S locks on x to be released

Consider the lost update problem presented earlier, amended to illustrate the use of locking. At time T3 there is no possibility of T1 acquiring an X lock on x, as there already exists an S lock on x, therefore it has to wait. Transaction T2 at time T4 also tries to get an X lock on x, but is unable to, as T1 itself has an S lock on it, therefore both wait fruitlessly for the other to release a lock. This situation is known as a deadly embrace or **deadlock**. The lost update problem does not occur, but the problem of deadlock now exists which we will discuss later.

The uncommitted dependency problem

Table 8.3: Uncommitted dependency with locking

Time	Transaction T1	Transaction T2	Comments
1		read_item(x); (request S lock on x)	
2		x:=x−20;	
3		write_item(x) (acquire X lock on x)	
4	read_item(x) (request S lock on x)		At time 4 a request for an S lock on data item x by T1, but T1 must wait for release of X lock by T2
5	Wait		
n	resume: read_item(x) (acquire S lock on x)	Commit (release X lock on x)	
n+1	...		

Table 8.3 shows what happens to the interleaved executions of the uncommitted dependency problem, but with the addition of a locking mechanism. Transaction T1's operation at time 4 is not accepted because it involves an implicit request for an S lock on x, and an X lock is already held by T2 so T1 goes into a wait state. It remains in that wait state until T2 reaches a synchronisation point (either commit or rollback) when T2's lock is released, and T1 is able to proceed. At that point T1 sees a committed value – the pre-T2 value if T2 terminates with a rollback, or the post-T2 value otherwise). Either way, T1 is no longer dependent on an uncommitted update. So in this case, locking solves the problem.

8.6 Guaranteeing serializability

Unlocking

To overcome the problem of deadlock it is tempting to allow **unlocking** to occur. If items to be used are locked, accessed and unlocked in a contiguous sequence of operations in a schedule, then the deadlocking impasse can be avoided. However, another important problem is then encountered: if unlocking is allowed, then the serializability of schedules in which transactions participate cannot be guaranteed. Thus, these schedules of transactions may result in incorrect states of the database. For example:

Transaction T1	Transaction T2
read_lock(y)	read_lock(x)
read_item(y)	read_item(x)
unlock(y)	unlock(x)
write_lock(x)	write_lock(y)
read_item(x)	read_item(y)
x:=x+y	y:=x+y
write_item(x)	write_item(y)
unlock(x)	unlock(y)

Initial values: x=20, y=30

Results of serial schedule **transaction T$_1$** followed by **transaction T$_2$**: x=50, y=80

Results of serial schedule **transaction T$_2$** followed by **transaction T$_1$**: x=70, y=50

Consider the interleaved schedule S:

T1	T2
read_lock(y)	
read_item(y)	
unlock(y)	
	read_lock(x)
	read_item(x)
	unlock(x)
	write_lock(y)
	read_item(y)
	y:=x+y
	write_item(y)
	unlock(y)
write_lock(x)	
read_item(x)	
x:=x+y	
write_item(x)	
unlock(x)	

Result of schedule S: x=50, y=50. This **schedule is not serializable** because the item y in transaction T_1, and x in transaction T_2, were unlocked too early.

Guaranteeing serializability

We have seen that using locks in themselves does not guarantee serializability. To guarantee serializability, an additional protocol must be included. This protocol concerns the positioning of locking and unlocking operations in every transaction and is known as **two-phase locking** (2PL).

There are a number of variations including:

- Basic 2PL
- Conservative 2PL
- Strict 2PL.

Basic two-phase locking (2PL)

A transaction is said to follow the **basic two-phase locking** protocol if, within a transaction, all locking operations (read_lock, write_lock) precede the first unlock operation. A transaction which follows the protocol has two phases: the **expanding phase** or growing phase (during which new locks on items can be acquired but none can be released), followed by a **shrinking phase** during which existing locks can be released but no new locks can be acquired. It can be proved that if every transaction in a schedule follows the two-phase locking protocol, then the schedule is guaranteed to be serializable. Unfortunately, this protocol may reintroduce the problem of deadlock.

Two-phase locking may limit the amount of concurrency that can occur in a schedule. This is because a transaction T may not be able to release an item x after it has finished using x – if T needs to lock an additional item y later on. Conversely, T must lock the additional item y before it needs it so that it can release x. Hence, x must remain locked by T until all items that the transaction needs have been locked – only then can x be released by T. Meanwhile, another transaction waiting to access x may be forced to wait, even though T has finished using x. Conversely, if y is locked earlier than it is needed, another transaction wanting to access y is forced to wait even though T is not using y yet. This is the price for guaranteeing serializability of all schedules without having to check the schedules themselves. The benefit is the guaranteed correctness of the resulting permanent values in the database.

Transactions T1 and T2 of the previous figure do not follow the two-phase locking protocol, as the write_lock(x) operation follows the unlock (y) operation in T1, and similarly, the write_lock(y) operation follows the unlock(x) operation in T2. If we enforce two-phase locking, the transaction can be rewritten as T1' and T2':

T1'	T2'
read_lock(y)	read_lock(x)
read_item(y)	read_item(x)
write_lock(x)	write_lock(y)
read_item(x)	read_item(y)
x:=x+y	y:=x+y
write_item(x)	write_item(y)
unlock(x)	unlock(y)
unlock(y)	unlock(x)

The two transactions that follow the basic 2PL protocol interleaved are as shown:

Table 8.4: Basic 2PL example

Time	Transaction T1	Transaction T2	Comments
1	read_lock(y)		
2	read_item(y)		
3		read_lock(x)	
4		read_item(x)	
5	write_lock(x)		At time step 5, it is not possible for T1 to acquire an X lock on x as there is already an S lock on x held by T2
6	Wait		
7		write_lock(y)	At time step 7, it is not possible for T2 to acquire an X lock on y as there is already an S lock on y held by T1
8		Wait	Both transactions are waiting for the other to release a lock
	.....		.....

These transactions could result in the schedule above which clearly terminates in a deadlock.

Preventing the lost update problem using basic 2PL

We have looked at the lost update problem earlier where another user can override an apparently successfully completed update operation. A solution to the problem using the lost update problem example which we considered earlier is shown next using 2PL:

Table 8.5: Solving lost update problem

Time	Transaction T1	Transaction T2	Comments
1	write_lock(x)		X lock on data item x by T1
2	read_item(x)	write_lock(x)	Read operation is performed in transaction T1 at time 2. Also at time 2 request for an X lock on data item x by T2, but T2 must wait for release of X lock by T1
3	x:=x−40	Wait	
4	write_item(x)	Wait	The value of data item x is modified by T1
5	Commit/unlock(x)	Wait	X lock on data item x by T1 released. T2's request for X lock now granted
6		read_item(x) (acquires S lock on x)	A read operation is performed in transaction T2
7		x:=x+20	
8		write_item(x) (acquires X lock on x)	The value of data item x is modified by T2
9		Commit/unlock(x)	

Conservative two-phase locking

Conservative 2PL is a deadlock-free protocol. It requires a transaction to lock all the data items it needs in advance. If at least one of the required data items cannot be obtained, then none of the items are locked. Rather, the transaction waits and then tries again to lock all the items it needs. Although conservative 2PL is a deadlock-free protocol, this solution further limits concurrency.

Strict two-phase locking

In practice, the most popular variation of 2PL is **strict 2PL**, which guarantees strict schedules. **Strict schedules** are those in which transactions can neither read nor write an item x until the last transaction that wrote x has committed or aborted. In this variation, a transaction T does not release any of its locks until after it commits or aborts. Hence, no other transaction can read or write an item that is written by T unless T has committed, leading to a strict schedule for recoverability. Strict 2PL is not deadlock free.

Notice the difference between **conservative** and **strict 2PL**. The former must lock all items before it starts, whereas the latter does not unlock any of its items until after it terminates (by committing or aborting). Strict 2PL is not deadlock free unless it is combined with conservative 2PL. In summary, all type 2PL protocols guarantee serializability (correctness) of a schedule, but limit concurrency. The use of locks can also cause the additional problem of deadlock. Conservative 2PL is deadlock free.

8.7 Dealing with deadlock

Locking mechanisms, including basic and strict two-phase locking, can cause the additional problem of deadlock. We have seen a number of examples of deadlock. Deadlock is the situation where one transaction is waiting for a resource which is locked by another transaction. This transaction in turn is waiting for a resource which is locked by the first transaction (or possibly yet another transaction).

Deadlock may involve more than two transactions. It may be dealt with by using one of two approaches: preventing deadlock from happening or allowing deadlock to occur and then resolving it.

Preventing deadlock from happening

There are a number of methods of achieving this which include:

- Locking all data items at the beginning of transaction (conservative two-phase locking which we looked at earlier)
- Ordering data items using transaction timestamps. With timestamping, a unique identifier is given to each transaction indicating its start time. When transactions are executing concurrently, older transactions are given priority. When accessing the same data, newer transactions are rolled back.

Resolving the deadlock

Some DBMSs allow deadlock to occur and then resolve the deadlock. If deadlock occurs, protocols for resolving it include: wait and retry, pre-empting one transaction in favour of another, aborting one or both transactions. A simple solution is based on **lock timeouts**. A transaction requesting a lock will wait for a system-defined period of time. If the request has not been granted within the period, the transaction is aborted and then restarted. The DBMS has assumed that there is a deadlock and is attempting to resolve it. This simple solution is used by a number of commercial DBMSs.

8.8 Oracle concurrency control

Oracle guarantees that users will see a consistent version of the database. If transactions are in progress which have not committed, then other transactions will not see any changes made by these uncommitted transactions.

Isolating transactions

We can use the following SQL SET TRANSACTION commands to isolate one transaction from other transactions.

- **SET TRANSACTION READ COMMITTED:** default command. Within a transaction a statement sees only the data which was committed before the statement started. This means that data may be changed by other transactions. This may cause inconsistent analysis problems
- **SET TRANSACTION SERIALIZABLE:** serialization is enforced at the transaction level. A transaction only sees data that was committed before the transaction began, as well as any changes made by the transaction through Insert, Update or Delete
- **SET TRANSACTION READ ONLY:** similar to the previous statement but data can be read only. A transaction only sees data that was committed before the transaction began.

The application of these commands can be seen with the following examples.

Airline reservation example

An airline reservation system might use the command SET TRANSACTION SERIALIZABLE. Assume we have two transactions running concurrently, each checking the availability of seats and making a reservation if possible. Assume that there is only one seat available.

Figure 8.3: SET TRANSACTION SERIALIZABLE

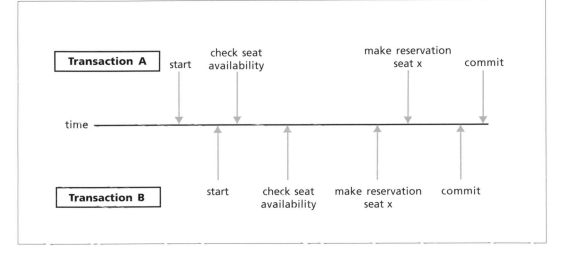

In figure 8.3, there is danger that the two transactions will double-book the same seat. However, if the transactions have been designated as SET TRANSACTION SERIALIZABLE it will not happen. Here, serialization is enforced at the transaction level. Both transactions only see data that was committed before the transaction began, as well as any changes made by that transaction through Insert, Update or Delete. Transaction B makes and commits a reservation on seat x before transaction A. When transaction A tries to commit, the database system recognises that data which it had used in its transaction has been changed (by transaction B). Transaction A will not be allowed to update seat x and therefore its changes will not be committed.

Online ordering example

Our second example, an online ordering system, might use the command SET TRANSACTION READ COMMITTED. Again we have two transactions running concurrently: one checking the price of an item and then making an order; the other changing the price of an item.

Figure 8.4: SET TRANSACTION READ COMMITTED

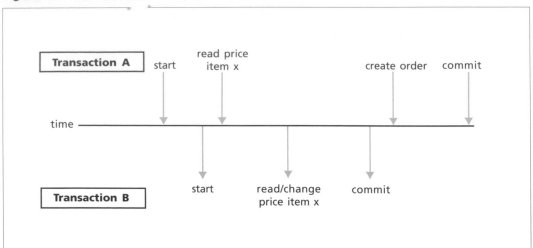

In figure 8.4, there is danger that in transaction A, an order will be created based on an old price for x. If the transactions have been designated as SET TRANSACTION READ COMMITTED, Oracle will allow this to happen. Here, serialization is enforced at the statement level. Therefore, transaction B changes price x and transaction A creates an order on the original price which user A has seen.

In our first example it is important that serializability is enforced at the transaction level, as it is critical that double-booking of airline seats is avoided. In the other applications, such as order entry, it may not be so important that transaction A in our example used an older price. In this case, increased concurrency of transactions might be more important.

Locks in Oracle

Locks are not placed on data for read operations – only for write operations. This means that a read operation never blocks a write operation. A user does not lock a data item explicitly – data locking will occur automatically for all SQL statements. A user is allowed, however, to lock data manually or change default-locking behaviour.

Deadlock in Oracle

Oracle will detect deadlock and it is automatically resolved when the statements involved in the deadlock are rolled back.

Serial schedules

Assuming that initially x=3, y=2:

Transaction T1	Transaction T2
read_lock(x)	read_lock(y)
read_item(x)	read_item(y)
x:=x+3	y:=2*y
write_lock(x)	write_lock(y)
write_item(x)	write_item(y)
unlock(x)	unlock(y)
read_lock(y)	read_lock(x)
read_item(y)	read_item(x)
y:= x+y	x:=x+y
write_lock(y)	write_lock(x)
write_item(y)	write_item(x)
unlock(y)	unlock(x)

Create all possible serial schedules and examine the values of x and y.

Checking for serializability

Assuming that initially x=3, y=2:

Transaction T1	Transaction T2
read_lock(x)	read_lock(y)
read_item(x)	read_item(y)
x:=x+3	y:=2*y
write_lock(x)	write_lock(y)
write_item(x)	write_item(y)
unlock(x)	unlock(y)
read_lock(y)	read_lock(x)
read_item(y)	read_item(x)
y:= x+y	x:=x+y
write_lock(y)	write_lock(x)
write_item(y)	write_item(x)
unlock(y)	unlock(x)

Create a non-serial interleaved schedule and examine the values of x and y. Is this schedule serializable?

The inconsistent analysis problem again

Consider the inconsistent analysis problem again. The example as before starts off with Account records having the following values:

ACC1	ACC2	ACC3
40	50	30

If 10 is transferred from ACC 3 to ACC 1 while concurrently calculating the total funds in the three accounts, the following sequence of events may occur:

Time	Transaction	Transaction T1	Comments T2
0	sum = 0	...	
1	read_item (ACC1)		
2	sum:= sum+ ACC1		
3	read_item (ACC2)		
4	sum:= sum+ACC2		Sum is now 90
5		read_item (ACC3)	
		(30)	
6		read_item(ACC1)	
		(40)	
7		ACC3=ACC3–10	
8		ACC1=ACC1+10	
9		write_item (ACC3)	ACC3 is now 20
10		write_item(ACC1)	ACC1 is now 50
11	COMMIT		
12	read_item (ACC3)		T1 has value 20 for ACC3
13	sum:= sum+ACC3		Sum is now 110 which is incorrect!

Rewrite the above transaction T1 and transaction T2 but with the addition of a locking mechanism (do not include unlock at this stage). Check to see if your new schedule is serializable.

Solving the inconsistent analysis problem with 2PL

Consider the inconsistent analysis problem discussed in activity 8.6. Use the basic 2PL protocol to see if you can solve this problem.

2PL example

Given the schedules and assuming that initially x=3, y=2:

T1	T2
read_lock(x)	read_lock(y)
read_item(x)	read_item(y)
x:=x+3	y:=2*y
write_lock(x)	write_lock(y)
write_item(x)	write_item(y)
unlock(x)	unlock(y)
read_lock(y)	read_lock(x)
read_item(y)	read_item(x)
y:= x+y	x:=x+y
write_lock(y)	write_lock(x)
write_item(y)	write_item(x)
unlock(y)	unlock(x)

Show how the basic two-phase locking protocol would generate a serializable schedule.

Activity 8.9

Deadlock example

Explain how deadlock would occur, given the following non-serial schedule:

Line no	T1	T2
1	read_lock(x)	
2	read_item(x)	
3	x:= x+7	
4		read_lock(x)
5		read_item(x)
6		x:= x+x*2
7	write_lock(x)	
8	write_item(x)	
9	unlock(x)	
10		write_lock(x)
11		write_item(x)
12		unlock(x)

8.9 Summary

This chapter examined the purpose of the transaction manager in a database management system and how concurrency was controlled when more than one transaction accessed a database at the same time. It was shown that, although transactions working on their own can be correct in themselves, interleaving can create databases with inconsistent data. A number of potential problems caused by concurrency were examined and various approaches to concurrency control were described.

8.10 Review questions

Review question 8.1 Discuss the reasons for designing database systems around transactions.

Review question 8.2 Describe the so-called 'ACID' properties of database transactions.

Review question 8.3 Discuss the meaning of transaction operations:

1. BEGIN_TRANSACTION

2. READ or WRITE

3. END_TRANSACTION

4. COMMIT_TRANSACTION

5. ROLLBACK (or ABORT)

6. UNDO

7. REDO

 Review question 8.4 Discuss the actions taken by the read_item and write_item operations on a database.

 Review question 8.5 Name and explain problems which can occur when transactions are scheduled.

 Review question 8.6 Explain the following terms:

1. Dirty read

2. Serial schedule

3. Serializability.

 Review question 8.7 Explain what is a locking mechanism, distinguishing between S (shared lock or read) locks and X (exclusive or write) locks.

Review question 8.8 What is two-phase locking protocol? How does it guarantee serializability? Distinguish between basic 2PL and conservative 2PL.

Review question 8.9 What is meant by the term 'deadlock'?

8.11 Answers to review questions

Answer to review question 8.1 A transaction is a logic unit of work on the database that is either completed in its entirety or not done at all.

A transaction is concerned with accessing or changing the contents of a database and may be the entire program, a portion of a program or a single command. A transaction has a clear start and finish. The assumption is that it will start its execution on a consistent database and if it runs to completion, then the transaction is said to be committed, and the database will be in a new consistent state. Once a transaction is committed, then the transaction manager knows that the database is in a consistent state again, and all of the updates made by that transaction can now be made permanent. If the changes are made permanent, then the database has reached a new synchronisation point. The other possibility is that the transactions do not commit satisfactorily (i.e. do not reach their end). In this case the transaction is aborted and the incomplete transaction is rolled back. The database is then restored to the consistent state it held before the transaction was started by the transaction manager.

Answer to review question 8.2 The acronym ACID indicates the properties of any well-formed transactions. Any transaction that violates these principles will cause failures of concurrency.

- **Atomicity:** a transaction is an atomic unit of processing; it is either performed in its entirety or not performed at all. A transaction does not partly happen

- **Consistency:** the database state is consistent at the end of a transaction

- **Isolation:** a transaction should not make its updates visible to other transactions until it is committed; this property, when enforced strictly, solves the temporary update problem, and makes cascading rollbacks of transactions unnecessary

- **Durability:** when a transaction has made a change to the database state, and the change is committed, this change is permanent and should be available to all other transactions.

Answer to review question 8.3 The states and operations include:

1. **BEGIN_TRANSACTION:** this marks the beginning of transaction execution.

2. **READ or WRITE:** these specify read or write operations on the database items that are executed as part of a transaction.

3. **END_TRANSACTION:** this specifies that read and write operations have ended, and marks the end limit of transaction execution. However, at this point it may be necessary to check whether the changes introduced by the transaction can be permanently applied to the database (committed), or whether the transaction has to be aborted because it violates concurrency control or for some other reason.

4. **COMMIT_TRANSACTION:** this signals a successful end of the transaction so that any changes (updates) executed by the transaction can be safely committed to the database and will not be undone.

5. **ROLLBACK (or ABORT):** this signals the transaction has ended unsuccessfully, so that any changes or effects that the transaction may have applied to the database must be undone.

6. **UNDO:** similar to rollback except that it applies to a single operation rather than to a whole transaction.

7. **REDO:** this specifies that certain transaction operations must be redone to ensure that all the operations of a committed transaction have been applied successfully to the database.

Answer to review question 8.4 This activity asks you to list all actions taken by the read and write operations.

Actions taken by the read_item operation on a database (assume the read operation is performed on data item x):

- Find the address of the disk block that contains item x

- Copy the disk block into a buffer in main memory, if that disk is not already in some main memory buffer

- Copy item x from the buffer to the program variable named x.

l Actions taken by the write_item operation on a database (assume the write operation is performed on data item x):

- Find the address of the disk block that contains item x

- Copy the disk block into a buffer in main memory, if that disk is not already in some main memory buffer

- Copy item x from the program variable named x into its correct location in the buffer. Store the updated block from the buffer back to disk (either immediately or at some later point in time).

Answer to review question 8.5

- **Lost update problem** – two transactions access the same database items (x) and have their operations interleaved in a way that makes the value of some database item incorrect

- **Uncommitted dependency problem** – occurs when one transaction can see intermediate results of another transaction before it has committed

- **Inconsistent analysis problem** – occurs when a transaction reads partial results of other incomplete transactions.

Answer to review question 8.6

1. **Dirty read** – data may be made available to one transaction from another before completion of the second transaction. If the second transaction does not complete successfully, and the original data is restored, the first transaction may continue with inaccurate data.

2. **Serial schedule** – a schedule S is serial if for every transaction T participating in the schedule, all of the operations of T are executed consecutively in the schedule.

3. **Serializability** – serializability identifies those executions of transactions guaranteed to ensure consistency. If a set of transactions executes concurrently, we say that the schedule is correct if it produces the same results as some serial execution. The objective of serializability is to find non-serial schedules that allow transactions to execute concurrently without interfering with one another. The result should be the same as if the database state had been produced by a serial execution. It is essential to guarantee serializability in order to ensure database correctness.

Answer to review question 8.7

S (shared locks or read): if a transaction has a read lock on a data item, it can read the item but not update it. It is permissible for more than one transaction to hold read locks simultaneously on the same item. If a read lock is requested on an item that already has a read lock on it, the request is granted; otherwise it has to wait.

X (exclusive or write): if a transaction has a write lock on a data item, it can both read and update the item. This transaction has excusive access to the data item. Other transactions must wait until the lock is released.

Answer to review question 8.8 A transaction is said to follow the basic two-phase locking protocol if all locking operations (read_lock, write_lock) precede the first unlock operation in the transaction. Such a transaction can be divided into two phases: an expanding (or growing) phase, during which new locks on items can be acquired, but none can be released; and a shrinking phase, during which existing locks can be released but no new locks can be acquired.

It can be proved that if every transaction in a schedule follows the two-phase locking protocol, the schedule is guaranteed to be serializable, because the protocols will prevent interference among different transactions. The lost update, uncommitted dependency and inconsistent analysis problems will not happen if 2PL is enforced. However, basic 2PL is prone to deadlock.

Conservative 2PL is a deadlock-free protocol. It requires all transactions to lock all the data items it needs in advance. If at least one of the required data items cannot be obtained, then none of the items are locked. Rather, the transaction waits and then tries again to lock all the items it needs. This solution further limits concurrency.

Answer to review question 8.9 Deadlock is the situation where one transaction is waiting for a resource which is locked by another transaction. This transaction, in turn, is waiting for a resource which is locked by the first transaction (or possibly yet another transaction).

8.12 Feedback on activities

Answer 8.1 A possible solution:

Transaction T1	Time	Transaction T2	x
read_item (x);	t1		5
x:=x−m;	t2	read_item (x);	5
write_item (x);	t3	x:=x+m;	−5
	t4	write_item (x);	15

Here, T1 and T2 start at nearly the same time; both read x as 5. T1 reduces x by m and stores the update in the database (−5). Meanwhile, T2 increases its copy of x by m, giving a result of 15, which it stores in the database. The previous update is therefore overwritten or lost.

Answer 8.2 A possible solution:

Transaction T1	Time	Transaction T2	x
	t1	read_item (x);	5
	t2	x:=x+m;	
	t3	write_item (x);	15
read_item (x);	t4		15
x:=x−n;	t5		15
write_item (x);	t6		0
	t7	**ROLLBACK**	5

This problem occurs when one transaction is allowed to see the intermediate results of another transaction before it is committed. T2 updates x to 15, but later it aborts the transaction so that x should be restored to its original value (5). In the meantime, T1 has read the new value of x and calculated the incorrect value of 0, instead of −10.

Answer 8.3 A possible solution:

Transaction T1	Time	Transaction T2	x	y	z	sum
	t1	sum:=0	5	20	30	
	t2	read_item(x);	5	20	30	
read_item (x);	t3		5	20	30	
read_item(y);	t4		5	20	30	
read_item(z)	t5		5	20	30	
y:=y*z	t6		5	20*	30	
write(y)	t7		5	600	30	
x:=x*z	t8		5*	600	30	
write(x)	t9		150	600	30	
COMMIT	t10		150	600	30	
	t11	sum:=sum+x;	150	600	30	
	t12	read_item (y);	150	600	30	
	t13	sum:=sum+y;	150	600	30	
	t14	write_item(sum)	150	600	30	605

Note: x, y and z in the fourth to sixth columns are the values of x, y, z on the database – not the internal values of the variables.

This problem occurs when a transaction reads values from the database (here T2 reads x), and a second transaction updates some of them during the execution of the first (here T1 updates x after T2 has read it). The result of sum is incorrect (the value of 605 should in fact be 750).

This is an example of a dirty read, where transactions are allowed to read partial results of incomplete transactions that are simultaneously updating the database.

Answer 8.4 A *serial schedule* is where transactions are performed one after another without interleaving. There are only 2 possible serial schedules: completing all operations of T1 and then all operations of T2, or vice versa. The first is given below:

Time	T1	T2	x	y
1	read_lock(x)			
2	read_item(x)		3	
3	x:=x+3			
4	write_lock(x)			
5	write_item(x)		6	
6	unlock(x)			
7	read_lock(y)			
8	read_item(y)			2
9	y:= x+y			
10	write_lock(y)			
11	write_item(y)			8
12	unlock(y)			
13		read_lock(y)		
14		read_item(y)		8
15		y:=2*y		
16		write_lock(y)		
17		write_item(y)		16
18		unlock(y)		
19		read_lock(x)		
20		read_item(x)	6	
21		x:=x+y		
22		write_lock(x)		
23		write_item(x)	22	
24		unlock(x)		

Answer 8.5 *Non-serial interleaved schedule* – there are many possible answers for this question. For example:

Time	T1	T2	x	y
1	read_lock(x)		3	2
2	read_item(x)		3	2
3	x:=x+3			
4	write_lock(x)			
5	write_item(x)		6	2
6	unlock(x)			
7		read_lock(y)	6	2
8		read_item(y)	6	2
9		y:=2*y		
10		write_lock(y)		
11		write_item(y)	6	4
12		unlock(y)	6	4
13		read_lock(x)	6	4
14		read_item(x)	6	4
15		x:=x+y		
16		write_lock(x)		
17		write_item(x)	10	4
18		unlock(x)	10	4
19	read_lock(y)		10	4
20	read_item(y)		10	4
21	y:= x+y			
22	write_lock(y)		10	10
23	write_item(y)		10	10
24	unlock(y)		10	10

This schedule gives an incorrect result at line 21: T1 has a value of 6 for x, but it had been changed by T2 to 10, so at line 21 y should have a value of 14.

Serializability – if a set of transactions executes concurrently, we say that the schedule is correct if it produces the same results as some serial execution. In this example the schedule is not serializable.

Answer 8.6 There are a number of solutions possible. For example:

Time	Transaction T1	Transaction T2	Comments
0	sum = 0		
1	read_item(ACC1) (40) (acquire S lock on ACC1)		
2	sum:= sum+ ACC1		
3	read_item(ACC2) (50) (acquire S lock on ACC2)		
4	sum:= sum+ ACC2		sum is now 90
5		read_item(ACC3) (30) (acquire S lock on ACC3)	
6		ACC3=ACC3–10	
7		write_item(ACC3): (20) (acquire X lock on ACC3)	
8		read_item(ACC1) (40) (acquire S lock on ACC1)	
9		ACC1=ACC1+10	
10		write_item(ACC1) (request X lock on ACC1)	X lock rejected as S lock acquired at time 1
11	read_item(ACC3) (20) (request S lock on ACC3)	Wait	S lock rejected as X lock acquired at time 7
12	Wait		

Transaction T2's update at time 10 is not accepted, because it is an implicit request for an exclusive lock on ACC1, and such a request conflicts with the shared lock already held by T1; so T2 goes into a wait state. Likewise, transaction T1's read at time 9 is also not accepted, because it is an implicit request for a shared lock on ACC3 and such a request conflicts with the exclusive lock already held by T2; so T1 also goes into a wait state. Once again therefore, locking solves the original problem by forcing a deadlock.

Answer 8.7 A possible solution:

Time	Transaction T1	Transaction T2	Comments
0	sum = 0		
1		write_lock (ACC3)	Acquire X lock on ACC3
2	read_lock(ACC3)	read_item(ACC3)	ACC3 is 30
3	wait	ACC3=ACC3-10	T1 must wait for S lock
4	wait	write_item(ACC3)	ACC3 is now 20
5	wait	write_lock (ACC1)	Acquire X lock on ACC1
6	wait	read_item(ACC1)	ACC1 is 40
7	wait	ACC1:= ACC1+10	
8	wait	write_item(ACC1):	ACC1 is now 50
9	wait	Commit/unlock (ACC1,ACC3)	
10	read_item(ACC3)		
11	sum:= sum+ ACC3		Sum is now 20
12	read_lock (ACC2)		Acquire S lock on ACC2
13	read_item(ACC2)		
14	sum:= sum+ ACC2		Sum is now 70
15	read_lock (ACC1)		Acquire S lock on ACC1
16	read_item(ACC1)		
17	sum:= sum+ ACC1		Sum is now 120 which is correct

Answer 8.8 A transaction is said to follow the two-phase locking protocol if, within a transaction, all locking operations (read_lock, write_lock), precede the first unlock operation. This protocol, however, is prone to deadlock but not in the example below.

Time	T1	T2	x	y
1	read_lock(x)		3	2
2	read_item(x)		3	2
3	x:=x+3			
4	write_lock(x)			
5	write_item(x)		6	2
6	read_lock(y)			
7	read_item(y)			
8	y:= x+y		6	2
9	write_lock(y)			
10	write_item(y)		6	8
11	unlock(x)	read_lock(y)		
12	unlock(y)	read_item(y)	6	8
13		y:=2*y		
14		write_lock(y)		
15		write_item(y)	6	16
16		read_lock(x)		
17		read_item(x)		
18		x:=x+y		
19		write_lock(x)		
20		write_item(x)	22	16
21		unlock(y)		
22		unlock(x)		

In the above solution the transactions are pretty much serial. Consider the following possible solution – would this work?

Time	T1	T2	x	y
1	read_lock(x)		3	2
2	read_item(x)			
3	x:=x+3			
4	write_lock(x)			
5	write_item(x)		6	2
6		read_lock(y)	6	2
7		read_item(y)	6	2
8		y:=2*y	6	2
9		write_lock(y)	6	2
10		write_item(y)	6	2
11	read_lock(y)			wait
12		read_lock(x)		wait

In this example we have a deadlock.

Answer 8.9 At line 7 there is already a read/shared lock on transaction x Definition of read lock: 'If a transaction has a shared lock on a database, it can read the item but not update it. If a transaction A holds a shared lock on record R, then a request from transaction B for an X lock on R will cause B to go into a wait state (and B will wait until A's lock is released). So at line 7 T1 will have to wait for the release of T2's read lock on x. The same applies at line 10. T2 cannot apply the write lock as T1 already has a read lock on it. It will have to wait.

Deadlock is the situation where one transaction (T1) is waiting for a resource which is locked by another transaction (T2). This transaction in turn is waiting for a resource which is locked by the first transaction. Deadlock may involve more than two transactions.

CHAPTER 9

Backup and recovery

OVERVIEW

Recovery techniques are intertwined with transaction management and concurrency control which were discussed in chapter 8. In this chapter we will look at some of the techniques that can be used to recover from transaction failures. We will first introduce some concepts that are used in recovery processes such as the **system log**, **checkpoints**, and **commit points**. After outlining the recovery procedures, the process of **rolling back** (undoing) the effect of a transaction will be discussed in detail. We will present recovery techniques based on **deferred update**, also known as NO-UNDO/REDO technique and **immediate update**, which is known as UNDO/REDO.

Learning outcomes	On completion of this chapter, you should be able to:

- Describe a range of causes of database failure and explain mechanisms available to deal with these

- Understand a range of options available for the design of database backup procedures

- Analyse the problems of data management in a concurrent environment.

9.1 Introduction

Database systems, like any other computer systems, are subject to failures. Despite this, any organisation that depends upon a database must have that database available when it is required. Therefore, any DBMS intended for a serious business or organisational user, must have adequate facilities for fast recovery after failure. In particular, whenever a transaction is submitted to a DBMS for execution, the system must ensure that either:

- All the operations in the transaction are completed successfully and their effect is recorded permanently in the database

or

- The transaction has no effect whatsoever on the database or on any other transactions.

The understanding of the methods available for recovering from such failures is therefore essential to any serious study of database systems. This chapter describes the methods for recovering from a range of problems that can occur throughout the life of a database system. These mechanisms include **automatic protection mechanisms** built into the database software itself, and **non-automatic actions** available to people responsible for the running of the database system, both for the backing up of data and recovery from a variety of failure situations. Certain recovery techniques are best used with specific concurrency control methods. Assume for the most part that we are dealing with large multi-user databases: small systems typically provide little or no support for recovery – in these systems, recovery is regarded as a user problem.

9.2 Transaction problems

There are a variety of causes of transaction failure.

These include:

- **Concurrency control enforcement:** concurrency control method may abort the transaction, to be restarted later, because it violates serializability (the need for transactions to be executed in an equivalent way as would have resulted if they had been executed sequentially) or because several transactions are in a state of deadlock

- **Local error detected by the transaction:** during transaction executions, certain conditions may occur that necessitate cancellation of the transaction (e.g. an account with insufficient funds may cause a withdrawal transaction from that account to be cancelled). This may be done by a programmed ABORT in the transaction itself

- **A transaction or system error:** due to some operation in the transaction that may cause it to fail, such as integer overflow, division by zero, erroneous parameter values or logical programming errors

- **System software errors:** that result in abnormal termination or destruction of the database management system

- **Crashes due to hardware malfunction:** resulting in loss of internal (main and cache) memory (otherwise known as system crashes)

- **Disk malfunctions:** such as read or write malfunction or a disk read/write head crash. This may happen during a read or write operation of the transaction

- **Natural physical disasters and catastrophes:** such as fires, earthquakes or power surges, sabotage, intentional contamination with computer viruses, or destruction of data or facilities by operators or users.

The last two types are far less common than the rest. Whenever a failure of the first five occurs, the system must keep sufficient information to recover from the failure. Disk failure or other catastrophic failures of the last two do not happen frequently. If these failures do occur, recovery is a major task.

9.3 A typical recovery problem

Data updates made by a DBMS are not automatically written to disk at each synchronisation point. Therefore, there may be some delay between the commit and the actual disk writing. If there is a system failure during this delay, the system must still be able to ensure that these updates reach the disk copy of the database. Conversely, data changes that may ultimately prove to be incorrect, made for example by a transaction that is later rolled back, can sometimes be written to disk. Ensuring that only the results of complete transactions are committed to disk is an important task, which if inadequately controlled by the DBMS may lead to problems, such as the generation of an inconsistent database. This particular problem can be clearly seen in the following example.

Suppose we want to enter a transaction into a customer order. The following actions must be taken:

START
1. Change the customer record with the new order data
2. Change the salesperson record with the new order data
3. Insert a new order record into the database
STOP

The initial values are shown in figure 9.1(a). If only operations 1 and 2 are successfully performed, this results in the values shown in figure 9.1(b).

Figure 9.1(a): Initial values of the database

CUSTOMER:

C-No	Order-No	Description	Cost
123	1000	400 Tennis balls	£2400

SALESPERSON:

Name	Total-Sales
Jones	£3200

ORDERS:

Order-No
1000
2000
3000
4000
5000

Figure 9.1(b): Values of the database after operations 1 and 2

CUSTOMER:

C-No	Order-No	Description	Cost
123	1000	400 Tennis balls	£2400
123	8000	250 Cricket balls	£6500

SALESPERSON:

Name	Total-Sales
Jones	£9700

ORDERS:

Order-No
1000
2000
3000
4000
5000

This database state is clearly unacceptable as it does not accurately reflect reality. For example, a customer may receive an invoice for items never sent, or a salesman may make commission on items never received. It is better to treat the whole procedure (i.e. from START to STOP) as a complete transaction and not commit any changes to the database until STOP has been successfully reached.

9.4 Transaction logging

System log

The recovery manager overcomes many of the potential problems of transaction failure by a variety of techniques. Many of these are heavily dependent upon the existence of a special file known as a **system log**, or simply log (sometimes called a journal or audit trail). This contains information about the start and end of each transaction, and any updates which occur in the transaction. The log keeps track of all transaction operations that affect the values of database items. This information may be needed to recover from transaction failure. The log is kept on disk (apart from the most recent log block that is in the process of being generated, this is stored in the main memory buffers). Thus, the majority of the log is not affected by failures, except for a disk failure, or catastrophic failure. In addition, the log is periodically backed up to archival storage to protect against such catastrophic failures.

The types of entries that are written to the log are described below – in these entries, T refers to a unique transaction identifier that is generated automatically by the system and used to uniquely label each transaction:

- **start_transaction(T):** this log entry records that transaction T starts the execution
- **read_item(T, X):** this log entry records that transaction T reads the value of database item X

- **write_item(T, X, old_value, new_value):** this log entry records that transaction T changes the value of the database item X, from old_value to new_value. The old value is sometimes known as **before image of X**, and the new value is known as an **after image of X**
- **commit(T):** this log entry records that transaction T has completed all accesses to the database successfully, and its effect can be committed (recorded permanently) to the database
- **abort(T):** this records that transaction T has been aborted
- **checkpoint:** this is an additional entry to the log. The purpose of this entry will be described in a later section.

Some protocols do not require that read operations be written to the system log, in which case the overhead of recording operations in the log is reduced, since fewer operations (only write) are recorded in the log. In addition, some protocols require simpler write entries that do not include new_value.

Because the log contains a record of every write operation that changes the value of some database item, it is possible to **undo** the effect of these write operations of a transaction T, by tracing backward through the log and resetting all items changed by a write operation of T to their old_values. We can also **redo** the effect of the write operations of a transaction T by tracing forward through the log, and setting all items changed by a write operation of T to their new_values. Redoing the operations of a transaction may be required if all its updates are recorded in the log, but a failure occurs before we can be sure that all the new_values have been written permanently in the actual database.

Committing transactions and force writing

A transaction T reaches its **commit point** when all its operations that access the database have been executed successfully – that is, the transaction has reached the point at which it will not abort (terminate without completing). Beyond the commit point, the transaction is said to be **committed**, and its effect is assumed to be permanently recorded in the database. Commitment always involves writing a commit entry to the log and writing the log to disk. At the time of a system crash, we search back in the log for all transactions T that have written a start_transaction(T) entry into the log but have not written commit(T) entry yet; these transactions may have to be rolled back to undo their effect on the database during recovery process. Transactions that have written their commit(T) entry in the log must also have recorded all their write operations in the log (otherwise they would not be committed), so their effect on the database can be redone from the log entries.

Notice that the log file must be kept on disk. At the time of a system crash, only the log entries that have been written back to disk are considered in the recovery process, because the contents of main memory may be lost. Hence, before a transaction reaches its commit point, any portion of the log that has not yet been written to the disk must now be written to it. This process is called **force writing** the log file before committing a transaction. A commit does not necessarily involve writing the data items to disk; this depends on the recovery mechanism in use.

A commit is not necessarily required to initiate writing of the log file to disk. The log may sometimes be written back automatically when the log buffer is full. This happens irregularly, as usually one block of the log file is kept in main memory until it is filled with log entries. Then it is written back to disk, rather than writing it to disk every time a log entry is added. This saves the overhead of multiple disk writes of the same information.

Checkpoints

In the event of failure, most recovery managers initiate procedures that involve redoing or undoing operations contained within the log. Clearly, not all operations need to be redone or undone, as many transactions recorded on the log will have been successfully completed and the changes written permanently to disk. The problem for the recovery manager is to determine which operations need to be considered, and which can safely be ignored. This problem is usually overcome by writing another kind of entry in the log, the **checkpoint entry**.

The checkpoint is written into the log periodically, and always involves the writing out to the database on disk the effect of all write operations of committed transactions. Hence, all transactions that have their commit(T) entries in the log before a checkpoint entry will not require their write operations to be redone in the case of a system crash. The recovery manager of a DBMS must decide at what intervals to take a checkpoint. The intervals are usually decided on the basis of the time elapsed, or the number of committed transactions since the last checkpoint.

Performing a checkpoint consists of the following operations:

- Suspending executions of transactions temporarily
- Writing (force-writing) all modified database buffers of committed transactions out to disk
- Writing a checkpoint record to the log
- Writing (force-writing) all log records in main memory out to disk.

A checkpoint record usually contains additional information, including a list of transactions active at the time of the checkpoint. Many recovery methods (including the deferred and immediate update methods) need this information when a transaction is rolled back, as all transactions active at the time of the checkpoint, and any subsequent ones, may need to be redone.

In addition to the log, further security of data is provided by generating backup copies of the database (held in a separate location). This guards against destruction in the event of fire, flood, disk crash etc.

Undoing

If a transaction crash does occur, then the recovery manager may **undo** transactions (that is, reverse the operations of a transaction on the database). This involves examining a transaction for the log entry write_item(T, x, old_value, new_value), and setting the value of item x in the database to old_value. Undoing a number of write_item operations from one or more transactions from the log must proceed in the reverse order from the order in which the operations were written.

Redoing

Redoing transactions is achieved by examining a transaction's log entry, and for every write_item(T, x, old_value, new_value) entry, the value of item x in the database is set to new_value. Redoing a number of transactions from the log must proceed in the same order in which the operations were written in the log. It is only necessary to redo the last update of x from the log during recovery, because the other updates would be overwritten by this last redo. The redo algorithm can be made more efficient by starting from the end of the log and working backwards towards the last checkpoint. Whenever an item is redone, it is added to a list of redone items. Before redo is applied to an item, the list is checked. If the item appears on the list, it is not redone, since its last value has already been recovered.

9.5 Recovery outline

Recovery from transaction failures usually means that the database is restored to some state from the past so that a correct state – one from close to the time of failure – can be reconstructed. To do this, the system must keep information about changes to data items during transaction execution outside the database. This information is typically kept in the system log. It is important to note that a transaction may fail at any point (e.g. when data is being written to a buffer or when a log is being written to disk). All recovery mechanisms must be able to cope with the unpredictable nature of transaction failure. Significantly, the recovery phase itself may fail and therefore the recovery mechanism must also be capable of recovering from failure during recovery. A typical strategy for recovery may be summarised, based on the type of failures.

Recovery from catastrophic failures

The main technique used to handle catastrophic failures, including disk crash, is that of **database backup**. The whole database and the log are periodically copied onto a cheap storage medium such as magnetic tapes. In case of a catastrophic system failure, the latest backup copy can be reloaded from the tape to the disk, and the system can be restarted. To avoid losing all the effects of transactions that have been executed since the last backup, it is customary to back up the system log by periodically copying it to magnetic tape. The system log is usually substantially smaller than the database itself, and so can be backed up more frequently. When the system log is backed up, users do not lose all transactions they have performed since the last database backup. All committed transactions recorded in the portion of the system log that has been backed up can have their effect on the database reconstructed. A new system log is started after each database backup operation. Hence, to recover from disk failure, the database is first re-created on disk from its latest backup copy on tape. Following that, the effects of all the committed transactions are reconstructed – those operations that have been entered in the backed-up copy of the system log.

Recovery from non-catastrophic failures

When the database is not physically damaged but has become inconsistent due to **non-catastrophic failure**, the strategy is to reverse the changes that caused the inconsistency, by undoing some operations. It may also be necessary to redo some operations that could have been lost during the recovery process (or for some other reason) in order to restore a consistent state to the database. In this case, a complete archival copy of the database is not required. Rather, it is sufficient that the entries kept in the system log are consulted during the recovery.

There are two major techniques for recovery from non-catastrophic transaction failures: **deferred updates** and **immediate updates**. The deferred update techniques do not actually update the database until after a transaction reaches its commit point. It is then that the updates are recorded in the database. Before commit, all transaction updates are recorded in the local transaction workspace. During commit, the updates are first recorded persistently in the log, and then written to the database. If a transaction fails before reaching its commit point, it will not have changed the database in any way, so UNDO is not needed. It may be necessary to REDO the effect of the operations of a committed transaction from the log, because their effect may not yet have been written in the database. Hence, deferred update is also known as the **NO-UNDO/REDO algorithm**. We will examine the deferred update technique in more detail later in this chapter.

In the immediate update techniques, the database may be updated by some operations of a transaction before the transaction reaches its commit point. However, these operations are typically recorded in the log on disk by force-writing before they are applied to the database, making recovery still possible. If a transaction fails after recording some changes in the database but before reaching its commit point, the effect of its operations on the database must be undone; that is the transaction must be **rolled back**. In the general case of immediate update, both undo and redo are required during recovery, so it is known as the **UNDO/REDO algorithm**.

Transaction rollback

If a transaction fails for whatever reason after updating the database, it may be necessary to roll back or UNDO the transaction. Any data item values that have been changed by the transaction must be returned to their previous values. The log entries are used to recover the old values of the data items that must be rolled back. If a transaction T is rolled back, any transaction S that has, in the interim, read the value of some data item X written by T, must also be rolled back. Similarly, once S is rolled back, any transaction R that has read the value of some item Y written by S must also be rolled back, and so on. This phenomenon is called **cascading rollback**. Cascading rollback, understandably, can be quite time-consuming. That is why most recovery mechanisms are designed so that cascading rollback is never required.

Figures 9.2(a), (b) and (c) show an example where cascading rollback is required. The read and write operations of three individual transactions are shown in figure 9.2(a). Figure 9.2(b) graphically shows the operations of different transactions along the time axis. Figure 9.2(c) shows the system log at the point of a system crash for a particular execution schedule of these transactions. The values of A, B, C, and D, which are used by the transactions, are shown to the right of the system log entries. At the point of system crash, transaction T3 has not reached its conclusion and must be rolled back. The write operations of T3, marked by a single * in figure 9.2(c), are the operations that are undone during transaction rollback.

Figure 9.2(a): The read and write operations of the three transactions

T1	T2	T3
read_item(A);	read_item(B);	read_item(C);
read_item(D);	write_item(B);	write_item(B);
write_item(D);	read_item(D);	read_item(A);
	write_item(D);	write_item(A);

Figure 9.2(b): Operations before the crash

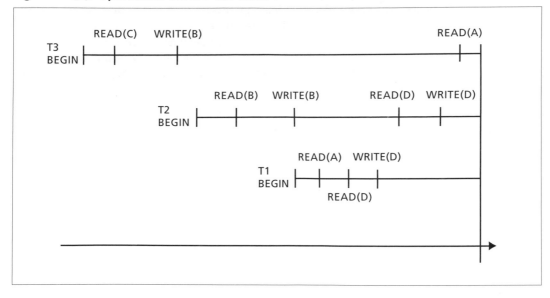

Figure 9.2(c): System log at point of crash

Log	A	B	C	D
	30	15	40	20
start_transaction(T3)				
read_item(T3, C)				
*write_item(T3, B, 15, 12)		12		
start_transaction(T2)				
read_item(T2, B)				
**write_item(T2, B, 12, 18)		18		
start_transaction(T1)				
read_item(T1, A)				
read_item(T1, D)				
write_item(T1, D, 20, 25)				25
read_item(T2, D)				
**write_item(T2, D, 25, 26)				26
read_item(T3, A)				
system crash				

* T3 is rolled back because it does not reach its commit point when system crash happens.

** T2 is rolled back because it reads the value of item B written by T3.

The rest of the write entries in the log are redone.

We must now check for cascading rollback. From figure 9.2(b) we see that transaction T2 reads the value B, which was written by T3. This can also be determined by examining the log. Because T3 is rolled back, T2 must also be rolled back. The write operations of T2, marked by ** in the log, are the ones that are undone. Note that only write operations need to be undone during transaction rollback. Read operations are only recorded in the log to determine whether cascading rollback of additional transactions is necessary.

9.6 Recovery techniques based on deferred update

Deferred update

The idea behind deferred update is to defer or postpone any actual updates to the database itself until the transaction completes its execution successfully and reaches its commit point. During transaction execution, the updates are recorded only in the log, and in the transaction workspace. After the transaction reaches its commit point and the log is force-written to disk, the updates are recorded in the database itself. If a transaction fails before reaching its commit point, there is no need to undo any operations, because the transaction has not affected the database in any way.

The steps involved in the deferred update protocol are as follows:

1. When a transaction starts, write an entry start_transaction(T) to the log.
2. When any operation is performed that will change values in the database, write a log entry write_item(T, x, old_value, new_value).
3. When a transaction is about to commit, write a log record of the form commit(T); write all log records to disk.
4. Commit the transaction; using the log to write the updates to the database, the writing of data to disk need not occur immediately.
5. If the transaction aborts, ignore the log records and do not write the changes to disk.

The database is never updated until after the transaction commits, and there is never a need to UNDO any operations. Hence, this technique is known as the NO-UNDO/REDO algorithm. The REDO is needed in case the system fails after the transaction commits, but before all its changes are recorded in the database. In this case, the transaction operations are redone from the log entries. The protocol, and how different entries are affected, can be best summarised as shown in figure 9.3.

Figure 9.3: How different entries are affected by deferred update protocol

Log entry	Log written to disk	Changes written to database buffer	Changes written on disk
start_transaction(T)	No	N/A	N/A
read_item(T, x)	No	N/A	N/A
write_item(T, x)	No	No	No
commit(T)	Yes	Yes	*Yes
checkpoint	Yes	Undefined	Yes(of committed Ts)

* Yes: writing back to disk may not occur immediately.

Deferred update in a single user environment

We will first discuss recovery based on deferred update in single user systems, where no concurrency control is needed. Hence we can understand the recovery process independently of any concurrency control method. In such an environment, the recovery algorithm can be rather simple. It works as follows. Use two lists to maintain the transactions: the **committed transactions list** which contains all the committed transactions since the last checkpoint, and the **active transactions list** (at most, one transaction falls in this category, because the system is a single user system). Apply the REDO operation to all the write_item operations of the committed transactions from the log, in the order in which they were written to the log. Restart the active transactions.

The REDO procedure is defined as follows: redoing a write_item operation consists of examining its log entry write_item(T, x, old_value, new_value) and setting the value of item x in the database to new_value. The REDO operation is required to be idempotent.

Notice that the transaction in the active list will have no effect on the database because of the deferred update protocol, and therefore is ignored completely by the recovery process. It is implicitly rolled back, because none of its operations were reflected in the database. However, the transaction must now be restarted, either automatically by the recovery process, or manually by the user.

The main benefit of the method is that any transaction operation need never be undone, as a transaction does not record its changes in the database until it reaches its commit point. The protocol is summarised in figure 9.4:

Figure 9.4: Deferred update protocol

Action	Entry in log	
	start_transaction(T)	commit(T)
Resubmit	Yes	No
Redo	Yes	Yes

Figures 9.5(a), (b) and (c) show an example of recovery in a single user environment, where the first failure occurs during execution of transaction T2, as shown in figure 9.5(b). The recovery process will redo the write_item(T1, D, 20) entry in the log by resetting the value of item D to 20 (its new value). The write(T2, ...) entries in the log are ignored by the recovery process because T2 is not committed. If a second failure occurs during recovery from the first failure, the same recovery process is repeated from start to finish, with identical results:

Figure 9.5(a): The read and write operations of two transactions

T1	T2
read_item(A)	read_item(B)
read_item(D)	write_item(B)
write_item(D)	read_item(D)
	write_item(D)

Figure 9.5(b): System log at the point of crash

start_transaction(T1)	
write_item(T1, D, 20)	
commit(T1)	
start_transaction(T2)	
write_item(T2, B, 10)	
write_item(T2, D 25)	system crash

Deferred update in a multi-user environment

For multi-user systems with concurrency control, the recovery process may be more complex, depending on the protocols used. In many cases, the concurrency control and recovery processes are interrelated. In general, the greater the degree of concurrency we wish to achieve, the more difficult the task of recovery becomes.

Consider a system in which concurrency control uses two-phase (basic 2-PL) locking, and prevents deadlock by pre-assigning all locks to items needed by a transaction before the transaction starts execution. To combine the deferred update methods for recovery with this concurrency control technique, we can keep all the locks on items in effect until the transaction reaches its commit point. After that, the locks can be released. This ensures strict and serializable schedules. Assuming that checkpoint entries are included in the log, a possible recovery algorithm for this case is given below.

Use two lists of transactions maintained by the system: the committed transactions list which contains all committed transactions since the last checkpoint, and the active transactions list. REDO all the write operations of the committed transactions from the log, in the order in which they were written into the log. The transactions in the active list that are active, and did not commit, are effectively cancelled and must be resubmitted. The REDO procedure is the same as defined earlier in the deferred update in the single user environment. Figure 9.6 shows an example schedule of executing transactions.

Figure 9.6: Example of recovery in a multi-user environment

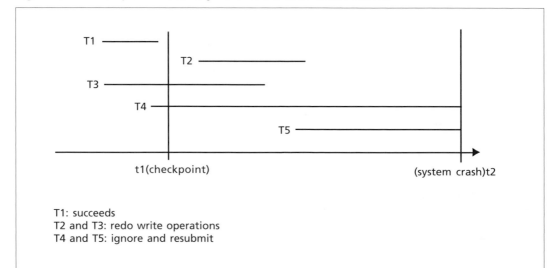

T1: succeeds
T2 and T3: redo write operations
T4 and T5: ignore and resubmit

In figure 9.6, when the checkpoint was taken at time t1, transaction T1 had committed, whereas transactions T3 and T4 had not. Before the system crash at time t2, T3 and T2 were committed, but not T4 and T5. According to the deferred update method, there is no need to redo the write operations of transaction T1, or any transactions committed before the last checkpoint time t1. Write operations of T2 and T3 must be redone, however, because both transactions reached their commit points after the last checkpoint. Remember that the log is force-written before committing a transaction. Transactions T4 and T5 are ignored: they are effectively cancelled and rolled back because none of their write operations were recorded in the database under the deferred update protocol.

Transaction actions that do not affect the database

In general, a transaction will have actions that do not affect the database – such as generating and printing messages, or reports, from information retrieved from the database. If a transaction fails before completion, we may not want the user to get these reports, since the transaction has failed to complete. Therefore, such reports should be generated only after the transaction reaches its commit point. A common method of dealing with such actions is to issue the commands that generate the reports, but keep them as batch jobs. The batch jobs are executed only after the transaction reaches its commit point. If the transaction does not reach its commit point because of a failure, the batch jobs are cancelled.

Activity 9.1

Deferred update protocol

Given the operations of the four concurrent transactions in (1), and the system log at the point of system crash in (2), discuss how each transaction recovers from the failure using the deferred update technique. Give yourself some time to do this before reading the answer for this exercise.

1. The read and write operations of four transactions:

T1	T2	T3	T4
read_item(A)	read_item(B)	read_item(A)	read_item(B)
read_item(D)	write_item(B)	write_item(A)	write_item(B)
write_item(D)	read_item(D)	read_item(C)	read_item(A)
	write_item(D)	write_item(C)	write_item(A)

cont...

2. System log at the point of crash:

start_transaction(T1)	
write_item(T1, D, 20)	
commit(T1)	
checkpoint	
start_transaction(T4)	
write_item(T4, B, 15)	
commit(T4)	
start_transaction(T2)	
write_item(T2, B, 12)	
start_transaction(T3)	
write_item(T3, A, 30)	
write_item(T2, D, 25)	system crash

Recovery management using deferred update with incremental log

Look at the schedule, below, of the five transactions A, B, C, D, and E. Assume the initial values for the variables are a=1, b=2, c=3, d=4, and e=5. Using an incremental log with deferred updates, for each operation in each of the transactions, show:

1. The log entries.

2. Whether the log is written to disk.

3. Whether the output buffer is updated.

4. Whether the DBMS on disk is updated.

5. The values of the variables on the disk.

Discuss how each transaction recovers from the failure.

cont...

A	B	C	D	E	Log entries	Log to disk	Buffer changed	DBMS on disk changed	a	b	c	d	e
									1	2	3	4	5
start A													
read value a													
a:=a*2													
write value a													
commit A													
	start B												
	read value b												
	b:=b*2												
	write value b												
		start C											
		read value c											
		c:=c*2											
		write value c											
					checkpoint								
	b:=0												
	write value b												
	commit. B												
			start D										
			read value d										
			d:=d*2										
			write value d										
			commit D										
				start E									
				read value e									
				e:=e*2									
				write value e									
					FAILURE								

9.7 Summary

Following on from the previous chapter on transaction management and concurrency control, this chapter introduces the student to recovery techniques and their importance in the management of large database systems. After reading this chapter, students will understand how system logs with before and after images, commit points and checkpoints are used to recover from different types of failures. The techniques of rollback and rollforward were also examined.

9.8 Review questions

 Review question 9.1 Unfortunately, transactions fail frequently and this is due to a variety of causes. Discuss the different causes of transaction failures.

 Review question 9.2 What is meant by system log? Discuss how a system log is needed in a recovery process.

 Review question 9.3 Discuss the actions involved in performing and writing a checkpoint entry.

 Review question 9.4 Discuss how UNDO and REDO operations are used in a recovery process.

 Review question 9.5 What is catastrophic failure? Discuss how a database can recover from catastrophic failure.

Review question 9.6 What is meant by transaction rollback? Why is it necessary to check for cascading rollback?

Review question 9.7 Compare deferred update with immediate update techniques by filling in the following blanks. The deferred update techniques do not actually update the database until .... a transaction reaches its commit point; then the updates are recorded in the database. Before commit, all transaction updates are recorded in the local transaction workspace.

During commit, the updates are first recorded persistently in the .... and then written to the .... If a transaction fails before reaching its commit point, it will not have changed the database in any way, so .... is not needed. It may be necessary to .... the effect of the operations of a committed transaction from the log, because their effect may not yet have been written in the database. Hence, deferred update is also known as .... algorithm.

In the immediate update techniques, the database may be updated by some operations of a transaction .... the transaction reaches its commit point. However, these operations are typically recorded in the log-on disk by ...., before they are applied to the database, making recovery still possible.

If a transaction fails after recording some changes in the database, but before reaching its commit point, the effect of its operations on the database must be .... ; that is, the transaction must be .... In the general case of immediate update, both .... and .... are required during recovery, so it is known as the .... algorithm.

Review question 9.8 Using your own words, describe the deferred update method for recovery management in a multi-user environment. Complete the following table to show how the deferred update protocol affects the log-on disk, database buffer, and database on disk:

Log entry	Log written to disk	Changes written to database buffer	Changes written on disk
start_transaction(T)			
read_item(T, x)			
write_item(T, x)			
commit(T)			
checkpoint			

9.9 Answers to review questions

Answer to review question 9.1 The practical aspects of transactions are about keeping control. There are a variety of causes of transaction failure. These may include:

1. Concurrency control enforcement: the concurrency control method may abort the transaction, to be restarted later, because it violates serializability, or because several transactions are in a state of deadlock.

2. Local error detected by the transaction: during transaction executions, certain conditions may occur that necessitate cancellation of the transaction (e.g. an account with insufficient funds may cause a withdrawal transaction from that account to be cancelled). This may be done by a programmed ABORT in the transaction itself.

3. A transaction or system error: some operation in the transaction may cause it to fail, such as integer overflow, division by zero, erroneous parameter values or logical programming errors.

4. User interruption of the transaction during its execution (e.g. by issuing a control-C in a VAX/VMS or UNIX environment).

5. System software errors that result in abnormal termination or destruction of the database management system.

6. Crashes due to hardware malfunction resulting in loss of internal (main and cache) memory (otherwise known as system crashes).

7. Disk malfunctions such as read or write malfunction or a disk read/write head crash. This may happen during a read or write operation of the transaction.

9. Natural physical disasters and catastrophes such as fires, earthquakes or power surges, sabotages, intentional contamination with computer viruses, or destruction of data or facilities by operators or users.

Answer to review question 9.2 The system log contains information about the start and end of each transaction, plus any updates which occur in the transaction. It keeps track of all transaction operations that affect the values of database items. This information may be needed to recover from transaction failure. The log is kept on disk. Thus, the majority of the log is not affected by failures, except for a disk failure or catastrophic failure. In addition, the log is periodically backed up to archival storage (e.g. tape) to protect against the effect of such catastrophic failures. The types of entries that are written to the log are described below – in these entries, T refers to a unique transaction identifier that is generated automatically by the system and used to uniquely label each transaction:

- **start_transaction(T):** this log entry records that transaction T starts the execution

- **read_item(T, X):** this log entry records that transaction T reads the value of database item X

- **write_item(T, X, old_value, new_value):** this log entry records that transaction T changes the value of the database item X from old_value to new_value. The old value is sometimes known as a **before image of X**, and the new value is known as an **after image of X**

- **commit(T):** this log entry records that transaction T has completed all accesses to the database successfully and its effect can be committed (recorded permanently) to the database

- **abort(T):** this records that transaction T has been aborted

- **checkpoint:** this is an additional entry to the log. The purpose of this entry will be described in the next review question answer.

Because the log contains a record of every write operation that changes the value of some database item, it is possible to undo the effect of these write operations of a transaction T, by tracing backward through the log and resetting all items changed by a write operation of T to their old_values. We can also redo the effect of the write operations of a transaction T, by tracing forward through the log and setting all items changed by a write operations of T to their new_values.

Answer to review question 9.3   This activity asked you to list all actions taken when a checkpoint entry is written in the system log:

- Suspending executions of transactions temporarily

- Writing (force-writing) all modified database buffers of committed transactions out to disk

- Writing a checkpoint record to the log

- Writing (force-writing) all log records in main memory out to disk.

Answer to review question 9.4

- **UNDO:** if a transaction crash does occur, then the recovery manager may undo transactions (that is, reverse the operations of a transaction on the database). This involves examining a transaction for the log entry write_item(T, x, old_value, new_value), and setting the value of item x in the database to old_value. Undoing a number of write_item operations from one or more transactions from the log must proceed in the reverse order from the order in which the operations were written

- **REDO:** is achieved by examining a transaction's log entry; and for every write_item(T, x, old_value, new_value) entry, the value of item x in the database is set to new_value. Redoing a number of transactions from the log must proceed in the same order in which the operations were written.

It is only necessary to redo the last update of x from the log during recovery, because the other updates are overwritten by this last redo.

Answer to review question 9.5 *Catastrophic failure* is extensive damage to a wide portion of the database, such as disk malfunctions, read or write malfunction or a disk read/write head crash. This may happen during a read or write operation of the transaction, and can be caused by natural physical disasters and catastrophes such as fires, earthquakes or power surges, sabotages, intentional contamination with computer viruses, or destruction of data or facilities by operators or users.

The main technique used to handle catastrophic failures, including disk crash, is that of **database backup**. The whole database and the log are periodically copied onto a cheap storage medium such as magnetic tapes. In case of a catastrophic system failure, the latest backup copy can be reloaded from the tape to the disk, and the system can be restarted.

Answer to review question 9.6 If a transaction fails, for whatever reason, after updating the database, it may be necessary to roll back or UNDO the transaction. Any data item values that have been changed by the transaction must be returned to their previous values. The log entries are used to recover the old values of data items that must be rolled back.

If a transaction T is rolled back, any transaction S that has, in the interim, read the value of some data item X written by T must also be rolled back. Similarly, once S is rolled back, any transaction R that has read the value of some item Y written by S must also be rolled back, and so on. This phenomenon is called **cascading rollback**. If cascading rollback is not checked, it may lead to an inconsistent database state. For example, when T is rolled back, S and R must also be rolled back, otherwise uncommitted dependency problems occur.

Answer to review question 9.7 The **deferred update** techniques do not actually update the database until after a transaction reaches its commit point; then the updates are recorded in the database. Before commit, all transaction updates are recorded in the local transaction workspace.

During commit, the updates are first recorded persistently in the log, and then written to the database. If a transaction fails before reaching its commit point, it will not have changed the database in any way, so UNDO is not needed. It may be necessary to REDO the effect of the operations of a committed transaction from the log, because their effect may not yet have been written in the database. Hence, deferred update is also known as the NO-UNDO/REDO algorithm.

In the **immediate update** techniques, the database may be updated by some operations of a transaction before the transaction reaches its commit point. However, these operations are typically recorded in the log-on disk, by force-writing, before they are applied to the database, making recovery still possible.

If a transaction fails after recording some changes in the database, but before reaching its commit point, the effect of its operations on the database must be undone; that is, the transaction must be rolled back. In the general case of immediate update, both UNDO and REDO are required during recovery, so it is known as the UNDO/REDO algorithm.

Answer to review question 9.8 Use two lists of transactions maintained by the system: the **committed transactions list** which contains all committed transactions since the last checkpoint, and the **active transactions list**. REDO all the write operations of the committed transactions from the log, in the order in which they were written into it. The transactions in the active list that are active and did not commit are effectively cancelled and must be resubmitted.

The REDO procedure is defined as follows: redoing a write_item operation consists of examining its log entry write_item(T, x, old_value, new_value), and setting the value of item x in the database to new_value. The REDO operation is required to be idempotent:

Log entry	Log written to disk	Changes written to database buffer	Changes written on disk
start_transaction(T)	No	N/A	N/A
read_item(T, x)	No	N/A	N/A
write_item(T, x)	No	No	No
commit(T)	Yes	Yes	*Yes
checkpoint	Yes	Undefined	Yes (of committed Ts)

*Yes: writing back to disk may not occur immediately.

9.10 Feedback on activities

Answer 9.1 T1 committed before the last checkpoint; its update has been successfully force-written to disk before the system crash. No action needs to be taken during the recovery process. T2 and T3 are ignored because they did not reach their commit points. They are in the active transaction list and will be resubmitted during the recovery process. T4 is redone because its commit point is after the last system checkpoint. As it is in the commit transaction list, its write operations will be redone. The following diagram will make things clearer.

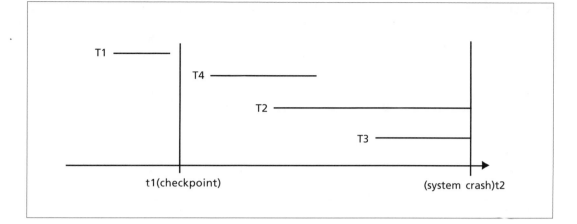

Answer 9.2

A	B	C	D	E	Log entries	Log to disk	Buffer changed	DBMS on disk changed	a	b	c	d	e
									1	2	3	4	5
start A					Start_transaction(A)	N	N	N	1	2	3	4	5
readvalue a					Read_item(A, a)	N	N	N	1	2	3	4	5
a:=a*2									1	2	3	4	5
writevalue a					Write_item(A, a, 1, 2)	N	N	N	1	2	3	4	5
commit A					Commit_transaction(A)	Y	Y	N	1	2	3	4	5
	start B				Start_transaction(B)	N	N	N	1	2	3	4	5
	readvalue b				Read_item(B, b)	N	N	N	1	2	3	4	5
	b:b*2								1	2	3	4	5
	writevalue b				Write_item(B, b, 2, 4)	N	N	N	1	2	3	4	5
		start C			Start_transaction(C)	N	N	N	1	2	3	4	5
		readvalue c			Read_item(C, c)	N	N	N	1	2	3	4	5
		c:=c*2							1	2	3	4	5
		writevalue c			Write_item(C, c, 3, 6)	N	N	N	1	2	3	4	5
					Checkpoint	Y	N	Y	2	4	6	4	5
	b:=0								2	4	6	4	5
	writevalue b				Write_item(B, b, 4, 0)	N	N	N	2	4	6	4	5
	commit. B				Commit_transaction(B)	Y	Y	N	2	4	6	4	5
			start D		Start_transaction(D)	N	N	N	2	4	6	4	5
			readvalue d		Read_item(D, d)	N	N	N	2	4	6	4	5
			d:=d*2						2	4	6	4	5
			writevalue d		Write_item(D, d, 4, 8)	N	N	N	2	4	6	4	5
			commit D		Commit_transaction(D)	Y	Y	N	2	4	6	4	5
				start E	Start_transaction(E)	N	N	N	2	4	6	4	5
				readvalue e	Read_item(E, e)	N	N	N	2	4	6	4	5
				e:=e*2					2	4	6	4	5
				writevalue e	write_item(E, e, 5, 10)	N	N	N	2	4	6	4	5
					FAILURE								

The recovery activities can be summarised in the following table:

Transaction	No need for action – changes irrevocably made to the database	Redo	Undo	Re-presented
A	Yes			
B		Yes		
C				Yes
D			Yes	
E				Yes

CHAPTER 10

Distributed database systems

OVERVIEW

In many organisations data is shared, often geographically. Typically, all personal computers are networked to support work-group computing and many previously (centralised) mainframe applications have been downsized for various reasons, including cost-effectiveness. Distributed databases are concerned with the efficient distribution of data across different platforms and networks. As far as users are concerned, the data is an integrated whole, even if it is geographically dispersed. Users may access a data item and be completely unaware that part of that data item resides on a machine in Tokyo, and that another component was recovered from Los Angeles.

Many of the issues considered in other chapters of this module require a degree of further consideration when translated into a distributed context. When it becomes a requirement to distribute data across a network, the processes of transaction processing, concurrency control, query optimisation, recovery, security and integrity control become significantly more involved. In this chapter we shall introduce some extensions to mechanisms which we have previously considered for non-distributed systems.

Learning outcomes On completion of this chapter, you should be able to:

- Describe the essential characteristics of distributed database systems

- Distinguish between client/server databases and distributed databases

- Understand the main design issues concerned with distributed DBMSs (fragmentation and replication).

10.1 Introduction

In previous chapters we assumed that databases are centralised where a single logical database is located at one site. We now discuss the concept and issues of **distributed database systems** where users can access data at both their own site, and remotely. We start by examining the various architectures for databases and show how distributed database systems have evolved from these earlier systems.

10.2 Centralised database

Figure 10.1: Centralised database

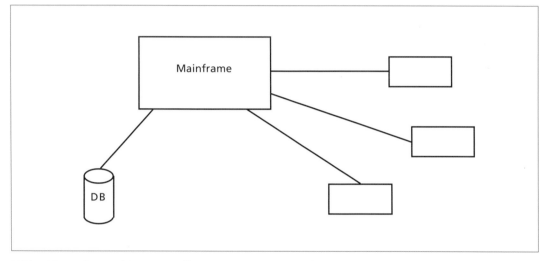

With this earlier architecture, all system components (i.e. the database and the DBMS), reside at a single mainframe computer or site. Users may be able to access the centralised database system remotely via terminals connected to the site; however, all the user interface processing, applications programs processing, as well as DBMS functionality, take place at the central site as in the figure 10.1.

Advantages:

- Cost – economies of scale (hardware, software and operations)
- Easier overall control over database (for backup, recovery and security).

Disadvantages:

- Data is not readily accessible to users at remote sites
- Data communication costs may be high
- The database system fails totally when the central system fails.

As the price of hardware fell, terminals were replaced with PCs and workstations. At first these were used just for interface processing, but gradually more of the processing was put on the user side. This led to client-side processing.

10.3 Client/server database

With client/server architecture we would expect many PCs and workstations, as well as a small number of mainframe computers, to all be connected by local area networks (LANs) and other types of computer networks. Application processing is divided (not necessarily evenly) between client and server. The client functions are performed on a separate computer from the database server functions. A client is a user machine and provides user interface and local processing capabilities. When the client requires functionality not available at the client, it connects to a server that provides additional functionality such as database access. This is shown diagrammatically as:

Figure 10.2: Client/server database

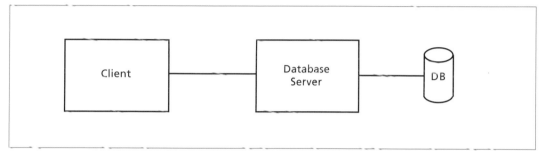

A client/server architecture is an example of a loosely coupled system which separates functions on specialised processors. The server and various clients may even run different operating systems. As the client functions are performed on a separate computer from the database server functions, neither the client nor the database server are complete application environments in themselves.

This approach is known as the **2-tier model of client/server computing**. This is because it is made up of the two types of component, **clients** and **servers**. It is also possible that a machine that acts as a server to some clients, may itself act as a client to another server. The distinction between a client and server machine is that the client is a device which initiates the connection, whereas the server is the device which accepts the connection.

Servers

The server is responsible for database storage, access and integrity checking, security, data dictionary maintenance and concurrent access management. Moreover, they also perform recovery and optimise query processing. The server controls access to the data by enforcing locking rules to ensure data integrity during transactions. The server can be a PC, mini- or mainframe computer and usually employs a multi-tasking operating system such as OS/2, Unix or MVS.

The server software is responsible for local data management at a site, much like centralised DBMS software. A number of relational products have taken the SQL server approach. Clients submit SQL to the SQL server to manipulate or retrieve data. Since SQL is a relational standard, various different SQL servers, possibly provided by different vendors, can accept SQL commands. In this approach, the SQL server has also been called a **database processor** or a **back-end machine**. The server responds to queries from clients, checks the syntax of these commands, verifies the access rights of the user, executes these commands, and responds with desired data or error messages. The server hides the server system from the client and from the end-user, so that the user is completely unaware of the server's hardware and software. The server of a client/server system may also include the part of the DBMS software responsible for handling data storage on disk pages, buffering and caching of disk pages and other such functions.

Clients

This is the front-end of the client/server system. It handles all aspects of the user interface – it is the 'front-end' of the system since the client presents the system to the user. It can also provide PC-based application development tools to enter, display, query and manipulate data on the central server and to build applications. The client operating system is usually Windows, OS/2 or Unix.

Clients send database commands to the database server for processing (usually as SQL queries). The client manages the user interface. This includes the programming language interface functions, presenting data, and handling all interactions with local devices (printer, keyboard, screen etc). The client has been called an **application processor** or a **front-end machine**. The client can be running any application system that is able to generate the proper commands to the server. For example, the application program might be written in Excel, a report writer, a sophisticated screen painter, or any fourth-generation language that has an application program interface (API) for the database engine. An API calls library routines that transparently manage SQL commands from the front-end client application to the database server. An API might work with existing front-end software, like a report generator, and it may include its own facilities for building applications. When APIs exist for several program development tools, there is considerable independence to develop client applications in the most convenient front-end programming environment, as well as drawing data from a common server database. APIs have evolved so that it is possible to have clients with heterogeneous operating systems (for example, DOS, OS/2, UNIX, and System 7 from Apple) running applications against a common database. Some APIs can interface to mainframe hosts running IBM's DB2 or SQL/DS as well as to Windows/NT and UNIX PC-based servers.

Advantages of the client/server approach

Here are some of the advantages of the client/server approach over centralised or stand-alone processing:

- It allows companies to maximise the benefits of microcomputer technology, delivering impressive computing power at a fraction of the costs of mainframes
- Users do not have to retain copies of corporate data on their own PCs, which would become quickly out of date. They can be assured that they are always working with the current data stored on the server machine. As the data is in one place, there is improved control of backup, recovery and security
- Processing can be carried out on the machine most appropriate to the task. Data-intensive processes can be carried out on the server, whereas data entry validation and presentation logic can be executed on the client machine. This reduces unnecessary network traffic and improves overall performance
- Scalability – if the number of users of an application grows, extra client machines can be added (up to a limit determined by the capacity of the network or server) without significant changes to the server.

Disadvantages of client/server computing

Some disadvantages of the client/server approach:

- Operating database systems over a local area network (LAN) or wide area network (WAN) brings extra complexities of developing and maintaining the network. The interfaces between the programs running on the client and server machines must be well understood. This usually becomes increasingly complex when the applications and/or DBMS software come from different vendors

- Security is a major consideration. Preventative measures must be in place to protect data theft or corruption on the client and server machines and during transmission over the network.

10.4 Distributed database management systems

Figure 10.3: Distributed database management system

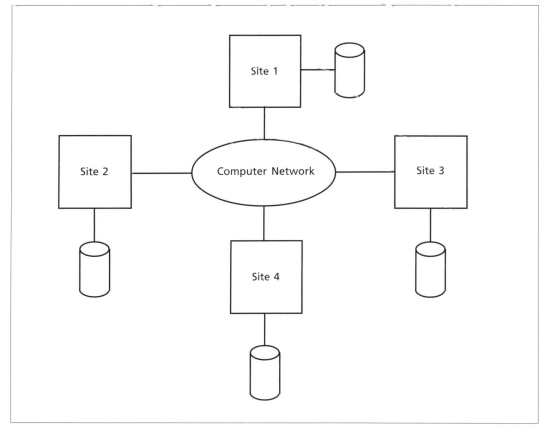

In a distributed database system the database is spread physically across computers or sites in different locations. These are usually connected with one another via high-speed networks or telephone lines. Typically, all personal computers are networked to support work-group computing, and many previously (centralised) mainframe applications have been downsized for various reasons, including for cost-effectiveness. Distributed databases are concerned with the efficient distribution of data across different platforms and networks.

A good working definition of a distributed database is that of Date (Date, 2000):

A **distributed database** consists of a collection of sites connected by some kind of communications network, in which:

> Each site is a database system in its own right, but the sites have agreed to work together so that a user at any site can access data anywhere in the network exactly as if the data were all stored at the user's own site.

Note that the generally understood description of a distributed database system given here is rather different from the client/server systems we examined earlier in the chapter. In client/server systems, the data is not itself distributed; it is stored on a server machine and accessed remotely from client machines. In a distributed database system, however, the data is itself distributed among a number of different machines. Decisions not only need to be made about the way in which the data is to be distributed, but also about how updates are to be propagated over multiple sites.

The sites of a distributed database may be spread over a large area (such as Britain or the world) connected via a wide area network (WAN), or over a small area (such as a building or a campus) connected via a local area network (LAN). It is not uncommon for the computers to vary in both technical specification and function, depending upon their importance and position in the system as a whole. For example, there may be IBM mainframes, VAXs, SUN workstations, PCs etc managed by different operating systems (such as VMS, UNIX, Windows NT). Each fragment of the database may be managed by a different DBMS (such as Oracle, Microsoft Access, O2).

As far as users are concerned, the data is an integrated whole, even if it is geographically dispersed. Users may access a data item and be completely unaware that part of that item resides on a machine in Tokyo, while another component was recovered from London. Users access the distributed database via applications. In a distributed database system, database applications running at any of the system's sites should be able to operate on any of the database fragments transparently (i.e. as if the data came from a single database managed by one DBMS). The software that manages a distributed database in such a way is called a **distributed database management system** (DDBMS).

Motivation for distributed database systems

So why have distributed databases become so desirable? There are a number of reasons that promote the use of a distributed database system. These can include such things such as:

- The sharing of data
- Local autonomy
- Data availability.

Furthermore, it is likely that the organisation which has chosen to implement the system will itself be distributed. By this we mean that there are almost always several departments and divisions within the company structure. An illustrative example is useful here in clarifying the benefits that can be gained by the use of distributed database systems:

Example scenario – banking system

Imagine a banking system that operates over a number of separate sites. For the sake of this example let us consider two offices, one in Piccadilly and another in Westminster.

Account data for Piccadilly accounts is stored in Piccadilly, while Westminster's account data is stored in Westminster. We can now see that two major benefits are afforded by the use of this system: efficiency of processing is increased due to the data being stored where it is most frequently accessed, while an improvement in the accessibility of account data is also gained.

Functions of a distributed database management system (DDBMS)

A distributed DBMS coordinates the access to data at the various sites where the distributed database resides. A DDBMS is required to perform the following functions in addition to the normal functions of a DBMS:

- **Extended communication services:** to provide access to remote sites and allow the transfer of queries and data among them
- **Extended system catalogue (global system catalogue):** to store data distribution details; this can determine the location from which to retrieve requested data
- **Distributed query processing:** if necessary, translate the request at one site using a local DBMS into the proper request to another site using a different DBMS and data model
- **Extended concurrency control:** to maintain consistency of replicated data
- **Extended recovery services:** to be able to recover from crashes at a particular site and failure of communication links.

DDBMS transparencies

Date (1999) gives the 'fundamental principle' behind a truly distributed database:

> To the user; a distributed system should look exactly like a NON distributed system.

In other words, the system should make the distribution transparent to the user.

In order to accomplish this fundamental principle, a number of transparencies, which hide the implementation details, can be identified as objectives for a DDBMS:

- Location transparency
- Copy transparency
- Fragmentation transparency
- Transaction transparency
- Performance transparency
- Schema change transparency
- Local DBMS transparency.

Location transparency

A user can submit a query that accesses distributed objects without having to know where the objects are.

Copy transparency

The system supports the optional existence of multiple copies of database objects. Hence, if a site is down, users can still access database objects by obtaining one of the copies from another site, and the user does not need to know either that the data is replicated or the source of the data.

Fragmentation transparency

A relation (class) can be divided into multiple pieces and stored at multiple sites according to specified distribution criteria. For example, the following distribution criteria might control the placement of tuples from an Employee relation:

- EMPLOYEE where dept = "accounts" at London
- EMPLOYEE where dept <> "accounts" at New York

In this way the tuples of a relation can be distributed, and users can subsequently query the relation as if the data were not fragmented at all. In the example, a user can access the Employee relation unaware of its distribution.

Transaction transparency

A user can run an arbitrary transaction that updates data at any number of sites (i.e. a distributed transaction) and the transaction behaves exactly like a local one. Atomicity is maintained.

Performance transparency

This requires the DDBMS to perform as if it were a centralised DBMS. In order to achieve this, the DDBMS must be able to determine the most cost-effective strategy to execute a request. For example, if you have one million objects in New York and ten objects in London, you want to perform the join by moving the ten objects to New York and not vice versa. Performance transparency loosely means that a query can be submitted from any node in a distributed DBMS and it will run with comparable performance.

Schema change transparency

A user who adds or deletes a database object from a distributed database need make the change only once (to the distributed dictionary) and does not need to change the catalogue at all sites that participate in the distributed database.

Local DBMS transparency

The distributed database system provides services without regard for which local DBMSs are actually managing local data. It hides the fact that the DBMSs at various sites may be different.

Advantages to distributed databases

There are numerous advantages to distributed databases. The most important of these are the following:

- Increased reliability and availability
- Local control
- Modular growth
- Lower communication costs
- Faster response.

Increased reliability and availability

When a centralised system fails, the database is unavailable to all. A distributed system continues to function at a reduced level even when a component fails. The reliability and availability will depend (among other things) on how the data is distributed.

Local control

Local groups exercise greater control over 'their' data, promoting improved data integrity and administration. At the same time, users can access non-local data when necessary. Hardware can be chosen for the local site to match local rather than other needs.

Modular growth

Suppose that an organisation expands to a new location and adds a new work group. It is often easier and more economical to add a local computer and its associated data to the distributed network than to expand a large central computer. Also, there is less chance of disruption to existing users than is the case when a central computer system is modified or expanded.

Lower communication costs

With a distributed system, data can be located closer to their point of use. This can reduce communication costs compared to a central system.

Faster response

Depending on how data is distributed, most requests for data by users at a particular site can be satisfied by data stored at that site. This speeds up query processing, because communication and central computer delays are minimised. It may also be possible to split complex queries and subqueries that can be processed in parallel at several sites, providing even faster response.

Disadvantages to distributed databases

The use of distributed database systems is not without its drawbacks. The main disadvantage is the added complexity that is involved in ensuring that proper coordination between the various sites is possible. This increase in complexity can take a variety of forms:

- Software cost and complexity
- Processing overhead
- Data integrity
- Slow response.

Software cost and complexity

More complex software (especially the DBMS) is required for a distributed database environment. There is a greater potential for bugs. With a number of databases operating concurrently, ensuring that algorithms for the operation of the system are correct becomes an area of great difficulty.

Processing overhead

The various sites must exchange messages and perform additional calculations to ensure proper coordination among the sites. This is a considerable overhead not present in centralised systems.

Data integrity

A by-product of the increased complexity and need for coordination is the additional exposure to improper updating and other problems of data integrity.

Slow response

If the data is not distributed properly according to its usage, or if queries are not formulated correctly, response to requests for data can be extremely slow.

10.5 Distributing data – strategies

A significant problem in physical database design is deciding at which nodes (or sites) in the network to physically locate the data. Data distribution is designed so that as much as possible of the locally required data is held at the local node, while minimising replication and data communication costs. But, how should a database be distributed among the sites (or nodes) of a network?

This section is about the way decisions are taken on where to store data, and how many copies are to be kept in different places.

There are four basic data distribution strategies:

1. Centralised

All data is located at a single site. Although this simplifies the implementation, there are at least three disadvantages:

- Data are not readily accessible to users at remote sites
- Data communication costs may be high
- The database system fails totally when the central system fails.

2. Fragmented

With this approach, the database is divided into disjoint (non-overlapping) fragments. Each fragment (also called a partition) is assigned to a particular site. The major advantage of this approach is that data is moved closer to local users and so is more accessible.

3. Replicated

A full copy of the database is assigned to more than one site in the network. This assignment maximises local access to data but creates update problems, since each database change must be reliably processed and synchronised at all of the sites.

4. Hybrid

With this strategy, the database is fragmented into critical and **non-critical fragments**.

Non-critical fragments are stored at only one site, while critical fragments are stored at multiple sites.

Fragmentation

A system can support data fragmentation if a given stored relation can be divided up into pieces, or **fragments**, for physical storage purposes. In this case there is no replication. All data is divided between nodes in logical units. When fragmented, each fragment, which may be a single relation or set of relations, is held at the node with the highest activity with regard to that partition. Fragmentation is desirable for performance reasons: data can be stored at the location where it is most frequently used, so that most operations are purely local and network traffic is reduced.

A fragment can be any arbitrary subrelation that is derivable from the original relation, via **restriction** (horizontal fragmentation) and **projection** (vertical fragmentation) operations. Note that the conceptual object is unchanged (e.g. there is still just one table), but it is stored in different places.

Horizontal fragmentation

With horizontal fragmentation, some of the rows of a table (or relation) are put into a base relation at one site, and other rows are put into a base relation at another site. More generally, the rows of a relation are distributed to many sites.

Horizontal fragmentation example

A bank has many branches. One of the base relations is the 'Customer' relation. Table 10.1 is the format for an abbreviated version of this relation. For simplicity, the sample data in the relation applies to only two of the branches (Piccadilly and Westminster). The primary key in this relation is account number (ACCT No.). 'Branch Name' is the name of the branch where customers have opened their accounts (and therefore where they presumably perform most of their transactions).

Table 10.1: Abbreviated version of Customer relation

ACCT No.	Customer name	Branch name	Balance
200	Jones	Piccadilly	1000.00
324	Smith	Westminster	250.00
426	Dorman	Piccadilly	796.00
153	Gray	Westminster	38.00
683	McIntyre	Piccadilly	1500.00
252	Elmore	Piccadilly	330.00
500	Green	Westminster	168.00

The next examples are the result of taking horizontal fragments of the Customer relation. Each row is now located at its home branch. If customers actually conduct most of their transactions at the home branch, the transactions are processed locally and response times are minimised. When a customer initiates a transaction at another branch, the transaction must be transmitted to the home branch for processing, and the response then transmitted back to the initiating branch (this is the normal pattern for persons using ATMs). If a customer's usage pattern changes (perhaps because of a move), the system may be able to detect this change and dynamically move the record to the location where most transactions are being initiated.

Table 10.2: Horizontal fragments of the Customer relation

Piccadilly Branch:

ACCT No.	Customer name	Branch name	Balance
200	Jones	Piccadilly	1000.00
426	Dorman	Piccadilly	796.00
683	McIntyre	Piccadilly	1500.00
252	Elmore	Piccadilly	330.00

Table 10.3: Horizontal fragments of the Customer relation

Westminster Branch:

ACCT No.	Customer name	Branch name	Balance
324	Smith	Westminster	250.00
153	Gray	Westminster	38.00
500	Green	Westminster	168.00

In summary, horizontal fragments for a distributed database have three major advantages:

- **Efficiency** – data is stored close to where it is used and separate from data used by other users or applications
- **Local optimisation** – data can be stored to optimise performance for local access
- **Security** – data not relevant to usage at a particular site is not made available.

Thus, horizontal fragments are usually used when an organisational function is distributed, but each site is concerned with only a subset of the entity instances (frequently based on geography).

Horizontal fragments also have two primary disadvantages:

- **Inconsistent access speed** – when data from several fragments is required, the access time can be significantly different from local-only data access
- **Backup vulnerability** – since data is not replicated, when data at one site becomes inaccessible or damaged, usage cannot switch to another site where a copy exists; data may be lost if proper backup is not performed at each site.

Vertical fragmentation

With vertical fragmentation, some of the columns of a relation are projected into a base relation at one of the sites, and other columns are projected into a base relation at another site (more generally, columns may be projected to several sites). The relations at each of the sites must share a common domain – the columns that define the primary key – so that the original table can be reconstructed.

Vertical fragmentation example

To illustrate vertical fragmentation, we use an application for the manufacturing company shown below in the 'Part' relation with 'Part no.' as the primary key. Some of the data is used primarily by manufacturing, while the other is used mostly by engineering. The data is distributed to the respective departmental computers using vertical fragmentation, as shown below. Each of the fragments shown is obtained by taking projections (that is, columns) from the original relation. The original relation in turn can be obtained by taking natural joins of the resulting fragments.

Table 10.4: Abbreviated version of Part relation

Part no.	Name	Cost	Drawing no.	Stock Level
P2	Widget	100.00	123-7	20.00
P7	Gizmo	550.00	621-0	100.00
P3	Thing	48.00	174-3	0.00
Pi	Whatsit	220.00	416-2	16.00
P8	Thumzer	16.00	321-0	50.00
P9	Bobbit	75.00	400-1	0.00
P6	Nailit	125.00	129-4	200.00

Table 10.5: Vertical fragments of the Part relation

Manufacturing:

Part no.	Name	Cost	Stock level
P2	Widget	100.00	20.00
P7	Gizmo	550.00	100.00
P3	Thing	48.00	0.00
Pi	Whatsit	220.00	16.00
P8	Thumzer	16.00	50.00
P9	Bobbit	75.00	0.00
P6	Nailit	125.00	200.00

cont...

Engineering:

Part no.	Drawing no.
P2	123-7
P7	621-0
P3	174-3
Pi	416-2
P8	321-0
P9	400-1
P6	129-4

In summary, the advantages and disadvantages of vertical fragments are identical to those for horizontal fragments. However, horizontal fragments support an organisational design in which functions are replicated, often on a regional basis, while vertical fragments are typically applied across organisational functions with reasonably separate data requirements.

Combinations of operations

To complicate matters further, there are almost unlimited combinations of the preceding strategies. Some data may be stored centrally, while other data is replicated at the various sites. Also, for a given relation, both horizontal and vertical fragments may be desirable for data distribution.

For example:

- Engineering parts, accounting, and customer data are each centralised at different locations
- Standard parts data are fragmented (horizontally) among the three locations
- The standard price list is replicated at all three locations.

The overriding principle in distributed database design is that data should be stored at the sites where they will be accessed most frequently (although other considerations, such as security, data integrity, and cost, are also likely to be important). The data administrator plays a critical and central role in organising a distributed database, in order to make it distributed, not decentralised.

Data replication

Data replication is the controlled duplication of data. A system supports data replication if a given stored relation – or, more generally, a given fragment – can be represented by many distinct copies or replicas, stored at many distinct sites. We can distinguish between **complete replication** where a complete copy of the database is maintained at each site (no fragmentation), and **selective replication** which is a combination of fragmentation and replication. The objective of this strategy is to have the advantages of the previous approaches without the disadvantages. However, this is subject to a good design.

There are two advantages to data replication:

- **Reliability** – if one of the sites containing the relation (or database) fails, a copy can always be found at another site
- **Faster and consistent access speeds** – applications can operate on local copies instead of having to communicate with remote sites.

There are also two primary disadvantages:

- **Storage requirements** – each site that has a full copy must have the same storage capacity that would be required if the data were stored centrally
- **Update propagation problem** – the major disadvantage of replication is that when a given replicated object is updated, all copies of that object must be updated – this is called the update propagation problem.

For these reasons, data replication is favoured where most transactions are read-only and where the data is relatively static, as in catalogues, telephone directories, train schedules and so on. CD-ROM storage technology has proved an economical medium for replicated databases. **Full replication** is where the whole database is replicated. **Partial replication** is where some data is replicated over several nodes – generally to achieve specific purposes, whether performance or recovery based.

Synchronous and asynchronous replication

As mentioned earlier, from the point of view of the user, a DDBMS should behave like a centralised DBMS. For example, as far as query processing is concerned, a user can ask a query of a database and be unaware of where the data is stored. When it comes to updates to data, transactions should appear to be atomic actions, regardless of data fragmentation and replication. With this view we refer to replication as **synchronous replication:** before an update transaction commits, it synchronises all copies of modified data. In other words, replicated data is updated immediately when the source data is updated, typically using the 2PL protocol that was discussed in chapter 7. However, this method comes at a significant cost. Before an updated transaction can commit, it must lock all copies of the modified data. The lock requests may be at remote sites. These sites may be unavailable and there may be communication failures.

Another approach to data replication is known as **asynchronous replication**. This method is gaining in popularity for commercial DDBMSs. Copies of an updated transaction are updated only periodically. This means that a transaction that reads different copies of the same relation may see different values for short periods of time. This method violates location transparency: users must now be aware of which copy is being accessed and that copies may be inconsistent. This method is, however, acceptable in many situations. The data eventually will synchronise at all the replicated sites.

Distributed database design

Consider the following scenario:

A bank has its head office in Central London. It has two branches, one in East Finchley and the other in Brent Cross. Each customer account belongs to one branch only. Currently, the company has one database located in the Head Office. Customers at branches access this database via a communication network for whatever data they need.

One of the relations in this centralised database system is the Account relation, where data about the accounts is kept. The attributes of the Account relation are: the account number (Acc no.), account type (Acc type), the customer's identification (assume Name), the branch where the account is held, the current balance for the account (balance) and an indicator which lets Head Office know if the publicity (information on updates to regulations, interest rates etc) for a particular account type for a customer has been sent out. An instance of the account relation is given below:

Acc no.	Acc type	Name	Branch	Balance	Publicity
191688	002	Jones	Brent Cross	2000	yes
779865	005	Smith	East Finchley	600	no
158756	002	Green	East Finchley	8	yes
125467	007	White	East Finchley	10000	no
124678	005	Black	Brent Cross	150	yes

The bank has decided to move to a distributed database system where each of the sites has its own database. Propose a fragmentation design of the Account relation that reflects the distribution of the company's sites and their functionality. Justify your proposal.

10.6 Summary

This chapter introduced the student to distributed database systems. It opened with a comparison with other architectures, namely centralised databases and client server systems. Distributed database transparencies were described, followed by a discussion of distributed database system advantages and disadvantages. Students were then introduced to various approaches to distributed database design, namely, vertical and horizontal fragmentation and replication.

10.7 Review questions

 Review question 10.1 Explain what is meant by the 2-tier model of client/server computing.

 Review question 10.2 Why is it sometimes said that client/server computing improves the scalability of applications?

 Review question 10.3 What additional security issues are involved in the use of a client/server system, compared with a traditional centralised mainframe database accessed via dumb terminals?

 Review question 10.4 Distinguish between the terms 'fragmentation' and 'replication' in a distributed database environment.

 Review question 10.5 Describe the main advantage and disadvantage of synchronous replication.

10.8 Answers to review questions

Answer to review question 10.1 The 2-tier model of client/server computing refers to the arrangement where the processing of an application is distributed across two types of machines:

- **Servers:** that handle the database functions of the application
- **Clients:** that handle the data entry and display and simple input validation tasks of the application.

In more complex applications, the way in which the processing is distributed between the two types of machines will vary depending on the power of the machines, volume of network traffic etc. There may be a number of client and server machines within any given network, though usually each server will support a number of client machines. It is possible in the 2-tier system to have a server which also behaves as a client with respect to another server machine.

Answer to review question 10.2 The client/server model provides a scalable solution because, within the limits of the available network and server machines, new client machines can be added to the network. In this way, more users can be added to the system.

Answer to review question 10.3 It is possible for data to be downloaded to client machines and taken away either on the machine or on other storage media such as disks or CD-ROMs. This is a major issue which needs to be addressed within organisations using client/server systems, requiring the development of policies about what data can be downloaded, and whether or not to allow removable storage media to be used on client machines.

A further major issue is the possibility of viruses being introduced to the system via client machines. Once more, policies need to be developed and enacted in order to establish protection against the introduction of viruses; these policies might disallow the introduction of external programs and data files by users via client machines.

Answer to review question 10.4

- **Fragmentation:** refers to the splitting up of relations in order that they may be stored in a distributed manner across a number of machines within the distributed system. The fact that the data itself is distributed distinguishes this type of system, known as a distributed database system, from a client/server system, in which only the processing is distributed. Relations may be fragmented horizontally and/or vertically

- **Replication:** refers to the process of keeping a number of distinct copies of data up to date although it is distributed across a network. Updates made at one of the sites containing data are propagated or replicated to other sites. A range of strategies are available to the designer to choose how updates will be propagated across the network.

Factors that will influence this choice include:

- How up to date it is necessary for the data to be in order for users at different sites to perform their tasks effectively

- The peak and average volumes of update transactions

- The amount of data updated by each transaction

- The available network bandwidth.

Answer to review question 10.5 The main advantage of synchronous replication is that it maintains all replicas of the data in synchronisation. This means that regardless of which site a person is using, they are guaranteed to be working with the most up-to-date version of the data.

The disadvantage of this approach is the overhead of the extra messages and data that needs to be transferred across the network in order for this synchronous updating process to take place. The effect of this extra network traffic is that the times to perform update transactions are increased.

10.9 Feedback on activity

Answer 10.1   A number of solutions are acceptable. For example, the relation is first fragmented vertically. The first fragment (Acc no., Acc type, Publicity), is stored at the Head Office. The second fragment (Acc No., Name, Branch, Balance) is then horizontally fragmented to two groups of tuples. The ones where Branch = 'Brent Cross' will be stored in Brent Cross, whereas those where Branch = 'East Finchley' will be stored in East Finchley.

In the vertical fragmentation, the attribute Acc no. is included in both the fragments, so that the original relation can be reconstructed. Note that it may also be necessary to replicate the Account type, and to hold this at the 'branch fragments', depending on the functions performed at the branch.

CHAPTER 11

Web database connectivity

OVERVIEW

Database technology has been around for a long time. For many organisations, database systems are an essential and integral part of their everyday operation. Prior to the advent of the Internet, these systems have only been accessible through company-based local area networks (LANs), or wide area networks (WANs). Now, the Internet has opened up new opportunities for developing and disseminating innovative database applications, and has made legacy systems available via the same paradigm. A multinational company, for example, can create a web-based database application to enable the effective sharing of information among offices around the world. A book company, such as Amazon, or computer company, like Dell, can reach a world-wide audience that can order their goods, track the status of orders and pay for the goods online without leaving their PC. Via the web, a database application can be made available, interactively, to users and organisations anywhere in the world.

In this chapter, we examine the impact that the web brings to the development and deployment of database applications. We will study the most commonly used approaches for creating and operating web databases, and discuss related issues such as dynamic updating of web pages online. In keeping with all aspects of web technology, which has been evolving at a considerable pace since it was first proposed in 1989, there are multiple, and sometimes conflicting ways of performing similar tasks.

The first part of this chapter introduces the concept and need for **web database connectivity**. This includes a discussion on the differences between traditional client/server and web-based applications and an examination of **dynamic web pages** and the role they play in web-based applications. We then look at the hardware and software architecture, in terms of a **3-tier model**, that is appropriate for both traditional and web-based applications. Next, each of the layers (components) of the architecture is looked at in depth, including **client-side database access** and **server-side database access**. As each layer is discussed, the concepts and approaches for **web server** management, **application logic** development and **database connectivity** are introduced.

- Distinguish between traditional and web-based database connectivity

- Understand the requirements for connecting database systems to the web

- Describe the 3-tier architecture, and functional components or layers, within the model which forms the essential building block for web database applications

- Identify the differences between client-side and server-side database access

- Critically compare a number of approaches that might be used to build a web-enabled database.

11.1 Differences between traditional client/server and web-based applications

Web-based database applications use a new type of client/server technology. Some of the traditional client/server database techniques, which we looked at in chapter 10, are still adopted. However, because of the incorporation of the web technology, there are important differences as set out in table 11.1.

Table 11.1: Traditional vs web server comparison

Traditional client/server applications	Web-based applications
Platform-dependent	Platform-independent
Client is natively compiled and therefore has fast execution speed	Client is an interpreter (e.g. HTML, Java, Java Script) and therefore is slower
Installation necessary	No need for installation
Complex client; high maintenance cost	Simple client; minimum maintenance
New, unfamiliar interface for users	One common, familiar interface across applications
Rich, custom GUI constructs possible	Limited set of GUI constructs; custom ones add to download time
Difficult to integrate with existing applications	Easy to integrate
Difficult to add multimedia	Easy to add multimedia
Persistent connection to database	Non-persistent connection

Platform independence

Web client logic (operating within any web browser) is platform-independent and does not require modification to be run on different operating systems. Traditional database clients, on the other hand, are frequently platform-specific and extensive porting effort is required to support multiple platforms. This is arguably one of the most compelling reasons for building a web-based client/server database application.

Interpreted applications

Web client logic is written in interpreted languages (e.g. HTML and Java). This has an adverse effect on performance. In many applications, however, this is a price worth paying to gain the advantage of platform independence. Time-critical applications may not be good candidates to be implemented on the web.

No need for installation

Another benefit of web database applications is that the need for installing special software is eliminated on the client's side. It is pretty safe to assume that the clients have already had a web browser installed, which is the only piece of software needed for the clients to run the applications. All web client logic (i.e. the HTML page) is automatically retrieved from the web servers when required.

Simple client

As a client needs just a browser to run a web-based database application, the potential complications are minimised.

Common interface across applications

Again, because there is no need for specialised software, users have the benefit of using a browser for possibly different applications.

Limited GUI (graphical user interface)

This is one area in which web-based database applications may fall short. Highly customised application interfaces and highly interactive clients may not translate well as web applications. This is because of HTML limitations. At the moment, HTML forms do not offer an extensive feature set, and GUI developers can resort to client-side scripting (e.g. JavaScript) or applets to provide better user interfaces. This can be complex, adds to downloading time, and degrades performance (although raw client power is still being doubled every two years through more powerful PCs).

Integrate with other applications

Because of the benefit of being platform-independent, different applications that adhere to the HTML standard can be integrated without many difficulties.

Multimedia support

HTML already provides easy-to-use constructs to present and manipulate multimedia contents, for example image files, and, with browser extensions (e.g. plug-ins), audio and video files.

Non-persistent connection to database

Persistent database connections are highly efficient data channels between a client and the

DBMS, and, therefore, are ideal for database applications. However, web-based applications do not have this benefit. A web-based client maintains its connection to a database only as long as is necessary to retrieve the required data, and then releases it. Thus, web application developers must address the added overhead for creating new database connections each time a client requires database access.

11.2 Web database connectivity

The term 'web database connectivity' describes the connection between a client machine and a remote database via the World Wide Web. Such a connection allows a web browser user to connect with a remote database, to both access and update the database content. Access and update of the database is, as with traditional systems, controlled by a layer of application logic. This is provided by the designers and developers of the database system. However, the manner in which a database connection is provided via the web, and the architecture and components that make up the solution, is very different from the traditional one and is the subject of this chapter.

In the first instance, web database connectivity is initiated through a web browser that understands HTML. In the second instance, web database connectivity involves database interaction via web servers on remote websites and results in 'dynamic' web pages that are returned to the browser user.

Static web pages

We will first of all consider the situation when a fixed HTML page with the standard '.html' file extension is requested:

- A web browser passes a URL reference to a remote website via the http protocol
- The web server on the website looks up the URL reference and retrieves the corresponding HTML file that is passed back, again via the http protocol, to the web browser
- The web browser displays the HTML page to the user.

This is an example of static web page access. What the end-user sees remains the same (unless the author puts an updated version of the HTML file on the server).

Dynamic web pages

The alternative to a static web page is a dynamic web page. The content of a dynamic web page is generated each time it is accessed, and it is server-side processing that handles the generation.

The flow is as follows:

- A web browser passes a URL reference to a remote website via the http protocol
- The web server sees that the URL reference is not a static '.html' reference but is a process or file reference with a different extension type
- The web server invokes an associated process, based on the URL name and extension type, that is responsible for generating the required HTML file
- The associated process generates the HTML file, accessing (and updating if necessary) one or more databases

- The HTML file is returned to the web server and is passed back, again via http protocol, to the web browser
- The web browser displays the HTML page to the user.

A conceptual diagram of this flow, including access to static HTML files, is shown in figure 11.1.

Figure 11.1: Dynamic HTML generation

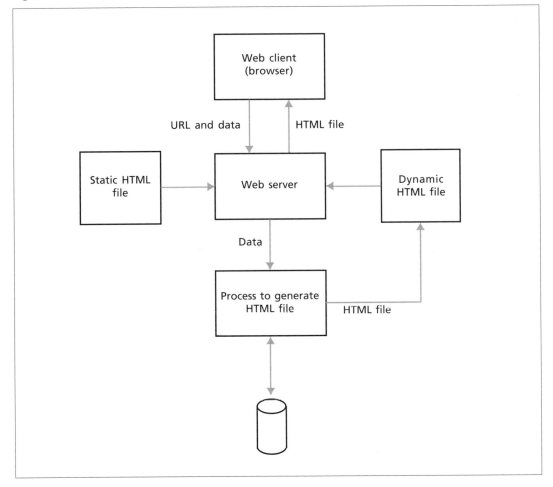

The need for web database connectivity is a natural extension of early limitations of the web. Initially, as we have already seen, websites were file-based where each document was stored in a separate HTML file. When items in a collection were to be presented on the web, a separate web page was created for each item or grouping of items. Such pages were difficult to organise and almost impossible to keep up to date and consistent over time. Increasingly, the huge volume and structure of data on the web warranted storing and organising into databases, and then generating web pages based on these databases. Any website that presents information about a collection of 'like items' is a candidate for using a web database. These items could be goods for sale, information about courses and modules at a university, or film clips. Organisations are now rapidly building new database applications, or changing existing ones, to take advantage of the web technologies.

Process to generate HTML file

What is the HTML generation process itself? What type of process is it? How does it get user input? What computer language is the application logic written in? How are underlying databases accessed and updated? In practice, there are multiple technologies addressing these questions, each handling the problem in slightly different ways.

Common Gateway Interface program (CGI program)

A common type of HTML generation process, and the one that has been around for the longest time, is a CGI program (often called a CGI script). A CGI program is identified by the URL passed from a web browser and it communicates with the web server via the CGI protocol (Common Gateway Interface protocol). CGI programs can be written in a number of languages, including C and Java, though very often they are written in the Perl scripting language, hence the name CGI script. The logic of a CGI program generates the entire HTML file that is returned to the web browser.

Java Servlets

Java Servlets, a more recent technology, perform a similar function to CGI programs. Java Servlets are Java programs that generate entire HTML files.

HTML 'template' approach

A further approach, typified by a number of technologies including Active Server Pages, Java Server Pages and Coldfusion Markup Language, involves template HTML files that are identified by the URL. The template files (with various extensions such as .asp, jsp, cfm as described later in this chapter) are a mixture of HTML code and programming (or 'scripting') code. The HTML code in the template forms the basis of the HTML document passed back to the web browser user, while the programming code specifies the logic that generates the remaining parts of the HTML page. This is illustrated in figure 11.2.

Figure 11.2: HTML generation from template

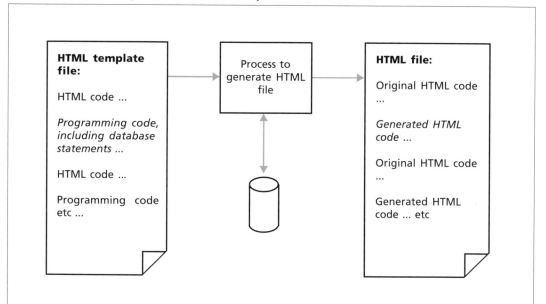

Example of HTML template and generated file

The programming code can be based around proprietary HTML tags (as is the case with Coldfusion template files). Alternatively, it can be written as a server-side scripting language (such as server-side JavaScript or server-side VBScript), or written in pure Java. An example of a Coldfusion template page and its dynamically generated HTML file is given below in figure 11.3. Here, a database called 'MDX University' is accessed, and the data items, module codes and titles are retrieved from the database. These are placed in an HTML file for subsequent display by a web browser.

Figure 11.3: Coldfusion template page example and generated HTML file

```
<CFQUERY NAME="ModuleList"
      DATASOURCE="MDX
University">
   SELECT * FROM Modules</
CFQUERY>

<HTML>
<HEAD>
<TITLE>Module List</TITLE>
</HEAD>
<BODY>
<H1>Middlesex Modules</H1>

<CFOUTPUT QUERY="ModuleList">
#Modulecode# $#Title# <BR>
</CFOUTPUT>

</BODY>
```

```
<HTML>
<HEAD>
<TITLE>Module List</TITLE>
</HEAD>
<BODY>
<H1>Middlesex Modules</H1>

BIS1000 Information Technology<BR>
BIS2020 Database Systems<BR>
BIS2030 Systems Analysis<BR>
BIS3021 Advanced Database
Systems<BR>

</BODY>
</HTML>
```

11.3 Web connectivity architecture

Business systems, whether or not they are delivered via the web, must have components that handle the user interface, the application logic and the database access and update. In a classic mainframe environment, most of these were packaged within the mainframe themselves. This gradually moved to a 2-tier client/server architecture, in which the user interface and some of the application logic was housed on a client machine (typically a PC), with the majority of the application logic and the database being on a server machine. Most business systems nowadays are built around a three-tier architecture that supports better distribution of processing, scalability and robustness.

3-tier architecture

There are three levels in the 3-tier architecture, as shown in figure 11.4.

Figure 11.4: 3-tier architecture

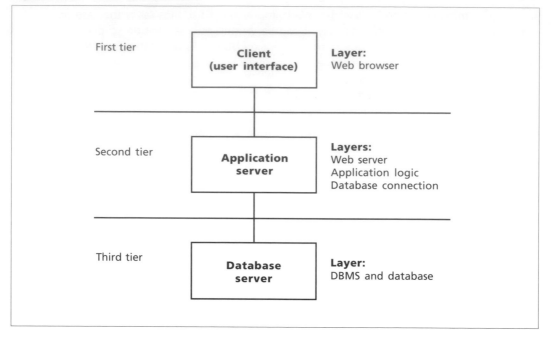

The first tier is the client machine that contains user interfaces. In a web-based system the client machine typically runs a web browser. The middle tier is the application server that provides application logic and data processing functions. In a web-based system, the application server runs the web server, which is a software component rather than a hardware one. The third tier, running on a separate server called a database server, contains the actual database management system (DBMS).

There may be variations on this theme in any particular implementation of a website. For example, there may be multiple, and possibly distributed, application server machines for multiple applications, and there may be multiple database servers each supporting a different database system within the organisation's operation.

Layers within the 3-tier model

Referring again to the 3-tier architecture diagram (figure 11.4), there are a number of functional components, or layers, that form essential building blocks for web database applications. These layers are summarised below and then described in more detail in subsequent sections:

- **Web browser layer:** this is in the first tier of the 3-tier model. Two of the best-known browsers are Netscape Navigator from the company Netscape, and Internet Explorer from Microsoft. The Netscape browser is available on both Windows and Unix-based operating systems, whereas Internet Explorer runs only under Windows. There are now a number of browsers competing with IE, including Firefox which is free, cross-platform and developed by Mozilla

- **Web server layer:** this is in the second tier of the 3-tier model. As with the web browser, there are a number of web server options. Both Netscape and Microsoft provide web servers, with the Microsoft version running exclusively on Windows-based operating systems (e.g. Windows 95/98, NT and 2000). There are also a number of 'freeware' or 'shareware' systems, such as Apache. Coldfusion sells a web server that supports its HTML extensions and, more recently, a number of web servers have appeared within transaction and session managers that are becoming the engines of eCommerce websites. Examples are WebSphere from IBM, and WebLogic from BEA Systems

- **Application logic layer:** this is in the second tier of the 3-tier model. The application logic layer is where the specifics of any web-based application are housed, containing all the business and data processing logic that makes up the application. It is this layer that is most important from an application developer's point of view, since this is where the features and functions of the application are built using the available web-based technologies. Examples of such technologies are CGI programs, Active Server Pages, ASP.NET, Java Servlets and Java Server Pages

- **Database connection layer:** this is in the second tier of the 3-tier model. The database connection layer is the set of communication protocols and APIs (application program interfaces) between the application logic and the database systems that hold all the data for an organisation. At one extreme, database connection can be provided through the native interfaces offered by the database management system(s) being used. However, this is not an ideal approach as it limits portability of the application, both from a hardware and software perspective. A preferred approach is to introduce a measure of database independence, through connection interfaces such as ODBC (open database connectivity) and JDBC (Java database connectivity)

- **Database layer:** this is in the third tier of the 3-tier model. The database layer holds the DBMS and the database(s), such as the Oracle DBMS, Microsoft Access and other DBMS solutions. This layer is not discussed further in this chapter.

11.4 Web browser layer

The browser is the client of a web database application and it has two major functions. First, it handles the layout and display of HTML documents. Second, it executes client-side extension functionality such as Java (in the form of Java Applets), client-side scripting, ActiveX (a Microsoft technology to extend a browser's capabilities) and plug-ins. An additional function of a web browser is to manage cookies, which are a way to overcome the stateless nature of the http protocol. Cookie functions are described later in this section. Currently, the three most popular browsers are Netscape Navigator (Netscape for short), Microsoft Internet Explorer (IE) and FireFox Web browser from Mozilla. In fact, FireFox is replacing Netscape as an alternative to IE. They have their own advantages and disadvantages with respect to web database applications:

- All three browsers support Java and JavaScript; IE also fully supports ActiveX and the VBScript scripting language (which is similar to Visual Basic)

- FireFox and Netscape is supported on numerous platforms, whereas IE runs only on Microsoft systems (e.g. Windows 98, 2000 and NT)

- IE offers compatibility with other Microsoft products, and can easily be integrated with existing tools such as Word, Excel and PowerPoint. The drawback is that IE is heavily dependent on the Windows platforms and other Microsoft proprietary systems

- ActiveX is designed to extend the functionality of IE, and works only on Windows platforms and Macintosh System 7+

- All three browsers support XML (extensible markup language), which is an open way to describe both the data structure and actual content of information displayed to an end-user.

Browsers are also responsible for providing forms for the collection of user input, packaging the input, and sending it to the appropriate server for processing. For example, input can include registration for site access, guest books and requests for information. HTML, Java Applets, scripting languages (JavaScript, VBScript) and ActiveX (for IE) may be used to implement forms.

Browsers, or more specifically the HTML pages rendered by browsers, most commonly access remote databases indirectly through the web server, application logic and database connectivity components. That is, access is indirect. Browsers can, via scripts and ActiveX controls, directly access local databases (those on the client machine). Browsers can also, via applets, ActiveX controls or plug-ins, directly connect to and access remote databases. This may be required when integrating a company's legacy applications into the web browser environment, but is not typical of most eCommerce systems accessed via the Internet.

In addition, some non-web applications, particularly if the GUI front-end is developed in a language such as Java, can be launched and run from within a browser environment, and operate in exactly the same way as if run from the operating system environment. Again, this might be due to integration of legacy systems but these will not be true web-based database applications.

Client-side scripting

Client-side scripting, in either JavaScript or VBScript, is embedded in standard HTML pages. It is used primarily to make the web page interface with the end-user more interactive. Objects within a web page can be dynamically moved, hidden or highlighted, user input can be received and validated, and user events (e.g. mouse over object) can be listened for. Scripts are programming languages in their own rights with computational, formatting and conditional capabilities, as well as methods to interact with applets and ActiveX controls.

Client-side scripting can reduce the load on the remote web server, for example, by doing input validation. This avoids having to use multiple web server requests to manage invalid data. Scripting can also reduce the load on the database server. For example, a web client request can result in a single database query on the server side that obtains a number of items (e.g. books by a given author). These items are then packaged into a JavaScript array or an XML document and are transmitted back to the client to be browsed locally.

Applets

An applet is a small bit of Java code that is downloaded from a web server host when referenced by an applet tag within a web page. Being Java programs, applets operate on any browser platform that supports a Java Virtual Machine, and can do most things that a Java program can do, including access and connection to remote databases. Such connections bypass the http protocol and web server path typically used for web database access, and make use of available connection mechanisms for standard Java programs. These include direct socket connections to databases via DBMS net protocols (such as SQL*Net for Oracle), and approaches such as Java DataBase Connectivity (JDBC), Open DataBase Connectivity (ODBC) and Remote Method Invocation (RMI).

Applets, working in this manner, do have an advantage over server-side solutions: they can be in full control over the user transaction and can utilise whatever transaction management capabilities are offered by the database management systems they connect to. Applets can also be used to lessen the load on the server-side processors, as they can be responsible for more of the application functionality. In practice, because of major concerns about remote programs creating havoc on a client's local machine, the Java applet package has in-built security constraints. One such constraint only allows connection to a database running on the server machine from which the applet was originally downloaded. Other constraints prohibit access to local files, invoking other programs and finding out local identities (e.g. usernames, passwords).

ActiveX controls

ActiveX is the name for a set of technologies and services based on Microsoft's Component Object Model (COM). An ActiveX control is a software component that performs a given function or set of functions. Typically, an ActiveX control is used to extend the functionality of a web browser, but controls are also used extensively in Microsoft's own web server systems (e.g. Internet Information Server – IIS).

Within a web page, controls can be used for almost anything a web page developer wants to do, from enhanced GUI, access to local or remote databases, database searches, graphical displays, multimedia file display, video and audio presentation and online games. As with applets, if an ActiveX control is used to access a remote database from within a web page, then the standard 'http/' web server path is bypassed. ActiveX controls have less in-built security mechanisms than applets, and can make use of the same database connection protocols such as direct sockets and ODBC. Any organisation or individual can develop controls, and there are more than a thousand available today. You can go to URL references such as http://www.active-x.com to look at the possibilities for yourself.

Note, of course, that ActiveX controls only operate on a Microsoft-compatible operating environment.

Plug-ins

Plug-ins are software programs that extend the capabilities of a browser in a specific way – giving you, for example, the ability to play audio samples or view video movies from within your browser. They are similar in concept to an ActiveX control, but must be separately installed before they can be used. Plug-ins can operate like any stand-alone applications on the client side.

Cookies

Cookies are not in the same category as applets, ActiveX controls and plug-ins, in that they do not offer mechanisms to connect to remote databases. However, they are an important web application concept as they support session persistence for a local web browser client connecting to a remote web-based application and database. Before we discuss what cookies are, we firstly need to look at why session persistence (overcoming the stateless nature of the http protocol) is necessary.

In a typical web application the client makes a request via the http protocol, which the web server honours by returning a dynamically generated web page. Once the page is returned, the web server and the web application have no further knowledge of the client, but the 'transaction' that the client is trying to do may not be complete. As an example, the end-user may be trying to buy one or more items in an eCommerce transaction, filling up a 'shopping cart' before completing the purchase. This involves multiple web browser/web server interactions.

Cookies are small bits of textual information that a web server sends back to the browser for storage locally. On the next interaction (i.e. http request) the web browser returns the cookie information to the server, which can then use the stored information to continue the transaction. The information stored in a cookie by a web application can be anything that the web application needs to identify the end-user and/or transaction. For example, a cookie can hold a user identity/password, and the current state of his/her shopping cart.

Cookies have a number of properties, including 'expiry date'. They can exist across multiple visits to a website. They also provide convenience to the user by remembering, for example, the user registration details, so that the user does not need to key in identity and password each time they visit a site. Cookies are not the only approach to session persistence, but they are one of the more widely used. Other approaches include extending the URL data and using 'hidden' form fields.

11.5 Web server layer

The web server layer is responsible for receiving client requests via the http protocol, for initiating appropriate action for each request, and for passing the end results back to the client. In its simplest form, a web server merely retrieves the static HTML file identified by a URL and sends it back to the web browser. No database interaction is required. Web servers became more sophisticated when CGI programs were introduced. In this case, the web server initiates the CGI program named in the URL, passes parameters to the program via the CGI protocol and receives the generated HTML file. The generated file is then transmitted to the web browser client, as shown in figure 11.5.

Figure 11.5: CGI processes

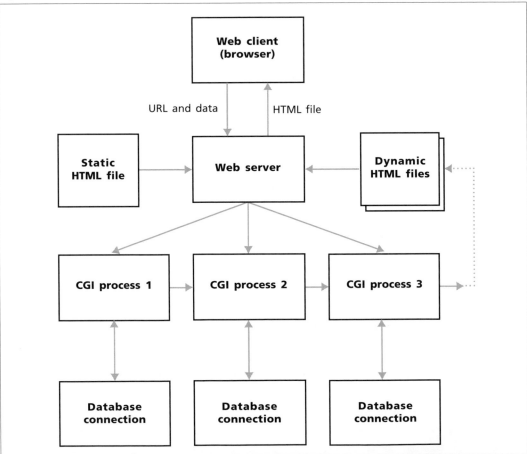

Although very widely used, there are problems with the CGI approach. In the first instance, each and every client request results in a new process being spawned. Then, if database interaction is required (and it very often will be), each new process has the overhead of logging onto and off the database management system. Finally, there is no form of transaction management that, if present, would allow more complex transactions perhaps over multiple databases to be handled. As a result, web server vendors have added capabilities to support more efficient passing of parameters between the server and the called processes, using, for example, multiple threads. One multi-thread process is spawned per named URL, and each client request is managed as a thread of this process. Database logon and other process overheads are done once rather than many times. Typical examples of web server extensions are provided by Netscape and Microsoft, through NSAPI, their Netscape Server application program interface (API) and Internet Information Server API (ISAPI) extensions respectively.

Most recently, web servers have evolved into more complicated and more fully functioned components called application servers. Application servers offer, in addition to the web server role, transaction and session management, access to multiple data sources and better security. Transaction management provides two-phase commit and rollback across multiple databases, such that either all of an end-user's transaction completes, or none of it does, ensuring the integrity of the transaction. Session management can keep the user session open across a number of separate http request/response actions, thereby minimising the user and database logon overhead.

These new application servers also support scalable solutions through distributed computing, combining technologies such as CORBA (Common Object Request Broker Architecture), EJB (Enterprise Java Beans) and others. Typical examples are IBM's WebSphere and BEA's WebLogic. A conceptual diagram of such a solution is shown in figure 11.6.

Figure 11.6: Application server processes

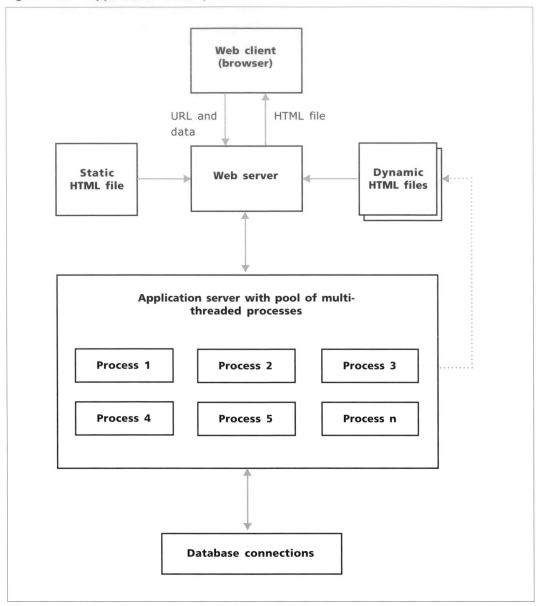

Most, if not all, web servers support standard URL file access and CGI programming. Increasingly, they should also support Java-based connectivity solutions such as Java Servlets and Java Server Pages. Microsoft's web servers, such as those operating on the Windows NT and 2000 environments, also support Microsoft-specific scripting languages, such as VBScript, and Microsoft-specific HTML templates, such as Active Server Pages (those with .asp file extensions). There are some 3rd party web servers that also support .asp files in a Unix (i.e. non-Microsoft) operating system environment.

11.6 Application logic layer

The application logic layer is the part of a web database application with which a developer will spend the most time. It is responsible for:

- Receiving and validating the input from the user request
- Collecting data for a query (e.g. an SQL statement)
- Preparing and sending the query to the database via the database connection layer
- Retrieving the results from the connection layer
- Formatting the data for display – most commonly in the shape of an HTML file
- Passing the data for display back to the web server layer.

Most of the application's business rules and functionality will reside in this layer, either in the form of server-side scripting logic (e.g. in JavaScript, VBScript, Perl or other scripting language) or Java code (packaged as Java Servlets or within Java Server Page templates). The browser client displays data as well as forms for user input, whereas the application logic component compiles the data to be displayed and processes user input as required. In other words, the application logic generates HTML that the browser renders. Also it receives, processes and stores user input that the browser sends.

As we have seen earlier, when we introduced the application logic layer, there are multiple ways in which it can be coded. Some solutions fall into the Microsoft camp; others tend towards the Sun and Java camp. Some are very proprietary, while others have been dominated by the early emergence of the CGI protocol standard. There is no 'right' way, and the application developer is free to pick and choose the approach that best fits the organisation for which they work. This will, of course, be heavily influenced by existing IT and IS strategy.

Application layer approaches

Some of the more popular approaches are summarised in table 11.2:

Table 11.2: Example approaches to application logic layer

Approach	Type*	URL reference	Scripting language	Database connection	Comment
CGI Script	All HTML is generated	File has .cgi extension or in cgi-bin directory	Primarily Perl but also many others including C, C++, Java and even Cobol	Native database API, CGI's DBI API** (Database Independent API)	
Active Server Pages (Microsoft)	HTML template	File has .asp extension	VBScript, Jscript	Microsoft Active Data Objects (ADO), which typically connects to ODBC	• Primarily available on Microsoft web servers, but some third party support is now appearing • Example given later in chapter (example web database display)
ASP.NET	HTML template	.aspx	Current C++, C#, VB.NET and others	ADO.NET	• Runs on any browser on any platform
Java Server Pages	HTML template	File has .jsp extension	Java	JDBC (plus other Java approaches) ODBC– (via ODBC-JDBC Bridge)	• JSP files are automatically generated into Java Servlets for processing • Advantage over servlets is that the number of print statements are minimised (i.e. a servlet has to generate all the HTML)
Java Servlet	All HTML is generated	Java program	Java	JDBC (plus other Java approaches) ODBC (via ODBC-JDBC Bridge)	

cont...

Approach	Type*	URL reference	Scripting language	Connection database	Comment
Coldfusion	HTML template	File has .cfm extension	Coldfusion Markup Extension tags	Native database API, ODBC	• Linked to the Coldfusion web server from Allaire Corporation • Example given at the start of this chapter (see figure 11.3)
PHP Hypertext	HTML template	File has .php3 extension	PHP Hypertext Preprocessor scripting language	Native database API, ODBC	• Freely supported, as part of the Apache Software Foundation
Web Server Extension API (e.g. Microsoft's Internet Database Connector approach within Microsoft's ISAPI web server)	HTML template	File has .idc extension	Standard HTML in a file with .htx extension, plus database query specified in .idc file	ODBC plus others	Netscape offers a similar approach with its NSAPI

* Type

 = HTML template if script embedded in an HTML template file referenced by the URL

 = All HTML is generated if all the resulting HTML is generated by the referenced URL file

** Database-independent API

ASP examples

In this section you are given some ASP examples, as it is generally agreed that one of the best ways to learn some new concepts of an unfamiliar technology is to look at concrete examples. However, you are not expected in this module to produce such code yourself, but to examine the code to understand the underlying concepts.

If, however, you wish to try the examples out for yourself, you can run ASP on your own PC without an external server. To do that, you must install Microsoft's personal web server (PWS) or Internet information server (IIS) on your PC. For information about installing the server, see the 'W3Schools' website:

 http://www.w3schools.com/default.asp

where you will find a number of tutorials for web-building. In particular, look at the ASP tutorial – here it is explained early on how to install IIS or PWS and run ASP on a number of Windows platforms. Creating these examples involves four fundamental steps:

- Create an ASP file using a text editor
- Add code to read the Access database and write corresponding HTML
- Copy the ASP file and the database onto the web server
- Run the page from a browser and view the results.

What is an ASP file?

- An active service page (ASP) is a program that runs inside IIS, the Microsoft server
- It is not a language; rather it is a framework that lets you combine one of a number of scripting languages, plus other software components
- An ASP file will have extension .asp and can contain text, HTML tags, XML and server scripts (VBScript and JavaScript being the most popular)
- Scripts in an ASP file are executed on the server, and can contain any expressions, statements, procedures, or operators that are valid for the scripting language used
- An ASP file can be used to access a database from a web page.

The code to access a database consists of a number of components, and examples of these are described below:

- **HTML:** hypertext markup language; markup tags tell the web browser how to display the page

- **Server-side VBScript:** scripts in an ASP file are executed on the server. VBScript is a version of MS's programming language 'Visual Basic'. Server-side scripting is a language which can be used for dynamically editing, changing or adding any content to a web page. It also responds to user queries or data submitted from HTML forms. It is the default scripting language for ASP

- **SQL (structured query language):** SQL statements are used to retrieve and update data in a database

- **ADO (ActiveX data object):** programming interface to access data in a database; in this case assessed from within an active server page.

We will look at these components using some examples.

ASP component – HTML

Example 11.1: ASP using server-side VBScript

```
<! — simple HTML example — >
<html>
<body>
This is what is displayed in your Browser: Hello World

</body>
</html>
```

- This is what is displayed in your browser: Hello World

```
<! – Another ASP example.  Note the HTML tags to format the text— >
<html>

<body>
Today's date is:
<%
Dim h
h = hour(now())

response.write("<p>" & now())
response.write(" </p>")

If h < 10 then
response.write("You can stay in bed!")
else
response.write("Time to get up!")
end if
%>
</body>
</html
```

- This is what is displayed in your Browser: Today's date is: 08.03.02 17:58:02
  Time to get up!

Notes:

- The delimiters <% and %> surround server scripts. In the foregoing example the VBScript is given in bold
- If you run this example from a browser, you cannot view the ASP code; you will only see the output from ASP, which is plain HTML. This is because the scripts are executed on the server before the result is sent to the browser
- Note the difference between an ASP and an HTML file:
  - when a browser requests an HTML file, the server returns the file
  - when a browser requests an ASP file, the web server passes the request to the ASP engine. The ASP engine reads the ASP file, line by line, and executes the scripts in the file. Finally, the ASP file is returned to the browser as plain HTML.

Connecting to a database using ADO and querying with SQL

Example 11.2: ASP connecting to a database using ADO and querying with SQL

```
1    <html>
2    <body>
3
4    <%
5    set conn=Server.CreateObject("ADODB.Connection")   'the connection
6    set rs = Server.CreateObject("ADODB.recordset")     'the recordset
7    conn.Open "busDepotsDatabase"              'this opens connection
8    sql=" select dname, bdname
9    from depot d, busdriver bd
10   where d.dno = bd.dno
11   order by dname;"
12   rs.Open sql, conn                         'store query result in rs
13   %>
14   <table border="1" width="100%">
15   <tr>
16   <%for each x in rs.Fields
17   response.write("<th>"& x.name & "</th>")
18   next%>
19   </tr>
20   <%do until rs.EOF%>
21   <tr>
22   <%for each x in rs.Fields%>
23   <td> <%Response.Write(x.value)%></td>
24   <%next
25   rs.MoveNext%>
26   </tr>
27   <%loop
28   rs.Close                                  'close recordset
29   conn.Close                                'close connection
30   %>
31   </table>
32   </body>
33   </html>
```

ADO stands for **ActiveX data objects** and is automatically installed with Microsoft IIS. It is a programming interface for accessing and manipulating data in a database. ADO is imbedded in the active service pages (ASP). ADO, VBScript and SQL are in bold in example 11.2. The results of example 11.2 are rendered to the browser in the form of a table:

dname	bdname
Holloway	Jane Brown
Holloway	Jack Jones
Hornsey	James Bond
Hornsey	John Peel
Hornsey	Maggie May
Islington	Peter Piper

Notes:

- ADO (ActiveX data object) – lines 5-12, lines 28-29. The SQL is embedded within the ADO
- The database name is specified at line 7
- To be able to read database data, the data must first be loaded into a recordset object. A recordset object is used to hold a set of records from a database table. It consists of records (rows) and columns. There are many methods that are associated with recordsets – in the example the methods 'open', 'close', 'movenext', 'eof' and 'fields' are used. A recordset object can process 'tables', 'records' and 'fields'.

The mechanism involved in accessing a database from inside an ASP page is to:

1. Create an ADO connection to the database   – line 5
2. Open the database connection   – line 7
3. Create an ADO recordset called here 'rs'   – line 6
4. Execute the query on the connection 'conn' and store result in the recordset called rs
    – line 12
5. Extract the data you need from the recordset   – lines 16-27
6. Close the recordset   – line 28
7. Close the connection   – line 29

11.7 Database connection layer

This is the component that actually links a database to the web. The connection layer within a web database application must accomplish a number of goals. It has to provide access to the underlying database, and it also needs to be easy to use, efficient, flexible, robust, reliable and secure. The database connection layer for a web database application is not different in principle to database connectivity for traditional client/server systems. In fact, the same approaches can be adopted, ranging from embedded database commands, through native database APIs to more open database APIs such as ODBC and JDBC.

Embedded database commands

The traditional way of providing database connectivity was to embed database commands within the programming language in which the application was constructed. The command set would be both database vendor specific, and programming language specific. Typically, a pre-compiler would be run before the compilation process, to translate the database commands into language-specific database function calls. Access to relational databases also started this way, though the ISO standards body introduced some standards. For example, the keywords 'EXEC SQL' normally started each database command. Again, each database/programming language combination required the corresponding pre-compiler. A simple C program to access all the rows of a BUSDRIVER table might look like the code in example 11.3:

Example 11.3: Embedded SQL

```
/* Program to access BUSDRIVER table */
#include <stdio.h>
#include <stdlib.h>
EXEC SQL INCLUDE sqlca;
Main()
{
/* Connect to database */
EXEC SQL CONNECT 'application_database';
/* Query database */
EXEC SQL SELECT * from BUSDRIVER;
Process query results ...
/* Disconnect from database */
EXEC SQL DISCONNECT;
```

As we have already discussed, the code in example 11.3 does not result in portable applications.

Native database APIs

Some database vendors improved upon the embedded database command approach by providing application program interfaces (APIs) to interact with their systems. Essentially, the APIs consist of a collection of functions, or object classes, that provide source code access to the databases. These functions enable the application developer to:

- Connect to the DBMS
- Create an SQL statement and send it to the DBMS
- Check for success
- For a query, retrieve each resultant row with call
- Disconnect from the DBMS.

Again, the APIs tended to be database specific, thus the name native database APIs, and therefore the result is code that is not immediately portable between operating platform and/or database vendor.

Open database API: ODBC

The ODBC standard (open database connectivity), pioneered by Microsoft, is an open database API that has been very successful in overcoming the problems of native database APIs. ODBC is not tied to any specific vendor, and drivers are available for over fifty DBMSs. ODBC provides:

- A library of function calls to connect to, access, update and disconnect from a database
- A representation of data type
- A standard set of error codes
- A standards-based SQL syntax.

ODBC has been ported to most popular computer platforms, including Windows, UNIX and Macintosh, and is so ubiquitous that you may be using it without knowing it. For example, database access within Active Server Pages is commonly conducted using active data objects (ADO), but ADO is merely an abstraction above ODBC. Similarly, open database connectivity from Java programs (using JDBC as discussed in the next section) often uses ODBC to connect to specific database types. To illustrate how ODBC works, we will use pseudocode rather than a real programming language (such as VBScript or server-side JavaScript), as in example 11.4:

Example 11.4: ODBC

```
1. /* Specify use of ODBC API */
2. use ODBC;
3. /* Connect to database */
4. Connection ("mydatabase");
5. /* Issue selection statement */
6. SqlStatement("SELECT * FROM BUSDRIVER);
7. /* Process resultant records */
8. .....
9. /* Close database connection and finish
10.    EndConnection("mydatabase");
11.    End;
```

Notes:

- In line 2, we indicate that the ODBC API is to be used
- In line 4, we connect to a specific database 'mydatabase', referring to the database as a string. If we wished to, we could dynamically connect to one of a number of databases governed by an input parameter, or to more than one database. Each database that we refer to in this way will have been registered to the operating environment that we are running in, as a data source with a given data name source (DNS). That is, 'mydatabase' will have been registered as a known DNS. In fact, the data source does not have to be a relational database, but we will be using SQL to access and update it
- Line 5, and those following, should be self-explanatory.

When the above program is executed, the ODBC driver manager process linked to the program automatically loads the appropriate ODBC driver, which then becomes a client of the database engine. This is shown in figure 11.7, in which two databases are being accessed (Oracle and Microsoft Access) through their respective ODBC drivers.

Figure 11.7: ODBC architecture

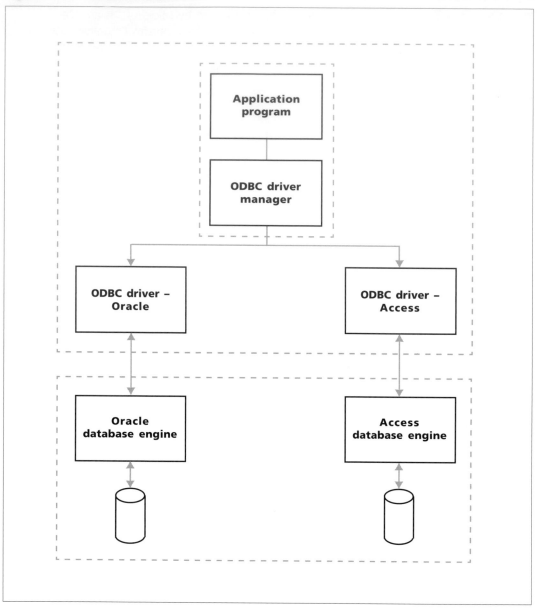

ODBC drivers are available from many sources and for many operating platforms. Typically, a database vendor (such as Oracle) will provide the drivers. The drivers are responsible for providing a level of indirection for the application program's interface to the database. Therefore a driver's role includes translation of database requests (in SQL) into the command set of the specific database (which may not have a SQL interface), and translation of result sets, and error conditions into the standard form.

One proviso, the drivers must be available on the machine that the application program is running on. The database engine that the driver connects to can be on the same machine, or on a separate database server machine. The beauty of the above arrangement is that the application is fully portable across any machine environment that supports ODBC. Also, one application can connect to multiple databases simultaneously if necessary, and the application program can dynamically establish the database to connect to at run time.

Open database API: JDBC

The JDBC database connection (JDBC unofficially stands for Java database connectivity) operates in a very similar way to the ODBC connection, but for Java programs. In a JDBC connection, the level of indirection is firstly provided by the set of classes and interfaces that is included within the java.sql package. A Java program uses these classes and interfaces to establish database-independent connections and access. In turn, a specific JDBC package is dynamically loaded to interact with a specific database. This is shown in figure 11.8.

Figure 11.8: JDBC architecture

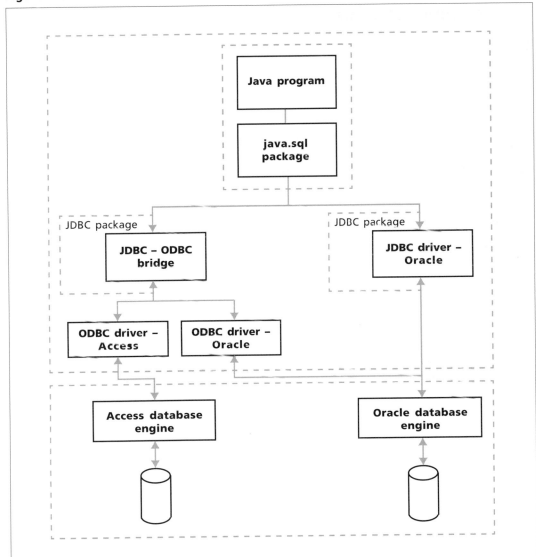

The diagram in figure 11.8 shows, on the left-hand side, a JDBC package that uses a JDBC-ODBC bridge for the connection. The bridge then uses appropriate ODBC drivers to connect to Access and Oracle databases respectively. On the right-hand side of the diagram, the JDBC package supports a direct connection to an Oracle database. Again, the database vendors, or third parties, supply the JDBC packages (the JDBC drivers). The JDBC-ODBC bridge approach makes use of the many existing drivers available with ODBC, and ensures wide Java connectivity to many types of databases.

11.8 Summary

After reading this chapter, students will understand some concepts relating to connecting a database to the World Wide Web. The 3-tier architecture and layers within the 3 tiers, which form the building blocks for connecting a database to the web, were described. A variety of methods for extending client-side functionality, for creating the application logic layer and for connecting to the database were described.

11.9 Review questions

 Review question 11.1 What are the major features of a web-based client/server application?

 Review question 11.2 What is meant by web database connectivity?

 Review question 11.3 What is a dynamic web page?

 Review question 11.4 What are the three general approaches to server-side processing?

 Review question 11.5 Many programming languages can be used to code a CGI program. Identify some of the languages that could be used.

 Review question 11.6 How can a 3-tier client/server architecture be used to implement a web database application?

 Review question 11.7 The 3-tier architecture consists of five layers. What are they? Briefly discuss the function of each.

 Review question 11.8 Name four ways that a browser can be extended to implement client-side processing.

Review question 11.9 Explain the role of an application server and list the main activities conducted within the application logic layer.

Review question 11.10 There are many ways in which the application logic layer can be coded, and this will depend on what best fits the target organisation. Give five examples of scripting languages that can be used.

 Review question 11.11 What is the fundamental difference between an ASP and an HTML file?

Review question 11.12 The following code has been saved as an active service page (ASP) file, which is to be used to access a database from a web page.

```
01      <html>
02      <body>

03      <%
04      set conn=Server.CreateObject("ADODB.Connection")
05
06      conn.Open "Customerdatabase"
07      set recset = Server.CreateObject("ADODB.recordset")
08      sql="SELECT CustomerNumber, Balance FROM
        Customer WHERE    CustomerName = 'Smith'"
09      recset.Open sql, conn
10      %>

11      <table border="1" width="100%">
12      <tr>
13      <%for each x in recset.Fields
14         response.write("<th>" & x.name & "</th>")
15      next%>
16      </tr>
17      <%do until recset.EOF%>
18         <tr>
19         <%for each x in recset.Fields%>
20            <td><%Response.Write(x.value)%></td>
21      <%next
22      recset.MoveNext%>
23            </tr>
24         <%loop
25         recset.close
26   conn.close
27   %>
28   </table>

29   </body>
30   </html>
```

The code consists of a number of components. Identify these components and explain what they are used for.

 Review question 11.13 Identify ways in which Coldfusion, ASP and JSP can connect to databases.

11.10 Answers to review questions

Answer to review question 11.1

- **Platform independence:** web clients are platform-independent and do not require modification to be run on different operating systems

- **Interpreted applications:** web applications are written in interpreted languages (e.g. HTML and Java). This has an adverse effect on performance

- **No need for installation:** it is pretty safe to assume that the clients already have a web browser installed, which is the only piece of software needed for the clients to run the applications

- **Simple client:** as a client needs just a browser to run a web-based database application, the potential complications are minimised

- **Common interface across applications:** again, because there is no need for specialised software, users have the benefit of using a browser for possibly different applications

- **Limited GUI (graphical user interface):** highly customised application interfaces and highly interactive clients may not translate well as web applications. This is because of the HTML limitations

- **Integrate with other applications:** because of the benefit of being platform-independent, different applications that adhere to the HTML standard can be integrated without many difficulties

- **Multimedia support:** HTML already provides easy-to-use constructs to present and manipulate multimedia contents

- **Non-persistent connection to database:** a web-based client maintains its connection to a database only as long as is necessary to retrieve the required data and then releases it.

Answer to review question 11.2 Web database connectivity is the connection between a client machine and a remote database via the World Wide Web. Such a connection allows a web browser user to connect to a remote database, to both access and update the database content.

Answer to review question 11.3 A dynamic web page is one whose contents are generated each time it is accessed. As a result, a dynamic web page can respond to user input from the browser by, for example, returning data requested by the completion of a form, or returning the result of a database query. A dynamic page can also be customised by, and for, each user. Once a user has specified some preferences when accessing a particular site or page, the information can be recorded, and appropriate responses can be generated according to those preferences.

Answer to review question 11.4

- Common Gateway Interface program (CGI program)

- Java Servlets

- HTML 'template' approach.

Answer to review question 11.5 CGI programs can be written in a number of languages, including C, Java and almost all the major compiled programming languages, though very often they are written in the Perl scripting language, hence the name CGI script.

Answer to review question 11.6 In the 3-tier client/server architecture, the first tier is the client which contains user interfaces. In a web-based system the client machine typically runs a web browser. The second tier is the application server that provides application logic and data processing functions. In a web-based system the application server runs the web server, which is a software component rather than a hardware one. The third tier contains the actual DBMS, which may run on a separate server called a database server.

Answer to review question 11.7 A web database application should comprise the following five layers:

1. **Browser layer:** the browser is the client of a web database application, and it has two major functions. First, it handles the layout and display of HTML documents. Second, it executes the client-side extension functionality such as Java, JavaScript, and ActiveX (a method to extend a browser's capabilities).

2. **Web server layer:** this is the software component. It is responsible for receiving client requests via the http protocol, for initiating appropriate action for each request, and for passing the end results back to the client.

3. **Application logic layer:** most of the application's business rules and functionality will reside in this layer. The browser client displays data as well as forms for user input, whereas the application logic component compiles the data to be displayed and processes user input as required. In other words, the application logic generates HTML that the browser renders. Also, it receives, processes, and stores user input that the browser sends.

4. **Database connection layer:** the database connection layer provides a link between the application logic layer and the DBMS.

5. **Database layer:** this is the place where the underlying database resides within the web database application.

Answer to review question 11.8 Client-side scripting, in either JavaScript or VBScript; plug-ins (on Netscape of IE); ActiveX controls (IE only); Java applets.

Answer to review question 11.9 An application server is a machine which is placed between the database server and client machines, in a client/server environment. It is used to provide a centralised point for the processing of application or business logic. It is used to relieve the load on the client and database server machines, enabling them to be used solely for interfacing, and data-intensive tasks respectively. Main activities:

- Receiving and validating the input from the user request

- Collecting data for a query (e.g. an SQL statement)

- Preparing and sending the query to the database via the database connection layer

- Retrieving the results from the connection layer
- Formatting the data for display; most commonly in the shape of an HTML file, and passing the data for display back to the web server layer.

Answer to review question 11.10

- CGI script (e.g. Perl)
- Active Server Pages (Microsoft)
- Java Server Pages
- Java Servlet
- Coldfusion.

Answer to review question 11.11 The difference between an ASP and an HTML file:

- When a browser requests an HTML file, the server returns the file
- When a browser requests an ASP file, the web server passes the request to the ASP engine. The ASP engine reads the ASP file, line by line, and executes the scripts in the file. Finally, the ASP file is returned to the browser as plain HTML.

Answer to review question 11.12

- **HTML** – bold text – (Hypertext Markup Language; markup tags tell the web browser how to display the page – in this case in the form of a table)
- **Server-side VBScript** – lines 13-25 (not including bold) – Scripts in an ASP file are executed on the server. VBScript is a version of MS's programming language 'Visual Basic'. Server-side scripting is a language which can be used for dynamically editing, changing or adding any content to a web page. Also responds to user queries, or data submitted from HTML forms. Default scripting language for ASP
- **SQL (structured query language)** – included in ADO line 8 – SQL statements are used to retrieve and update data in a database
- **ADO (ActiveX data object)** – lines 4-9, lines 25-26 – programming interface to access data in a database; in this case assessed from within an active server page.

Answer to review question 11.13

Approach	DB connection
Coldfusion	Native database API, ODBC
Active Server Pages	Microsoft Active Data Objects (ADO),which typically connects to ODBC
Java Server Pages	JDBC (plus other Java approaches)

CHAPTER 12

Data warehousing

OVERVIEW

Rapid developments in information technology have resulted in the construction of many business application systems in numerous areas. Within these systems, databases often play an essential role. Data have become a critical resource in many organisations. Efficient access to data, sharing data, extracting information from data, and making use of the information stored, have become an urgent need. As a result, there have been many efforts to integrate the various data sources (e.g. databases) scattered across different sites, and to build a corporate data warehouse from which to extract information in the form of patterns and trends.

A **data warehouse** is very much like a database system, but there are certain distinctions between them. A data warehouse brings together the essential data from the underlying heterogeneous databases, so that a user only needs to make queries to the warehouse instead of accessing individual databases. The cooperation of several processing modules to process a complex query is hidden from the user. Essentially, a data warehouse is built to provide decision support functions of an enterprise or organisation. For example, while the individual data sources may have the raw data, the data warehouse will have correlated data, summary reports, and aggregate functions applied to the raw data. Thus, the warehouse is able to provide useful information that cannot be obtained from any individual databases. The differences between the data warehousing system and operational databases are discussed later in the chapter.

We will also see what a data warehouse looks like – its architecture and other design aspects will be studied. Important issues include the role of **metadata**, as well as various access tools. Data warehouse development issues are discussed with an emphasis on **data transformation** and **data cleansing**. **Star schema**, a popular data modelling approach, is introduced.

Data mining is a process of extracting information and patterns, which are previously unknown, from large quantities of data using various techniques ranging from machine learning and statistical methods. Here we will introduce basic data mining concepts, look at some areas in which data mining is being used for strategic benefits and examine the combination of technologies used in data mining.

Learning outcomes On completion of this chapter, you should be able to:

- Appreciate the needs for developing a data warehouse for large corporations

- Distinguish between a data warehouse and an operational database system

- Understand the general architecture of a data warehouse system

- Describe user access tools for data warehousing

- Explain the importance of data mining.

12.1 Introduction

The term 'data warehousing' is now commonly used in industry. It refers to a kind of heterogeneous information system – one in which the focus is on gathering together the data from the different operational databases within an organisation, and making it available for decision-making purposes. This chapter explains the differences between the type of information one can obtain from a data warehouse compared with a traditional database. We look at the problems and steps involved in building a data warehouse, and examine some of the techniques that have been proposed for constructing them.

Data warehousing takes from, and builds on, the material we have covered in the design of relational systems. Data warehouses usually contain large amounts of aggregated data, and so pose a number of additional problems regarding design and performance tuning. In this chapter, we will cover new concepts required for the design of data warehouses, and consider how to develop a warehouse to support strategically or tactically oriented queries across very large sets of data.

12.2 General introduction to data warehousing

What is a data warehouse?

A data warehouse is an environment, not a product. The motivation for building a data warehouse is that corporate data is often scattered in different databases and possibly in different formats. In order to obtain a complete piece of information, it is necessary to access these heterogeneous databases, obtain bits and pieces of partial information from each, and then put them together to produce an overall picture. Attempting this process without a data warehouse is a cumbersome task, inefficient, ineffective, error-prone, and usually will involve huge efforts from system analysts. All these difficulties deter the effective use of complex corporate data, which usually represents a valuable resource within an organisation.

In order to overcome these problems, it is considered necessary to create an environment that can bring together the essential data from the underlying heterogeneous databases. In addition, the environment should also provide facilities for users to carry out queries on all the data, without worrying where it actually resides. Such an environment is called a data warehouse. All queries are issued to the data warehouse as if it is a single database, and the warehouse management system handles the evaluation of the queries. The different techniques used in data warehouses are aimed at effective integration of operational databases into an environment that enables strategic use of data. These techniques include: relational and multidimensional database management systems; client/server architecture; metadata modelling and repositories; graphical user interfaces and much more.

A data warehouse system has the following characteristics:

- It provides a centralised utility of corporate data or information assets
- It is contained in a well-managed environment
- It has consistent and repeatable processes defined for loading operational data
- It is built on an open and scalable architecture that will handle future expansion of data
- It provides tools that allow its users to effectively process the data into information, without a high degree of technical support.

Building data warehouses has become a rapidly expanding requirement for most information technology departments. The reason for growth in this area stems from many sources:

- **Progressive accumulation of data** – most companies now have access to more than 20 years of data on managing the operational aspects of their business
- **Improvements in technology** – the technology of user computing has reached a point where corporations can now effectively allow the users to navigate corporation databases without causing a heavy burden for technical support
- **Modern corporate management strategy** executives are realising that the only way to sustain and gain an advantage in today's economy is to better leverage information.

Operational systems vs data warehousing systems

Before we proceed to detailed discussions of data warehousing systems, it is beneficial to briefly overview, and note some of the major differences between operational and data warehousing systems.

Operational systems

Operational systems are those that assist a company or organisation in its day-to-day business to respond to events or transactions. As a result, operational system applications and their data are highly structured around the events they manage. These systems provide an immediate focus on business functions and typically run in an online transaction processing (OLTP) computing environment. The databases associated with these applications are required to support a large number of transactions on a daily basis. Typically, operational databases are required to work as fast as possible. Strategies for increasing performance include:

- Keeping these operational data stores small
- Focusing the database on a specific business area or application
- Eliminating database overheads in areas such as indexes.

Data warehousing systems

Most companies today usually have relatively sophisticated operational systems, and are now focusing on putting together information contained within these systems. The aim is to define what they have done right (and therefore should continue to do) as well as what they have done wrong (and should not be allowed to happen again). This data is being captured and stored in data warehouses.

Operational system applications and their data are highly structured around the events they manage. Data warehouse systems are organised around the trends or patterns in those events. Operational systems manage events and transactions in a similar fashion to manual systems utilised by clerks within a business. These systems are developed to deal with individual transactions according to the established business rules. Data warehouse systems focus on business needs and requirements. These needs are established by managers, who need to reflect on events, and develop ideas for changing the business rules to make these events more effective.

Operational systems and data warehouses provide separate data stores. The data store of a data warehouse is designed to support queries and applications for decision making. The separation of a data warehouse from operational systems serves multiple purposes:

- It minimises the impact of reporting and complex query processing on operational systems
- It preserves operational data for reuse after that data has been purged from operational systems
- It manages the data based on time, allowing the user to look back and see how the company looked in the past compared to the present
- It provides a data store that can be modified to conform to the way the users view the data
- It unifies the data within a common business definition, offering one version of reality.

A data warehouse assists a company in analysing its business over time. Users of data warehouse systems can analyse data to spot trends, determine problems, and compare business techniques in a historical context. The processing that these systems support includes complex queries, ad hoc reporting, and static reporting (such as the standard monthly reports that are distributed to managers). The data that is queried tends to be of historical significance, and provides its users with a time-based context of business processes.

Differences between operational and data warehousing systems

While a company can better manage its primary business with operational systems, through techniques that focus on cost reduction, data warehouse systems allow a company to identify opportunities for increasing revenues, and, therefore, for growing the business. From a business point of view, this is the primary way to differentiate these two mission-critical systems. However, there are many other key differences between these two types of systems:

- **Size and content:** the goals and objectives of a data warehouse differ greatly from an operational environment. While the goal of an operational database is to stay small, a data warehouse is expected to grow large in order to contain a good history of the business. The information required to assist us in better understanding our business can grow quite large over time, and we do not want to lose this data
- **Performance:** in an operational environment, speed is of the essence. However, in a data warehouse some requests – 'meaning-of-life' queries – can take hours to fulfil. This may be acceptable in a data warehouse environment, because the true goal is to provide better information, or 'business intelligence'. For these types of queries, users are typically given a personalised extract of the requested data. This is so they can further analyse and query the information package provided by the data warehouse

- **Content focus:** operational systems tend to focus on small work areas, not the entire enterprise; a data warehouse, on the other hand, focuses on cross-functional subject areas. For example, a data warehouse could help a business understand who its top twenty at-risk customers are – those who are about to drop its services – and what type of promotions will assist in not losing these customers. To fulfil this query request, the data warehouse needs data from the customer service application, the sales application, the order management application, the credit application, and the quality system

- **Tools:** typically, operational systems are structured, offering only a few ways to enter or access the data they manage, and lack a large amount of tools accessibility for users. With a data warehouse, various tools are available to support the different types of data requests. These tools provide many features that transform and present the data from a data warehouse as business intelligence. These features offer a high flexibility over the standard reporting tools that are offered within an operational systems environment.

Benefits of data warehousing systems

The successful implementation of a data warehouse can bring benefits to an organisation, including:

- Providing a single manageable structure for data used in decision making
- Enabling users of an organisation to run complete queries on data from a number of business areas
- Producing more timely data reports. With an operational system, monthly reports can take so long to create and distribute that they may be out of date with user requirements
- Allowing a number of business intelligence applications to be used. These include online analytical processing and data mining.

12.3 Data warehouse architecture

Data warehouses provide a means to make information available for decision making. An effective data warehousing strategy must deal with the complexities of modern enterprises. Data is generated everywhere, and controlled by different operational systems and data storage mechanisms. Users demand access to data anywhere and anytime, and data must be customised to their needs and requirements. The function of a data warehouse is to convert the current transactions from operational systems into data with a historical context required by the users of the data warehouse.

Overall architecture

The general data warehouse architecture is based on a relational database management system server that functions as the central repository for informational data. In the data warehouse architecture, operational data and processing is completely separate from data warehouse processing. This central information repository is surrounded by a number of key components, designed to make the entire environment functional, manageable and accessible, by both the operational systems that source data into the warehouse, and by end-user query and analysis tools. Figure 12.1 depicts such a general architecture.

Typically, the source data for the warehouse comes from the operational applications. As the data enters the data warehouse, it is transformed into an integrated structure and format. The transformation process may involve conversion, summarisation, filtering, and condensation of data. Because data within the data warehouse contains a large historical component (sometimes over five to ten years), the data warehouse must be capable of holding and managing large volumes of data, as well as different data structures for the same database over time.

Figure 12.1: A general data warehouse architecture

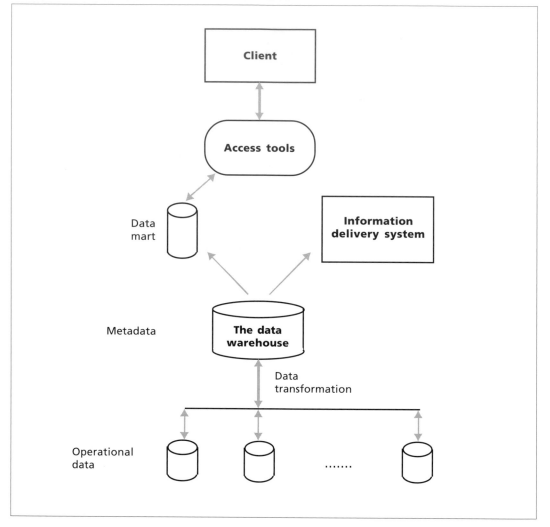

The data warehouse

The central data warehouse database is a cornerstone of the data warehousing environment. This type of database is mostly implemented using a relational DBMS (RDBMS). However, a warehouse implementation, based on traditional RDBMS technology, is often constrained by the fact that traditional RDBMS implementations are optimised for transactional database processing. Certain data warehouse attributes, such as very large database size, ad hoc query processing, and the need for flexible user-view creation including aggregates, multi-table joins, and drill-downs, have become the motivation for different technological approaches to the data warehouse database.

Data transformation

A significant portion of the data warehouse implementation effort is spent extracting data from operational systems, and putting it in a format suitable for information applications that will run off the data warehouse. The data sourcing, clean-up, transformation, and migration tools perform all of the conversions, summarisation, key changes, structural changes, and condensations needed to transform disparate data into information that can be used by the decision support tool. It also maintains the metadata. The functionality of data transformation includes:

- Removing unwanted data from operational databases
- Converting to common data names and definitions
- Calculating summaries and derived data
- Establishing defaults for missing data
- Accommodating source data definition changes.

Metadata

A crucial area of data warehouse is metadata, which is a kind of data that describes the data warehouse itself. Within a data warehouse, metadata describes and locates data components, their origins (which may be either the operational systems or the data warehouse), and their movement through the data warehouse process. The data access, data stores, and processing information will have associated descriptions about the data and processing – the inputs, calculations, and outputs – documented in the metadata. This metadata should be captured within the data architecture, and managed from the beginning of a data warehouse project. The metadata repository should contain information such as:

- Description of the data model
- Description of the layouts used in the database design
- Definition of the primary system managing the data items
- A map of the data, from the system of record to the other locations in the data warehouse, including the descriptions of transformations and aggregations
- Specific database design definitions
- Data element definitions, including rules for derivations and summaries.

It is through metadata that a data warehouse becomes an effective tool for an overall enterprise. This repository of information will tell the story of the data: where it originated, how it has been transformed, where it went, and how often. One important functional component of the metadata repository is the information directory. The content of the information directory is the metadata that helps users exploit the power of data warehousing. This directory helps integrate, maintain, and view the contents of the data warehousing system. From a technical requirement point of view, the information directory and the entire metadata repository should:

- Be a gateway to the data warehouse environment, and, therefore, should be accessible from any platform via transparent and seamless connections
- Support an easy distribution and replication of its content for high performance and availability
- Be searchable by business-oriented keywords
- Act as a launch platform for end-user data access and analysis tools
- Support the sharing of information objects such as queries, reports, data collections, and subscriptions between users

- Support a variety of scheduling options for requests against the data warehouse, including on-demand, one-time, repetitive, event-driven, and conditional delivery (in conjunction with the information delivery system)
- Support the distribution of query results to one or more destinations in any of the user-specified formats (in conjunction with the information delivery system)
- Support and provide interfaces to other applications, such as email, spreadsheet, and schedules
- Support end-user monitoring of the status of the data warehouse environment.

At a minimum, the information directory components should be accessible by any web browser, and should run on all major platforms, including MS Windows, Windows NT, and UNIX. Also, the data structures of the metadata repository should be supported on all major relational database platforms. These requirements define a very sophisticated repository of metadata information. In reality, however, existing products vary in the extent to which these requirements are implemented.

Access tools

The principal purpose of data warehousing is to provide information to business users for strategic decision making. These users interact with the data warehouse using front-end tools. Although ad hoc requests, regular reports, and custom applications are the primary delivery vehicles for the analysis done in most data warehouses, many development efforts of data warehousing projects are focusing on exceptional reporting also known as alerts. These alert a user when a certain event has occurred. For example, if a data warehouse is designed to assess the risk of currency trading, an alert can be activated when a certain currency rate drops below a predefined threshold. When an alert is well synchronised with the key objectives of the business, it can provide warehouse users with a tremendous advantage. The front-end user tools can be divided into five major groups:

- Data query and reporting tools
- Application development tools
- Executive information systems (EIS) tools
- Online analytical processing (OLAP) tools
- Data mining tools.

Query and reporting tools

This category can be further divided into two groups:

- **Reporting tools** – these comprise production reporting tools and desktop report writers. Production reporting tools will let companies generate regular operational reports, or support high-volume batch jobs, such as calculating and printing pay cheques. Report writers, on the other hand, are affordable desktop tools designed for end-users
- **Managed query tools** – shield end-users from the complexities of SQL and database structures, by inserting a metalayer between users and the database. The metalayer is the software that provides subject-oriented views of a database, and supports point-and-click creation of SQL. Some of these tools proceed to format the retrieved data into easy-to-read reports, while others concentrate on on-screen presentations. These tools are the preferred choice of the users of business applications such as segment identification, demographic analysis, territory management, and customer mailing lists. As the question complexity grows, these tools may rapidly become inefficient.

Application development tools

Often, the analytical needs of the data warehouse user community exceed the built-in capabilities of query and reporting tools. Organisations will mostly rely on a true and proven approach of in-house application development, using graphical data access environments designed primarily for client/server systems. Some of these application development platforms integrate well with popular OLAP tools, and can access all major database systems, including Oracle, Sybase, and Informix.

Executive information systems (EIS) tools

EIS tools tend to give their users a high-level summarisation of key performance measures to support decision making. The target users, therefore, are the senior management of a company. The tools are used to transform information, and present it to users in a meaningful and usable manner. They support advanced analytical techniques and free-form data exploration, allowing users to easily transform data into information.

OLAP (online analytical processing)

These tools are based on the concepts of multidimensional database, and allow a sophisticated user to analyse the data using elaborate, multidimensional, and complex views. Typical business applications for these tools include:

- Product performance and profitability
- Effectiveness of a sales programme or a marketing campaign
- Sales forecasting
- Capacity planning.

These tools assume that the data is organised in a multidimensional model, which is supported by a special multidimensional database, or by a relational database designed to enable multidimensional properties.

Data mining tools

Data mining can be defined as: the process of discovering meaningful new correlations, patterns, and trends, by digging (mining) large amounts of data stored in the warehouse, using artificial intelligence (AI) and/or statistical/mathematical techniques. The major attraction of data mining is its ability to build predictive rather than retrospective models. Using data mining to build predictive models for decision making has several benefits:

- The model should be able to explain why a particular decision was made
- Adjusting a model on the basis of feedback from future decisions will lead to experience accumulation, and true organisational learning
- A predictive model can be used to automate a decision step in a larger process. For example, using a model to instantly predict whether a customer will default on credit card payments will allow automatic adjustment of credit limits, rather than depending on expensive staff making inconsistent decisions.

12.4 Data warehouse development

Data warehouse blueprint

The data warehouse blueprint should include clear documentation of the following items:

- **Requirements** – what does the business want from the data warehouse?
- **Architecture blueprint** – how will you deliver what the business wants?
- **Development approach** – what is a clear definition of phased delivery cycles, including architectural review and refinement processes?

The blueprint document essentially translates an enterprise's mission, goals and objectives for the data warehouse, into a logical technology architecture. This is composed of individual sub-architectures for the application, data and technology components of a data warehouse, as shown in figure 12.2.

Figure 12.2: Areas of an architecture blueprint

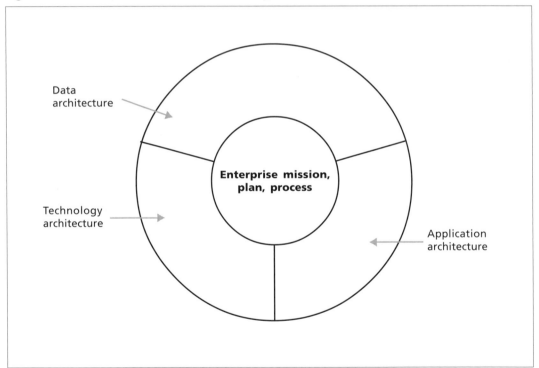

An architecture blueprint is important, because it serves as a road map for all development work and as a guide for integrating the data warehouse with legacy systems. When the blueprint is understood by the development staff, decisions become much easier. The blueprint should be developed in a logical sense rather than in a physical sense. With reference to the database components, for example, you will state things like 'the data store for the data warehouse will support an easy-to-use data manipulation language that is standard in the industry, such as SQL'. This is a logical architecture-product requirement. When you implement the data warehouse, this could be Sybase SQL Server or Oracle. The logical definition allows your implementations to grow as technology evolves. If your business requirements do not change in the next three to five years, neither will your blueprint.

Data architecture

As shown in figure 12.1, a data warehouse is presented as a network of databases. The sub-components of the data architecture will include the enterprise data warehouse, metadata repository, data marts, and multidimensional data stores. These sub-components are documented separately, because the architecture should present a logical view of them. It is for the data warehouse implementation team to determine the proper way to physically implement the recommended architecture. This suggests that the implementation may well be on the same physical database rather than separate data stores (see figure 12.1).

Transformation

A data architecture needs to provide a clear understanding of the transformation requirements that must be supported, including logic and complexity. This is one area in which the architectural team will have difficulty finding commercially available software to manage or assist with the process. Transformation tools and standards are currently immature. Many tools were initially developed to assist companies in moving applications away from mainframes. Operational data stores are vast and varied. Many data stores are unsupported by these transformation tools, and writing tools support the popular database engines.

Data cleansing

In addition to finding tools to automate the transformation process, the developers should also evaluate the complexity behind data transformations. Most legacy data stores lack standards and have anomalies that can cause enormous difficulties. Again, tools are evolving to assist in automating transformations.

Data architecture requirements

As a summary of the data architecture design, this section lists the main requirements placed on a data warehouse:

- **Subject-oriented data** – data that is contained within a data warehouse should be organised by subject. For example, if your data warehouse focuses on sales and marketing processes, you need to generate data about customers, prospects, orders, products, and so on. To completely define a subject area, you may need to draw upon data from multiple operational systems. To derive the data entities that clearly define the sales and marketing process of an enterprise, you might need to draw upon an order entry system, a sales force automation system, and various other applications

- **Time-based data** – data in a data warehouse should relate to a specific time span, allowing users to capture data that is relevant to their analysis period. Consider an example in which a new customer was added to an order entry system with a primary contact of Jo Bloggs on 2/11/05. This customer's data was changed on 4/11/05 to reflect a new primary contact of Jane Bloggs. In this scenario, the data warehouse would contain the two contact records shown in the following table:

Cust_ID	Contact_ID	Last_Name	First_Name	Time_Stamp
1999120601	01	Bloggs	Jo	2/11/05
1999120601	01	Bloggs	Jane	4/11/05

- **Update processing** – a data warehouse should contain data that represents closed operational items, such as fulfilled customer orders. In this sense, the data warehouse will usually contain little or no update processing. Typically, incremental or mass loading processes are run to insert data into the data warehouse. Updating individual records that are already in the data warehouse will rarely occur
- **Transformed and scrubbed data** – data that are contained in a data warehouse should be transformed, scrubbed, and integrated into user-friendly subject areas
- **Aggregation** – data needs to be aggregated into and out of a data warehouse. Thus, computational requirements will be placed on the entire data warehousing process
- **Granularity** – a data warehouse typically contains multiple levels of granularity. It is normal for the data in the warehouse to be summarised and contain less detail than the original operational data; however, some data warehouses require dual levels of granularity. For example, a sales manager may need to understand how sales representatives in their area perform a forecasting task. In this example, monthly summaries that contain the data associated with the sales representatives' forecast, and the actual orders received are sufficient; there is no requirement to see each individual line item of an order. However, a retailer may need to wade through individual sales transactions to look for a correlation which may show that people tend to buy soft drinks and snacks together. This need requires more details associated with each of the individual purchases. The data required to fulfil both of these requests may exist, and therefore the data warehouse might be built to manage both summarised data to fulfil a very rapid query, and the more detailed data required to fulfil a lengthy analysis process
- **Metadata management** – because a data warehouse pools information from a variety of sources, and the data warehouse developers will perform data gathering on both current and new data stores, it is required that storage and management of metadata be effectively done through the data warehouse process.

Application architecture

An application architecture determines how users interact with a data warehouse. To determine the most appropriate application architecture for a company, the intended users and their skill levels should be assessed. Other factors that may affect the design of the architecture include the technology currently available, and budget constraints. In any case, the architecture must be defined logically rather than physically.

Technology architecture

It is in the technology architecture section of the blueprint that hardware, software, and network topology are specified to support the implementation of the data warehouse. This architecture is composed of three major components – clients, servers and networks – and the software to manage each of them:

- **Clients** – the client technology component comprises the devices that are utilised by users. These devices can include workstations, personal computers, personal digital assistants, and even beepers for support personnel. Each of these devices has a purpose in being served by a data warehouse
- **Servers** – the server technology component includes the physical hardware platforms, as well as the operating systems that manage the hardware. Other components, typically software, can also be grouped within this component, including database management software, application server software, gateway connectivity software, replication software, and configuration management software

- **Networks** – the network component defines the transport technologies needed to support communication activities between clients and servers. This component includes requirements and decisions for wide area networks (WANs), local area networks (LANs), communication protocols, and other hardware associated with networks, such as bridges, routers, and gateways.

12.5 Star schema design

Data warehouses can best be modelled using a technique known as star schema modelling. It defines data entities in a way that supports the view of the decision maker in a business, as well as data entities that reflect the important operational aspects of the business. A star schema contains three logical entities: dimension, measure and category detail (or category for short).

A star schema (figure 12.3) is optimised to queries, and therefore provides a database design that is focused on rapid response to users of the system. Also, the design that is built from a star schema is not as complicated as traditional database designs. Hence, the model will be more understandable to users of the system. Also, users will be better able to understand the navigation paths available to them through interpreting the star schema.

The star schema defines the join paths for how users access the facts about their business. In figure 12.3, for example, the centre of the star could represent product sales revenues that could have the following items: actual sales, budget, and sales forecast. The true power of a star schema design is to model a data structure that allows filtering, or reduction in result size, of the massive measure entities during user queries and searches. A star schema also provides a usable and understandable data structure, because the points of the star, or dimension entities, provide a mechanism by which a user can filter, aggregate, drill down, and slice and dice the measurement data in the centre of the star.

Figure 12.3: Star schema design

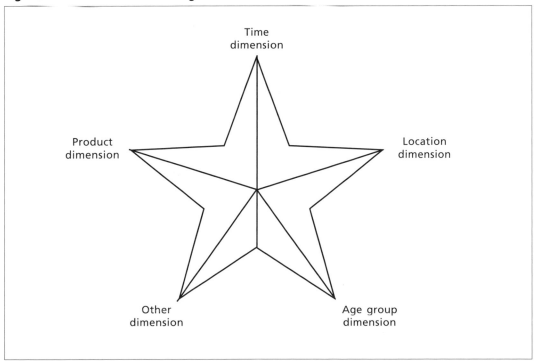

Entities within a data warehouse

A star schema, like the data warehouse it models, contains three types of logical entities: measure, dimension, and category detail. It is a logical structure which has one measure entity at the centre containing factual data, and this is surrounded by dimension entities containing reference data. We will now look at each of these entities.

Measure entities

Within a star schema, the centre of the star – and often the focus of the users' query activity – is the measure entity (or fact table). A measure entity is represented by a rectangle and is placed in the centre of a star schema diagram (not shown in figure 12.3).

A sample of raw measure data is shown in figure 12.4. The data contained in a measure entity is factual information from which users derive 'business intelligence'. The measurement data provides users with quantitative data about a business. This data is numerical information that the users wish to monitor, such as pounds, degrees, counts and quantities. The data contained within measure entities grows large over time, and therefore is typically of greatest concern to the technical support personnel, database administrators and system administrators.

Figure 12.4: Measure entity data

Month	Branch	Product	Sales forecast	Sales actual	Variance
199901	ABC	COLA	200000	1900000	−10000
199901	XYZ	COLA	150000	1550000	50000
199901	PQR	COLA	125000	1050000	−20000
....					......

Dimension entities

Dimension entities are graphically represented by diamond-shaped squares, and placed at the points of the star. Dimension entities are much smaller entities than measure entities. The dimensions and their associated data allow users of a data warehouse to browse measurement data with ease of use and familiarity. These entities assist users in minimising the rows of data within a measure entity, and in aggregating key measurement data. In this sense, these entities filter data, or force the server to aggregate data, so that fewer rows are returned from the measure entities. With a star schema model, the dimension entities are represented as the points of the star, as demonstrated in figure 12.3, by the time, location, age group, product and other dimensions. Figure 12.5 illustrates an example of dimension data, and a hierarchy representing the contents of a dimension entity.

Figure 12.5: Dimension entity data

Country key	Area key	Region key	District key	Country	Area	Region	District
USA	EAST	CEN	NC	USA	Eastern	Central	N-Central
USA	EAST	CEN	SC	USA	Eastern	Central	S-Central
USA	EAST	NE					
USA	WEST	SE					
CANADA							
FRANCE							
GERMANY							

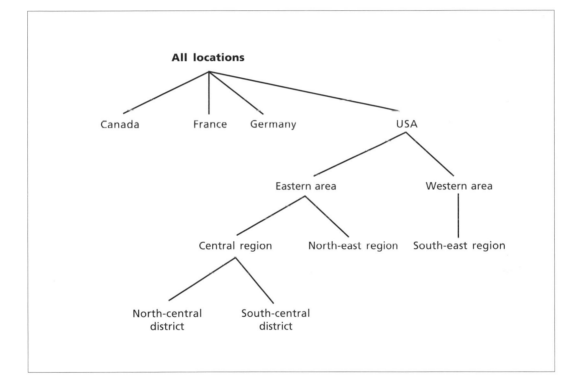

Category detail entities

Each element in a dimension is a category, and represents an isolated level within a dimension that might require more detailed information to fulfil a user's requirement. These categories that require more detailed data are managed within category detail entities. These entities have textual information that supports the measurement data and provides more detailed or qualitative information to assist in the decision-making process. Figure 12.6 illustrates the need for a client category detail entity within the 'All clients' dimension. Category entities are represented on other diagrams as an octagonal shape.

Figure 12.6: Category detail entity data

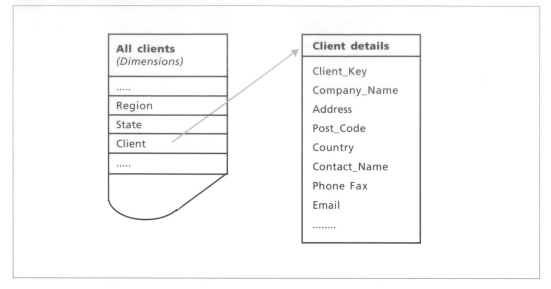

Translating information into a star schema

During the data-gathering process, an information package can be constructed, based on which a star schema is formed. Figure 12.7 shows an information package diagram ready for translation into a star schema. As can be seen from the diagram, there are six dimensions, and within each there are different numbers of categories. For example, the 'All locations' dimension has five categories while 'All genders' has one. The number within each category denotes the number of instances the category may have. For example, the 'All time periods' will cover five different years with twenty quarters and sixty months. Gender will include male, female, and unknown.

Figure 12.7: Information package diagram ready for translation into star schema

All time periods	All locations	All products	All age groups	All economy classes	All genders
Year 5	Country 20	Classifi-cation 8	Age group 8	Class 10	Gender 3
Quarter 20	Area 80	Group 40			
Month 60	Region 400	Product 200			
	District 2000				
	Store 200000				

Dimensions →

Categories ↓

Measures/facts:
Forecast sales, budget sales, actual sales, forecast variance (calc.), budget variance (calc.)

To define the logical measure entity, take the lowest category, or cell, within each dimension (the shaded cells in figure 12.7) along with each of the measures, and take them as the measure entity. For example, the measure entity translated from figure 12.7 would be Month, Store, Product, Age Group, Class, and Gender with the measures Forecast Sales, Budget Sales, Actual Sales, Forecast Variance (calculated), and Budget Variance (calculated). They could be given a name 'Sales Analysis' and put in the centre of the star schema in a rectangle. Each column of an information package in figure 12.7 defines a dimension entity, and is placed on the periphery of the star of a star schema, symbolising the points of the star (figure 12.8). Following the placement of the dimension entities, you want to define the relationships that they have to the measure entity. Because dimension entities always require representation within the measure entity, there is always a relationship.

Figure 12.8: Star schema relationships between dimension and measure entities

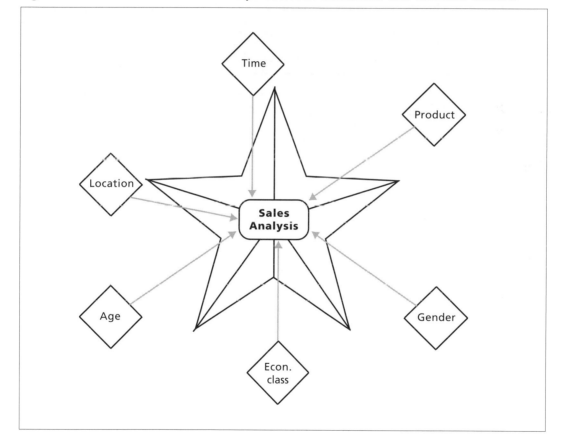

The relationship is defined over the lowest-level detail category for the logical model; that is the last cell in each dimension. These relationships possess typically one-to-many cardinality; in other words, one dimension entity exists for many within the measures. For example, you may hope to make many product sales (Sales Analysis) to females (Gender) within the star model illustrated in figure 12.8. In general, these relationships can be given an intuitive explanation such as: 'Measures based on the dimension'. In figure 12.8, for example, the relationship between Location (the dimension entity) and Sales Analysis (the measure entity) means 'Sales Analysis based on Location'.

The final step in forming a star schema is to define the category detail entity. Each individual cell in an information package diagram must be evaluated and researched to determine if it qualifies as a category detail entity. If the user has a requirement for additional information about a category, this formulates the requirement for a category detail entity. These detail entities become extensions of dimension entities as illustrated in figure 12.9. We need to know more detailed information about data such as Store, Product, and customer categories (i.e. Age, Class and Gender). These detail entities (Store detail, Product detail and Customer detail), having been added to the current star schema, now appear as shown in figure 12.10.

Figure 12.9: Category detail entity translation

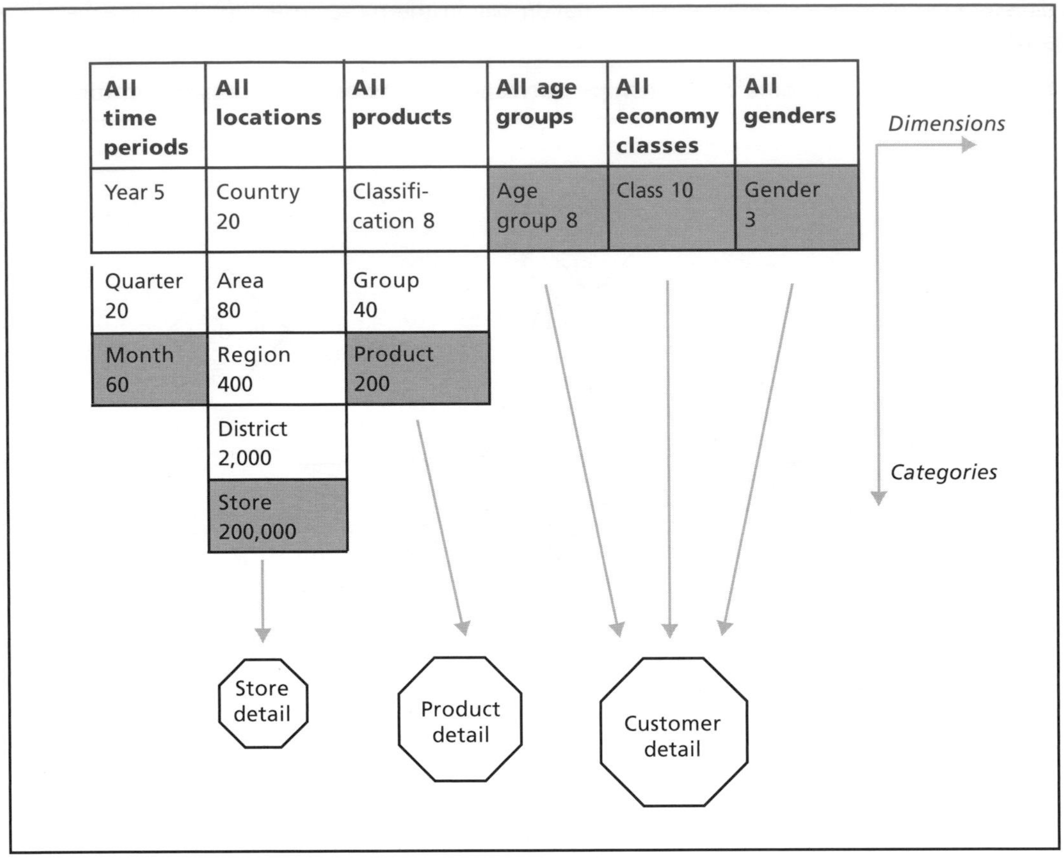

Figure 12.10:   Extended star schema

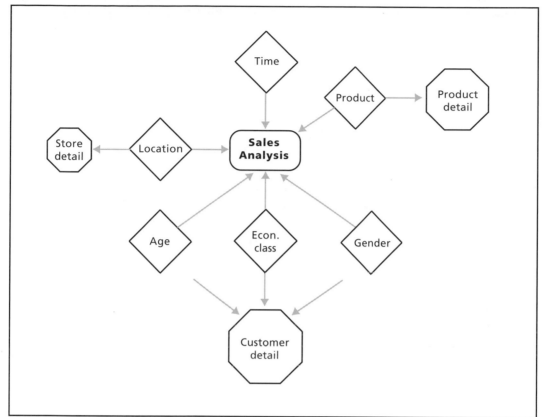

12.6 Data extraction, cleansing and loading

The construction of a data warehouse begins with careful considerations on architecture and data model issues, and with their sizing components. It is essential that a correct architecture is firmly in place that supports the activities of a data warehouse. Having solved the architecture issue and built the data model, the developers of the data warehouse can decide what data they want to access, in which form, and how it will flow through an organisation. This phase of a data warehouse project will actually fill the warehouse with goods (data). This is where data is extracted from its current environment and transformed into the user-friendly data model managed by the data warehouse. Remember, this is a phase that is all about quality. A data warehouse is only as good as the data it manages.

Extraction specifications

The data extraction part of a data warehouse is a traditional design process. There is an obvious data flow, with inputs being the operational systems and output being the data warehouse. However, the key to the extraction process is how to cleanse the data and transform it into usable information that the user can access and make into business intelligence. Thus, techniques such as data flow diagrams may be beneficial to defining extraction specifications for the development. An important input to such a specification may be the useful reports that you collected during user interviews. In these kinds of reports, intended users often tell you what they want and what they do not, and then you can act accordingly.

Loading data

Data needs to be processed for extraction and loading. An SQL select statement shown below is normally used in the process:

select	Target Column List
from	Source Table List
where	Join & Filter List
group by	
or **order by**	Sort & Aggregate List

Multiple passes of data

Some complex extractions need to pull data from multiple systems, and merge the resultant data while performing calculations and transformations for placement into a data warehouse. For example, the sales analysis example mentioned in the star schema modelling section might be such a process. We may obtain budget sales information from a budgetary system, which is different from the order entry system where we get actual sales data, and this in turn is different from the forecast management system from which we get forecast sales data. In this scenario, we would need to access three separate systems to fill one row within the Sales Analysis measure table.

Staging area

Creating and defining a staging area can help the cleansing process. This is a simple concept that allows the developer to maximise up-time of a data warehouse while extracting and cleansing the data. A staging area, which is simply a temporary work area, can be used to manage transactions that will be further processed to develop data warehouse transactions.

Checkpoint restart logic

The concept of checkpoint restart has been around for many years. It was originated in batch processing on mainframe computers. This type of logic states that if there is a long-running process that fails prior to completion, then restart the process at the point of failure rather than from the beginning. Similar logic should be implemented in the extraction and cleansing process. Within the staging area, define the necessary structures to monitor the activities of transformation procedures. Each of these programming units has an input variable that determines where in the process it should begin. Thus, if a failure occurs within the seventh procedure of an extraction process that has ten steps, assuming the right rollback logic is in place, it would only require that the last four steps (seven through to ten) be conducted.

Data loading

After data has been extracted, it is ready to be loaded into a data warehouse. In the data loading process, cleansed and transformed data that now complies with the warehouse standards is moved into the appropriate data warehouse entities. Data may be summarised and reformatted as part of this process, depending on the extraction and cleansing specifications and the performance requirements of the data warehouse. After the data has been loaded, data inventory information is updated within the metadata repository to reflect the activity that has just been completed.

Star schema design

An information package of a promotional analysis is shown below. To evaluate the effectiveness of various promotions, brand managers are interested in analysing data for the products represented, the promotional offers, and the locations where the promotions ran. Construct a star schema based on the information package diagram, and discuss how the brand manager or other analysts can use the model to evaluate the promotions.

All time periods	All products	All locations	All promotions
Years	Category	Region	Type
Quarters	Subcategory	District	Subtype
Months	Brand	Store	Name
	Package size		

Measures/facts: units, revenue, cost, margin (calculated).

Data warehousing

Based on your experience (the areas you are familiar with), give a number of examples to illustrate how businesses may benefit from applying data warehousing and data mining techniques.

12.7 Data mining

Data warehousing has been the subject of discussion so far. A data warehouse assembles data from various databases so that users need only query a single system. The response to a user's query depends on the contents of the data warehouse. In general, the warehouse system will answer the query as it is and will not attempt to extract further/implicit information from the data. While a data warehousing system formats data and organises data to support management functions, data mining attempts to extract useful information as well as predict trends and patterns from the data.

It should be noted that a data warehouse is not exclusive for data mining; data mining can be carried out in traditional databases as well. However, because a data warehouse contains quality data, it is highly desirable to have data mining functions incorporated in the data warehouse system. In general, a data warehouse comes up with query optimisation and access techniques to retrieve an answer to a query – the answer is explicitly in the warehouse. Some data warehouse systems have built-in decision-support capabilities. They do carry out some of the data mining functions like predictions. For example, consider a query like 'How many BMWs were sold in London in 2004?'. The answer can clearly be in the data warehouse. However, for a question like 'How many BMWs do you think will be sold in London in 2010?', the answer may not explicitly be in the data warehouse. Using certain data mining techniques, the selling patterns of BMWs in London can be discovered, and then the question can be answered. Essentially, a data warehouse organises data effectively so that the data can be mined. As shown in figure 12.11, however, a good DBMS that manages data effectively could also be used as a mining source.

Figure 12.11: Databases, data warehousing and data mining

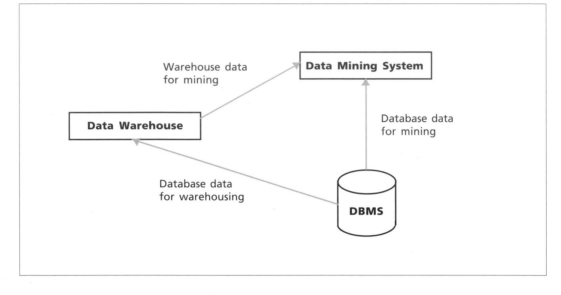

Data mining concepts

Data mining can be defined as a process of extracting previously unknown, valid and actionable information from large sets of data and then using the information to make crucial business decisions. The key words in the above definition are **unknown, valid and actionable**.

Firstly, **the information discovered must have been previously unknown**. That is, the data miner is looking for something that is not intuitive. The further away the information is from being obvious, potentially the more value it has. A classical example here is the anecdotal story of the beer and nappies. Apparently a large supermarket used data mining to analyse customer purchasing patterns and discovered that there was a strong association between the sales of nappies and beer, particularly on Friday evenings. It appeared that male shoppers who stocked up on baby requisites for the weekend decided to include some of their own shopping requirements at the same time. If true, this shopping pattern is so counter-intuitive that the supermarket's competitors probably do not know about it, and the management could profitably exploit it.

Secondly, **the new information must be valid**. This element of the definition relates to the problem of over-optimism in data mining; that is, if data miners look hard enough in a large collection of data, they are bound to find something of interest sooner or later. For example, the potential number of associations between items in customers' shopping baskets rises exponentially with the number of items. Some supermarkets have in stock up to 300,000 items at all times, so the chances of getting false associations are quite high. The possibility of spurious results applies to all data mining and highlights the constant need for post-mining validation and sanity checking.

Thirdly, and most critically, **the new information must be actionable**. That is, it must be possible to translate it into some business advantage. In the case of the retail store manager, clearly he could leverage the results of the analysis by placing the beer and nappies closer together in the store or by ensuring that two items were on sale at the same time. In many cases, however, the actionable criterion is not so simple. For example, mining of historical data may indicate a potential opportunity that a competitor has already seized. Equally, exploiting the apparent opportunity may require use of data that is not available or not legally usable.

Benefits of data mining

Various applications may need data mining, but many of the problems have existed for years.

Furthermore, data has been around for centuries. Why is it that we are talking about data mining now?

The answer to this is that we are using new tools and techniques to solve problems in a new way. We have large quantities of data computerised. The data could be in files, relational databases, multimedia databases, and even on the World Wide Web. We have very sophisticated statistical analysis packages. Tools have been developed for machine learning. Parallel computing technology is now established for improving performance. Visualisation techniques improve the understanding of the data. Decision support tools are also getting mature. Here are a few areas in which data mining is being used for strategic benefits:

- **Direct marketing** – the ability to predict who is most likely to be interested in what products can save companies immense amounts in marketing expenditures. Direct mail marketers employ various data mining techniques to reduce expenditures; reaching fewer, better qualified potential customers can be much more cost-effective than mailing to your entire mailing list

- **Trend analysis** – understanding trends in the marketplace is a strategic advantage, because it is useful in reducing costs and timeliness to market. Financial institutions desire a quick way to recognise changes in customer deposit and withdraw patterns. Retailers want to know what product people are likely to buy with others (market basket analysis). Pharmaceuticals ask why someone buys their product over another. Researchers want to understand patterns in natural processes

- **Fraud detection** – data mining techniques can help discover which insurance claims, mobile phone calls, or credit card purchases are likely to be fraudulent. Most credit card issuers use data mining software to model credit fraud. The Inland Revenue, MasterCard, and Visa are a few of the organisations who have been mentioned as users of such data mining technology. Banks are among the earliest adopters of data mining

- **Forecasting in financial markets** – data mining techniques are extensively used to help model financial markets. The idea is simple: if some trends can be discovered from historical financial data, then it is possible to predict what may happen in similar circumstances in the future. Enormous financial gains may be generated this way

- **Mining online** – websites today find themselves competing for customer loyalty. It costs little for a customer to switch to competitors. The electronic commerce landscape is evolving into a fast, competitive marketplace where millions of online transactions are being generated from log files and registration forms every hour of every day, and online shoppers browse by electronic retailing sites with their finger poised on their mouse, ready to buy or click/move on should they not find what they are looking for – that is, should the content, wording, incentive, promotion, product, or service of a website not meet their preferences. In such a competitive marketplace, the strategic use of customer information is critical to survival. As such, data mining has become crucial to doing business in fast-moving crowded markets.

Data mining tasks

The most common types of data mining tasks, classified by the kind of knowledge they are looking for, are listed as follows:

- **Classification** – data records are grouped into some meaningful subclasses. For example, suppose a car sales company has some information that all the people on its list who live in City X own cars worth more than 20K. They can then assume that even those who are not on their list, but live in City X, can afford to own cars costing more than 20K. This way the company classifies the people living in City X

- **Sequence detection** – by observing patterns in the data, sequences are determined. Here is an example: after John goes to the bank, he generally goes to the supermarket

- **Data dependency analysis** – potentially interesting relationships between data items are detected. For example, if people buy X, they tend to buy Y

- **Deviation analysis** – for example, John went to the bank on Saturday, but he did not go to the supermarket after that. Instead he went to a football game. With this task, anomalous instances and discrepancies are found.

Techniques for data mining

Data mining is a combination of many technologies. These include data management, data warehousing, statistics, decision support, and others such as visualisation and parallel computing. Many of these technologies have existed for many decades. The ability to manage and organise data effectively has played a major role in making data mining possible.

Database management researchers are taking advantages of work on **deductive and intelligent query processing** for data mining. One of the areas of interest is to extend query processing techniques to facilitate data mining. Data warehousing is another key data management technology for integrating the various data sources and organising the data so that it can be effectively mined.

Researchers in **statistical analysis** are integrating their techniques with those of machine learning to develop more sophisticated statistical techniques for data mining. Various statistical analysis packages are now being marketed as data mining tools. There is some dispute over the value of this approach. Nevertheless, statistics is a major area contributing to data mining.

Machine learning is an area of artificial intelligence that has been around for a while. It is concerned with the development of techniques which allow computers to learn. The idea is for the machine to learn various rules from observed patterns and then apply these rules to solve problems. While the principles used in machine learning and data mining are similar, data mining usually considers large quantities of data to mine. Therefore, integration of database management and machine learning techniques are needed for data mining.

Researchers from the computing **visualisation** field are approaching the area from another perspective. One of their focuses is to use visualisation techniques to aid the mining process. In other words, interactive data mining is a goal of the visualisation community.

Decision support systems are a collection of tools and processes to help managers make decisions and guide them in management – for example, tools for scheduling meetings and organising events.

Finally, researchers in high-performance computing are also working on developing appropriate algorithms in order to make large-scale data mining more efficient and feasible. There is also interaction with the hardware community so that appropriate architectures can be developed for high-performance data mining.

Data mining directions and trends

While significant progresses have been made, there are still many challenges. For example, due to the large volumes of data, how can the algorithms determine which technique to select and what type of data mining to do? Furthermore, the data may be incomplete and/or inaccurate. At times, there may be redundant information, and at times there may not be sufficient information. It is also desirable to have data mining tools that can switch to multiple techniques and support multiple outcomes. Some of the current trends in data mining are illustrated in figure 12.12.

Figure 12.12: Data mining trends

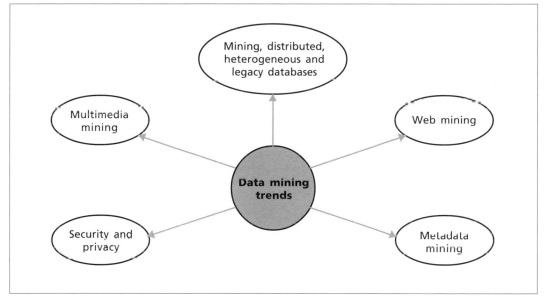

12.8 Oracle Warehouse Builder 10g (OWB)

Oracle's Warehouse Builder 10g allows developers to design, create, and manage data warehouses for an enterprise. It is a component of Oracle's Business Intelligence Suite. OWB enables users to create their own Business Intelligence applications with the Warehouse Builder at the heart of the design. Along with Oracle Database 10g, the DBMS, which includes ETL (Extract, Transform, Load), OLAP, and Data Mining built into the data server, OWB allows the development and creation of data warehouses, with facilities for querying, reporting, analysing, and management of data warehouse data. It includes a graphical environment for designing and creating the data warehouse.

Warehouse Builder architecture

The architecture consists of two main components: the design environment and the run-time environment, with the former controlling the **metadata repository**, and the latter controlling the **physical warehouse database**. The metadata is the abstract representations of the warehouse objects. The metadata repository contains design objects like source definitions. The run-time environment is responsible for the metadata and turns it into physical database objects and process flows.

The design environment

The design environment consists of the metadata repository (part of the Oracle database) and a number of tools used for setting up the run-time environment and reporting on the metadata repository. OWB comes with a Web-based environment to provide reports against the metadata in the repository. For example, one component of the reporting environment is the Impact Analysis function which allows the developer to gauge the impact of possible or intended changes to the metadata repository prior to implementing them. For example, we might want to know the impact of a change to the Bus Type data file to our Bus Depots' application. The Warehouse Builder design browser provides graphical impact analysis reports to find out where this change may have to be distributed.

Run-time component

The design in the Warehouse Builder metadata repository is logical. The OWB run-time component is used after the logical model has been built in the repository to create physical database objects, together with scripts to extract data from source system, and populate the warehouse objects. This enables the developer to set up the design in multiple different environments (e.g. development, test, production) without making any changes to the design. OWB generates 'extraction specific languages' (such as for the SQL*Loader control files for flat files and PL/SQL) for the extract, transform, load (ETL) processes and SQL Data Definition statements for the database objects. The ETL process then loads the source data into the target database.

12.9 Summary

After reading this chapter, students will understand the purpose of data warehouses, their benefits and the difference between operational and data warehouse data. Students were introduced to the general architecture of a data warehouse and its various components and processes including metadata, data transformation, cleansing and tools to access the data. The star schema design was introduced as a technique for modelling data warehouses. One important access tool is data mining and this was examined in more detail. Finally, Oracle's Warehouse Builder 10g was briefly examined.

12.10 Review questions

 Review question 12.1 Analyse the differences between data warehousing and operational systems, and discuss the importance of the separation of the two systems.

 Review question 12.2 Discuss the functionality of data transformation in a data warehouse system.

 Review question 12.3 What is metadata? How is it used in a data warehouse system?

Review question 12.4 Describe the three components of the technology architecture of a data warehousing system.

Review question 12.5 What are the three types of entities in a star schema and how are they used to model a data warehouse?

Review question 12.6 How can a staging area help the cleansing process in developing a data warehousing system?

Review question 12.7 Why is checkpoint restart logic useful? How can it be implemented for the data extraction and cleansing process?

12.11 Answers to review questions

Answer to review question 12.1 While a company can better manage its primary business with operational systems through techniques that focus on cost reduction, data warehouse systems allow a company to identify opportunities for increasing revenues, and therefore for growing the business. From a business point of view, this is the primary way to differentiate these two mission-critical systems. However, there are many other key differences between these two types of systems. These include·

- **Size and content** – the goals and objectives of a data warehouse differ greatly from an operational environment. While the goal of an operational database is to stay small, a data warehouse is expected to grow large – to contain a good history of the business. The information required to assist us in better understanding our business can grow quite large over time, and we do not want to lose this data

- **Performance** – in an operational environment, speed is of the essence. However, in a data warehouse some requests – 'meaning-of-life' queries – can take hours to fulfil. This may be acceptable in a data warehouse environment, because the true goal is to provide better information, or 'business intelligence'. For these types of queries, users are typically given a personalised extract of the requested data, so they can further analyse and query the information package provided by the data warehouse

- **Content focus** – operational systems tend to focus on small work areas, not the entire enterprise; a data warehouse, on the other hand, focuses on cross-functional subject areas. For example, a data warehouse could help a business understand who its top twenty at-risk customers are – those who are about to drop their services – and what type of promotions will assist in not losing these customers. To fulfil this query request, the data warehouse needs data from the customer service application, the sales application, the order management application, the credit application and the quality system

- **Tools** – typically, operational systems are structured so as to offer only a few ways to enter or access the data they manage, and lack a large amount of tools accessibility for users. A data warehouse is the land of user tools. Various tools are available to support the types of data requests. These tools provide many features that transform and present the data from a data warehouse as business intelligence. These features offer a high flexibility over the standard reporting tools that are offered within an operational systems environment.

Operational systems and data warehouses provide separate data stores. The data store of a data warehouse is designed to support queries and applications for decision making.

The separation of a data warehouse and operational systems serves multiple purposes, including:

- It minimises the impact of reporting and complex query processing on operational systems

- It preserves operational data for reuse after that data has been purged from operational systems

- It manages the data based on time, allowing the user to look back and see how the company looked in the past versus the present

- It provides a data store that can be modified to conform to the way the users view the data

- It unifies the data within a common business definition, offering one version of reality.

A data warehouse assists a company in analysing its business over time. Users of data warehouse systems can analyse data to spot trends, determine problems, and compare business techniques in a historical context. The processing that these systems support include complex queries, ad hoc reporting, and static reporting (such as the standard monthly reports that are distributed to managers). The data that is queried tends to be of historical significance and provides its users with a time-based context of business processes.

Answer to review question 12.2 A significant portion of the data warehouse implementation effort is spent extracting data from operational systems, and putting it in a format suitable for information applications that will run off the data warehouse. The data sourcing, clean-up, transformation, and migration tools perform all of the conversions, summarisation, key changes, structural changes, and condensations needed to transform disparate data into information that can be used by the decision-support tool. It also maintains the metadata. The functionality of data transformation includes:

- Removing unwanted data from operational databases

- Converting to common data names and definitions

- Calculating summaries and derived data

- Establishing defaults for missing data

- Accommodating source data definition changes.

Answer to review question 12.3 Metadata is a kind of data that describes the data warehouse itself. Within a data warehouse, metadata describes and locates data components, their origins (which may be either the operational systems or the data warehouse), and their movement through the data warehouse process. The data access, data stores and processing information will have associated descriptions about the data and processing – the inputs, calculations and outputs – documented in the metadata. This metadata should be captured within the data architecture and managed from the beginning of a data warehouse project. The metadata repository should contain information such as that listed below:

- Description of the data model

- Description of the layouts used in the database design

- Definition of the primary system managing the data items

- A map of the data from the system of records to the other locations in the data warehouse, including the descriptions of transformations and aggregations

- Specific database design definitions

- Data element definitions, including rules for derivations and summaries.

It is through metadata that a data warehouse becomes an effective tool for an overall enterprise. This repository of information will tell the story of the data: where it originated, how it has been transformed, where it went, and how often – that is, its genealogy or artefacts. Technically, the metadata will also improve the maintainability and manageability of a warehouse by making impact analysis information and entity life histories available to the support staff.

Equally important, metadata provides interactive access to users to help them understand content and find data. Thus, there is a need to create a metadata interface for users.

Answer to review question 12.4 The technology architecture is composed of three major components – clients, servers and networks – and the software to manage each of them.

- **Clients** – the client technology component comprises the devices that are utilised by users. These devices can include workstations, personal computers, personal digital assistants, and even beepers for support personnel. Each of these devices has a purpose in being served by a data warehouse. Conceptually, the client either contains software to access the data warehouse (this is the traditional client in the client/server model and is known as a 'fat client'), or it contains very little software, and accesses a server that contains most of the software required to access a data warehouse. The latter approach is the evolving Internet client model known as a 'thin client and fat server'

- **Servers** – the server technology component includes the physical hardware platforms as well as the operating systems that manage the hardware. Other components, typically software, can also be grouped within this component, including database management software, application server software, gateway connectivity software, replication software, and configuration management software. (Some of the concepts are related to web database connectivity and were discussed in chapter 11.)

- **Networks** – the network component defines the transport technologies needed to support communication activities between clients and servers. This component includes requirements and decisions for wide area networks (WANs), local area networks (LANs), communication protocols and other hardware associated with networks, such as bridges, routers and gateways.

Answer to review question 12.5 A star schema consists of three types of logical entities: measure, dimension and category detail. Within a star schema, the centre of the star – and often the focus of the users' query activity – is the measure entity. The data contained in a measure entity is factual information from which users derive 'business intelligence'. This data is therefore often given synonymous names to measure, such as key business measures, facts, metrics, performance measures and indicators.

Dimension entities are much smaller entities than measure entities. The dimensions and their associated data allow users of a data warehouse to browse measurement data with ease of use and familiarity. These entities assist users in minimising the rows of data within a measure entity, and in aggregating key measurement data. In this sense, these entities filter data, or force the server to aggregate data so that fewer rows are returned from the measure entities.

Each element in a dimension is a category, and represents an isolated level within a dimension that might require more detailed information to fulfil a user's requirement. These categories that require more detailed data are managed within category detail entities. These entities have textual information that supports the measurement data, and provides more detailed or qualitative information to assist in the decision-making process.

Answer to review question 12.6 Creating and defining a staging area can help the cleansing process. This is a simple concept that allows the developer to maximise up-time (minimise the down-time) of a data warehouse, while extracting and cleansing the data. A staging area, which is simply a temporary work area, can be used to manage transactions that will be further processed to develop data warehouse transactions.

Answer to review question 12.7 The checkpoint restart logic states that if there is a long-running process that fails prior to completion, then restart the process at the point of failure rather than from the beginning. If used properly, it can help improve efficiency of a complex process, while maintaining consistency and integrity. Similar logic should be implemented in the extraction and cleansing process. Within the staging area, define the necessary structures to monitor the activities of transformation procedures. Each of these programming units has an input variable that determines where in the process it should begin. Thus, if a failure occurs within the seventh procedure of an extraction process that has ten steps, assuming the right rollback logic is in place, it would only require that the last four steps (seven through to ten) be conducted.

12.12 Feedback on activities

Answer 12.1

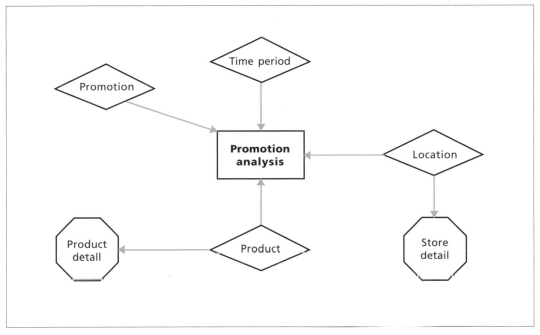

The star schema model can be used to analyse the effectiveness of the promotion, answering questions such as those listed below:

- Was a promotion profitable?
- What was the cost of developing the brand name over time?
- Was the promotion more successful in some locations than others?
- Based on historical data, how long does it take to build a brand name?
- Is the time to achieve name recognition decreasing or increasing?
- Does the product appear to have a seasonal trend; if so, do promotions assist in altering such trends?

Answer 12.2 Some examples of data warehousing and data mining applications:

- A supermarket analyses the purchases made by various people, and arranges the items on the shelves in such a way as to improve sales
- A credit agency analyses the credit history of various people, and determines who are at risk and who are not
- An investigation agency analyses the behaviour patterns of people, and determines who can be potential threats to protected information
- A pharmacy determines which physicians are likely to buy their products by analysing the prescription patterns of physicians
- An insurance company determines which patients might be potentially expensive by analysing various patient records
- A car sales company analyses the buying patterns of people living in various locations, and sends them brochures that are most likely to be of interest to them

- An employment agency analyses the employment history of employees, and sends them information of potentially lucrative jobs
- An educational institution analyses student records, determines who are likely to attend their institution, and sends them promotional brochures
- By analysing travel patterns of various groups of people, an investigation agency determines the associations between the groups
- By analysing patient history and current medical conditions, doctors not only diagnose the medical conditions, but also predict potential problems
- The Inland Revenue office examines the tax returns of various groups of people, and finds abnormal patterns and trends
- An investigation agency analyses the records of criminals, and determines who are likely to commit terrorism and mass murder.

THE BUS DEPOTS' DATABASE

Middlesex Transport is responsible for running a fleet of buses throughout North London. The buses are housed in one of three depots: Holloway, Hornsey and Islington. Each depot is identified by its depot number; in addition, the depot name and address are recorded.

Each bus is identified by its registration number. Details of the buses' models are also held, for example Routemaster and Spirit of London. The buses run on various routes which are described by their starting and finishing point, for example Camden Town/Hendon. Each route is identified by its route number. Only buses from particular depots will travel on a particular route, so, for example, only buses from the Islington depot will travel on the Camden Town/Hendon route. Buses are classified by various types such as doubledecker, bendy-bus etc. There are restrictions on some bus types for some of the routes, for example those with low bridges may exclude doubledecker buses, and bendy-buses may be unable to operate around some corners. For this reason, buses are designated to particular routes.

The bus company employs bus drivers to operate the buses and cleaners who help maintain them. Both the bus drivers and cleaners work at one particular depot. Drivers and cleaners have an employee number, name, and salary. In addition, the company holds information on the date that the driver passed his/her PCV (Passenger Carrying Vehicle) driving test.

For cleaning purposes, the depots are organised with cleaners being responsible for a number of buses; each bus has one cleaner who is particularly responsible for that bus. In the case of bus drivers, they can only drive buses where they have completed training for that type of bus, and the date when training is completed is recorded. In addition, bus drivers can only drive buses where they have had practice on particular routes.

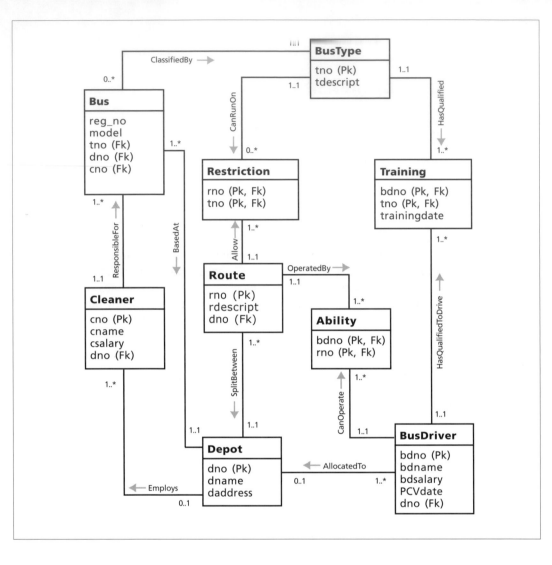

The Depot table

describe depot;

Name	Null?	Type
DNO	NOT NULL	VARCHAR2(5)
DNAME		VARCHAR2(20)
DADDRESS		VARCHAR2(20)

select * from Depot;

DNO	DNAME	DADDRESS
101	Holloway	Camden Road
102	Hornsey	High Road
104	Islington	Upper Street

The BusType table

describe bustype;

Name	Null?	Type
TNO	NOT NULL	VARCHAR2(5)
TDESCRIPT		VARCHAR2(20)

select * from bustype;

TNO	TDESCRIPT
1	doubledecker
2	metrobus
3	midibus
4	bendy-bus
5	open top

The BusDriver table

describe busdriver;

Name	Null?	Type
BDNO	NOT NULL	VARCHAR2(5)
BDNAME		VARCHAR2(20)
BDSALARY		NUMBER(6,2)
PVCDATE		DATE
DNO		VARCHAR2(5)

select * from busdriver;

BDNO	BDNAME	BDSALARY	PVCDATE	DNO
001	Jane Brown	1800	09-FEB-85	101
006	Sally Smith	1750	09-MAR-96	
007	James Bond	1500	09-JAN-99	102
008	Maggie May	2200	09-JAN-00	102
009	Jack Jones	1400	09-AUG-01	101
010	Peter Piper	3500	09-JUN-04	104
011	John Peel	2000	09-FEB-05	102

The Cleaner table

describe cleaner;

Name	Null?	Type
CNO	NOT NULL	VARCHAR2(5)
CNAME		VARCHAR2(20)
CSALARY		NUMBER(6,2)
DNO		VARCHAR2(5)

select * from cleaner;

CNO	CNAME	CSALARY	DNO
110	John	2550	101
111	Jean	2500	101
112	Betty	2400	102
113	Vince	2800	102
114	Jay	3000	102
115	Doug	2000	102
116	Geeta	4000	

The Route table

describe route;

Name	Null?	Type
RNO	NOT NULL	VARCHAR2(5)
RDESCRIPT		VARCHAR2(30)
DNO		VARCHAR2(5)

select * from route;

RNO	RDESCRIPT	DNO
10	Tottenham/Angel	102
11	Islington/Highgate	102
6	Camden/Golders Green	101
7	Finchley/Tottenham	101
8	Hendon/Muswell Hill	101

The Bus table

describe bus;

Name	Null?	Type
REG_NO	NOT NULL	VARCHAR2(10)
MODEL		VARCHAR2(20)
TNO		VARCHAR2(5)
DNO		VARCHAR2(5)
CNO		VARCHAR2(5)

select * from bus;

REG_NO	MODEL	TNO	DNO	CNO
A123ABC	Routemaster	1	101	113
D678FGH	Volvo 8700	2	101	114
D345GGG	Volvo 8500	1	101	112
H259IJK	Daf SB220	3	102	114
P200IJK	Mercedes 709D	2	102	110
P300RTY	Mercedes Citaro	4	102	111
R678FDS	Daf SB220	1		110

The Ability table

describe ability;

Name	Null?	Type
BDNO	NOT NULL	VARCHAR2(5)
RNO	NOT NULL	VARCHAR2(5)

select * from ability;

BDNO	RNO
001	6
001	7
001	8
007	10
007	6
008	10
008	11
009	7

The Training table

describe training;

Name	Null?	Type
BDNO	NOT NULL	VARCHAR2(5)
TNO	NOT NULL	VARCHAR2(5)
TRAININGDATE		DATE

select * from training;

BDNO	TNO	TRAININGDATE
001	1	09-JAN-06
001	2	09-JAN-06
006	2	09-FEB-06
007	1	09-FEB-06
007	2	09-FEB-06
007	3	09-MAR-06
008	2	09-MAR-06
008	3	09-MAR-06
008	4	09-APR-06
009	3	09-APR-06
009	4	09-MAY-06
011	1	09-MAY-06
011	2	09-MAY-06
011	3	09-JUN-06
011	4	09-JUN-06
011	5	09-JUN-06

The Restriction table

describe restriction;

Name	Null?	Type
RNO	NOT NULL	VARCHAR2(5)
TNO	NOT NULL	VARCHAR2(5)

select * from restriction;

RNO	TNO
10	1
10	2
10	3
10	4
11	1
11	2
11	3
11	4
6	1
6	2
6	3
6	4
7	1
7	2
8	3
8	4

Atkinson, Malcolm P, Bancilhon, Francois, DeWitt, David J, Dittrich, Klaus R, Maier, David and Zdonik, Stanley B, *The Object-Oriented Database System Manifesto*, DBLP, http://dblp.uni-trier.de, 1989.

Beynon-Davies P, *Database Systems,* third edition, Palgrave, 2004.

Bowman J, Emerson L, Darnovsky M, *The practical SQL using Structured Query Language*, Addison Wesley, 2000.

Buyens J, *Web Database Development*, Step by Step, Microsoft, 2000.

Connolly, T and Begg, C, *Database Systems, A Practical Approach to Design, Implementation & Management*, Pearson Education Ltd, 4th edition, 2005.

Date, C J, *Introduction to Database Systems*, 7th edition, Addison Wesley, 1999.

Eaglestone, B, Ridley M, *Web Database Systems*, McGraw-Hill, 2001.

Hall, M, *Core Servlets and JavaServer Pages*, Prentice-Hall, 2000.

Khoshafian, Setrag and Abnous, Razmik, *Object orientation: concepts, languages, databases, user interfaces*, John Wiley & Sons, Inc., 1990.

Kusnetzky, D and Olofson, C W, *Oracle 10g: Putting Grids to Work*, White Paper by IDC sponsored by Oracle, 2004.

Loney K, Koch G, *Oracle9i: The Complete Reference,* Osborne McGraw-Hill, 2002.

Morrison J, Morrison M, Conrad R, *Guide to Oracle 10g*, Thomson, 2006.

Oracle Corp Oracle 9i Application Developer's Guide – Object Relational Features, 2002.

Oracle Corp Solving Business Problems with Oracle Data Mining, http://www.oracle.com/technology/obe/obe10gdb/bidw/odm/odm.htm

Oracle Corp Oracle Data Warehousing http://www.oracle.com/solutions/business_intelligence/dw_home.html

Riccardi, G, *Principles of Database Systems with Internet and Java Applications*, Addison Wesley, 2001.

Rittman, M, *An Introduction to Oracle Warehouse Builder 10g*, The Online Community for Database Issues and Solutions, dbazine.com, 2005.

Silberschatz A, Korth H, Sudarshan S, *Database System Concepts*, 4th edition, McGraw-Hill, 2002.

Smith W, *Systems Building with Oracle*, Palgrave Macmillan, 2004.

Sunderraman R, *Oracle 9i Programming*, Addison Wesley, 2004.

Watson R, *Data Management Databases and Organizations*, 3rd edition, Wiley 2002.

INDEX